The Widening of
God's Mercy

The Widening of God's Mercy

*Sexuality Within
the Biblical Story*

CHRISTOPHER B. HAYS
and RICHARD B. HAYS

Yale UNIVERSITY PRESS

New Haven and London

Published with assistance from the Louis Stern Memorial Fund.

Yale University Press books may be purchased in quantity for educational, business, or promotional use. For information, please e-mail sales.press@yale.edu (U.S. office) or sales@yaleup.co.uk (U.K. office).

Set in type by Integrated Publishing Solutions.
Printed in the United States of America.

Library of Congress Control Number: 2024937265
ISBN 978-0-300-27342-7 (hardcover : alk. paper)

Unless otherwise noted, scripture quotations are from New Revised Standard Version of the Bible, copyright 1989, and New Revised Standard Version Updated Edition, copyright 2021 National Council of the Churches of Christ in the United States of America. Used by permission. All rights reserved worldwide.

A catalogue record for this book is available from the British Library.

This paper meets the requirements of ANSI/NISO Z39.48-1992 (Permanence of Paper).

10 9 8 7 6 5 4 3 2 1

To our children and grandchildren

There's a wideness in God's mercy like the wideness of
the sea.
There's a kindness in God's justice which is more than
liberty.

—FREDERICK WILLIAM FABER, "THERE'S A
WIDENESS IN GOD'S MERCY"

God's mercy is not like that of flesh and blood.

—SIFRE TO NUMBERS §133

Go and learn what this means, "I desire mercy, not sacrifice."

—MATTHEW 9:13, QUOTING HOSEA 6:6

Every single one of us could use some mercy now.

—MARY GAUTHIER

Contents

Acknowledgments

We do not remember ever writing anything that made us conscious of the limitations of our own perspective to the degree that this book did. That being the case, we feel more indebted than ever to the friends and colleagues who generously read the book in draft form, offered comments, and in many cases continued to engage us in dialogue about it. These included Kutter Callaway, Cathy Eskew, Tommy Givens, Michael Gorman, Jesse Huddleston, Jeremy Hutton, Robert Johnston, Karen Keen, Monica Miller, and Barry Seltser. In some cases the engagement took the form of disagreement—we are responsible for the book that has emerged—but it is certainly the product of collegial energy that inspired us and challenged us to think more deeply and argue more clearly.

We are grateful to Jennifer Banks at Yale University Press, who immediately saw the book's potential, but also brought an editorial perspective that helped to shape its form. We also thank Margaret Otzel and Jessie Dolch for their kind editorial work; Enid Zafran for compiling the indices; Brenda King, Amanda Cordero, and Stephen Cebik for ensuring the book found its readers; and Kristy Leonard and Eva Skewes for their attention to many details along the way.

As we note in the Introduction, this book began from conversations within the family, and we are grateful to have, within that nucleus, formidable minds, voracious readers, and gracious interlocutors such as Judy, Carly, Maddie, and Sandy, who think for themselves and possess strong moral visions that enrich our own.

The Widening of God's Mercy

Introduction

In 1 Samuel, the great prophet Samuel comes to announce to King Saul that the Lord has torn the kingdom of Israel from him and given it to David. Saul begs him to reconsider and to pardon him, to which Samuel thunders: "the Glory of Israel does not recant or change his mind! He is not a mortal, that he should change his mind!" (1 Sam 15:29).[1]

This is a satisfying and important-sounding thing to say. If there were red-letter Hebrew Bibles, it would probably be printed in red. If it were posted on an internet chat board, it would likely appear as ALL CAPS.

It's also a lie. How do we know? Because God said so, earlier in the same chapter: "I regret that I made Saul king" (1 Sam 15:11). And if that weren't clear enough, the omniscient narrator summarizes at the end of the chapter, "And the LORD regretted that he had made Saul king over Israel" (15:35).[2]

English translations obscure the connection, but the Hebrew verb translated "change his mind" twice in 15:29 (*nacham*) is the same one translated "regret" in the surrounding verses.[3] It's a challenging term to translate consistently, but it's also possible that English translators aren't much more comfortable with the contradiction than Samuel was.

For Samuel and many readers of the Bible today, it is a comfort and a bedrock idea that God "is the same yesterday and today and forever" (Heb 13:8), and that, as Isaiah put it, "The grass withers, the flower fades; / but the word of our God will stand forever" (Isa 40:8). We suggest that for those who would like to make sense of the Bible, these statements about God's unchanging word must somehow be held together with a long tradition of examples where God *does* in fact change his mind—and so do faithful people. In particular, God repeatedly changes his mind in ways that expand the sphere of his love, preserve his relationship with humankind, and protect and show mercy toward them.

Because of that, we are forced to conclude that many religious conservatives, however well-intentioned, are wrong about the most essential point of theology: the character of God. In recent years, this is nowhere more apparent than in ecclesiastical debates about sexuality. The church's inability to recognize the God it claims to worship, and to free itself from incessant bickering over sexual orientation, has become profoundly toxic. It has not only harmed individuals, but it has impeded the church's broader mission and cast a pall over everything else that we do. This book invites us all to move on in peace and harmony.

The repetitive arguments about the same set of verses, and the meaning of specific words, have reached an impasse; they are superficial and boring. We have lost the forest for the trees, and we need to return to a more expansive reading of the biblical story as a story about the wideness of God's mercy:

- Contrary to the common idea that biblical law was written once, in stone, and is unchangeable, the actual biblical story of God and humanity is one in which laws are under constant negotiation and revision. Often different law collections in the Torah say different things about the same topics. There are also stories of Moses rethinking laws when he was pressed by people with a good cause.

- Contrary to the common idea that "God's people" was a clearly defined entity based on ethnic or national boundaries, various texts from the beginning of the Bible onward show that God's plan was always wider, and that new groups were regularly being invited in from the margins, even when existing biblical laws expressly excluded and condemned them.
- Contrary to the common idea that God's decisions are eternal and immutable, there are numerous stories of God changing God's mind in the Bible, and others in which God declares that past judgments were too extreme. God even admits that some of the laws were not good: "I gave them statutes that were not good and ordinances by which they could not live" (Ezek 20:25).
- Contrary to the common idea that the New Testament brings complete and final closure to God's revelation, the New Testament itself promises that the Holy Spirit will continue to lead the community of Jesus's followers into new and surprising truths. In Jesus's final discourse with his disciples in the Gospel of John, he puts it like this: "I still have many things to say to you, but you cannot bear them now. When the Spirit of truth comes, he will guide you into all the truth, for he will not speak on his own but will speak whatever he hears, and he will declare to you the things that are to come" (John 16:12–13).

In sum, there is an ongoing conversation *within* the Bible in which rules, boundaries, and theologies are repeatedly rethought. If God's Spirit is still at work in the communities of faith that are grounded in the Bible, then that process must surely continue even now. As Karl Barth wrote, the theologian does not just ask "what the apostles and prophets said, but what we must say on the basis of the apostles and prophets."[4]

On the basis of the apostles and prophets, we conclude that the story of God and humanity is meant to be one of ever-expanding grace. God's mysterious plan, in "the fullness of time," is "to gather up all things in him" (Eph 1:10). The Bible is the story of that grace—its expansion to the world as a whole, to men and women alike, to foreign nations, and to those who were previously expressly banned from the community's worship.

Those who do not conform to traditional expectations for sexual orientation should be the next to be explicitly included, as an extension of this ancient and traditional process.

This is a book about basic issues of biblical theology. We envision it as a popular book for the broad audience of readers interested in what the Bible has to say. It is written for laypeople in the pews. It is written for clergy who have to lead congregations. It is written for our students—past, present, and future. The reader will find few footnotes. Although we are informed by our years of scholarship, there are few new or controversial ideas here from the standpoint of biblical studies, and academic issues are not at the forefront. Rather, we are trying to retell the biblical story in a way that it is often not told, and offering a reading of the literary and moral universes that the texts create.

We hope that this book will provide a different ethical and moral "map" of the Bible—a way of guiding readers through the texts.

This is not just another "how my mind has changed" book about human sexuality—although it's no secret that one of us wrote a book that has been a touchstone for "compassionate conservatives" for decades. Instead, this book is a fresh attempt to trace the Bible's portrayal of the dynamic and gracious character of God and to offer a proposal about how that portrayal should impact our contemporary reflections about sexuality.

This book also starts from the recognition of the harm that modern conservative Christianity has done by fighting battles that God doesn't call us to fight, and from the recognition that faithful LGBTQ Christians are all around us. Many of those who oppose the full inclusion of sexual minorities in the sacramental life of the church understand themselves as defenders of the Christian tradition. There is dignity to a theological tradition, but there is greater dignity in every human being (Ps 8:5–6 [ET 4–5]). Any religious tradition that makes its peace with harming people is to be feared. And any religious tradition that fails to grow and respond to the ongoing work of the Spirit will stagnate or die. There are riches in the tradition, but there is always the danger, as Jesus warned us in Matthew 25:14–30, of burying our treasure in the ground so that it cannot grow.

Our Stories

We are two family members, father and son, who speak from different perspectives but find ourselves not terribly far apart. We are also two faculty members who come from different fields: Old Testament and New Testament studies. Here is a brief introduction to the perspective from which each of us speaks.

RICHARD'S STORY

Five years ago, my brother Whis told me that he would refuse to attend our mother's funeral. Why? He had not been alienated from her. Far from it: His relationship with her had always been warm and loving. I was stunned by his announcement.

The problem: In making the preliminary plans, without consulting him, I had arranged for the funeral service to be held in a United Methodist church our mother had formerly attended, more than thirty years before, in her home city. That congregation, as it turned out, had very recently voted to declare itself a "reconciling church" and to display a rainbow banner alongside the church sign in front of the building. For my brother, this was, he declared, "a deal-breaker." Even though there would have been no reference to the issue of same-sex relationships in the service, he felt he would be publicly endorsing the church's stand—and compromising both his faith and his leadership position—by participating in a funeral service there. (He was and is the executive director of a youth ministry program. That program had included "*non-practicing* same-sex and bisexually attracted individuals" but firmly opposed same-sex unions.)

I was incredulous. "Do you really believe that a church's decision on welcoming gay people is a matter on which the faith stands or falls?" I asked. "This isn't about the doctrine of the Trinity or justification by faith. It's not about Nazism's 'German Christianity' or apartheid. Surely you don't really think that a congregation's decision to offer hospitality to gay and lesbian folks is a heretical betrayal of the Christian faith?" He said the movement to advocate LGBTQ inclusivity in the church, as he had experienced it, had (paradoxically) turned ruthless and divisive, excluding those who didn't get on board with "the cause." He said his objection was primarily to the movement's open claims to know better than the Bible when it comes to knowing good from evil. So he remained unmoved.

After much discussion, our family decided it would be a painful outcome to bury our mother with one of her sons boycotting the funeral, and so we moved the service to a different church building.

My brother's adamant stand was based on his commitment to the authority of scripture as he understood it. I saw that his position had integrity, given his understanding of *how* the Bible speaks to us today. But it also seemed to me troublingly wrong.

The present book proposes that advocacy for welcoming sexual minorities in the church need not be based on claiming "to know better than the Bible." Instead, the argument for inclusion can be grounded in a broader understanding of *how* the biblical narratives can inform moral judgments: Rightly understood, they can shape and reshape communities of faith as visible signs of God's mercy.

My brother and I have moved on from this disagreement and continue our brotherly relationship. Nonetheless, our unexpected conflict dramatized the tragic controversy that is currently fracturing churches and families everywhere. In a manner that would have been unimaginable a generation ago, decisions about the ordination of LGBTQ people and the acceptance of same-sex marriage have become identity-defining issues—one way or the other—for Protestant churches.

For me, this argument with my brother was a tipping point. Here is the backstory:

In 1996 I published a book titled *The Moral Vision of the New Testament.* That book includes a chapter on homosexuality that has been widely cited and discussed in the ensuing debates about sexuality—usually by voices defending the church's traditional teaching, which categorized acts of same-sex intercourse as sinful.[5] My chapter argued that most of the then-current proposals to explain away the Bible's condemnation of such activity were exegetically unsustainable and that "though only a few biblical texts speak of homoerotic activity, all that

do mention it express unqualified disapproval" (389). As a judgment about what these very few biblical texts say, that statement
still seems to me to be correct.

Nevertheless, in the ensuing years, I have been deeply
troubled by the way my chapter has been appropriated as am-
munition by some individuals and groups taking the uncom-
promising "conservative" position exemplified by my brother's
stern stance against attending our mom's funeral. At the same
time, I have been privileged more recently to belong to a grace-
filled church community where gay and lesbian Christians participate fully as members and as leaders, without making it into
a church-defining issue.

And so my thinking about the issues of sexuality has developed significantly in recent years. Even in *Moral Vision*, I
had argued emphatically that gay and lesbian people should be
welcome in the church. I put it like this:

> Unless we think that the church is a community of
> sinless perfection, we must acknowledge that per-
> sons of homosexual orientation are welcome along
> with other sinners in the company of those who trust
> in the God who justifies the ungodly (Rom 4:5). If
> they are not welcome, I will have to walk out the
> door along with them, leaving in the sanctuary only
> those entitled to throw the first stone. (400)

But now I think that clear statement in favor of inclusion was,
and is, inadequate. It was accompanied by my equally clear
judgments that scripture's disapproval of same-sex *acts* was
univocal and that the Bible's symbolic world portrays heterosexual marriage as the definitive norm. I summed up my interpretation of the evidence in this way:

> Thus, in view of the considerable uncertainty sur-
> rounding the scientific and experiential evidence,
> in view of our culture's present swirling confusion
> about gender roles, in view of our propensity for
> self-deception, I think it prudent and necessary to
> let the univocal testimony of Scripture and the
> Christian tradition order the life of the church on
> this painfully controversial matter. We must affirm
> that the New Testament tells us the truth about our-
> selves as sinners and as God's sexual creatures: mar-
> riage between man and woman is the normative
> form for human sexual fulfillment, and homosex-
> uality is one among many tragic signs that we are
> a broken people, alienated from God's loving pur-
> pose. (399–400)

From that constellation of judgments, it followed that gay and
lesbian Christians, while welcome in the church, were summoned to lives of singleness and celibacy: "Perhaps for many
the best outcome that is attainable in this time between the
times will be a life of disciplined abstinence" (403).

I offered those judgments—alongside deliberations about
other ethical issues such as nonviolence, divorce and remar-
riage, ethnic conflict, and abortion—as my *proposals* about
how best to discern the New Testament's relevance for difficult
and contested questions in our time. I thought that those judgments could *start* a conversation rather than end one, but subsequent developments have shown that I was naïve. Many traditionalists and conservatives have seized upon that one chapter
as the final word, as a cover for exclusionary attitudes and practices wrapped in more "compassionate" packaging. I fear that
the rhetoric of my chapter left itself open to such uses. I ac-

knowledge that I bear responsibility for the pain such developments have caused to many believers who belong to sexual minorities. And for that I am deeply sorry.

Much has changed since 1996. When *Moral Vision* was published, same-sex marriage was illegal everywhere in the United States. Few congregations were openly affirming of gay and lesbian folks, though an unofficial "don't ask, don't tell" policy was becoming more common. In view of the subsequent developments over the past quarter century, both in the church and in the wider culture, we now have much more lived experience of the ways in which the Spirit may be at work to expand our vision. My own experience of participating in a church where gay and lesbian members were a vital part of the congregation's life and ministry has caused me to stop and reconsider what I wrote before.

What is needed now is a comprehensive rethinking of the way in which the Bible might speak to these matters. In this book I want to start over—to repent of the narrowness of my earlier vision and to explore *a new way of listening to the story that scripture tells about the widening scope of God's mercy.*

CHRIS'S STORY

Like many families, ours has been thrown into turmoil by church teachings about human sexuality. Unlike most others, ours has played a leading role in those debates. We've been guilty of a failure of moral vision, and it's time to set that right.

My father was a Methodist church organist's kid from Oklahoma who made his way to the Ivy League. His *Moral Vision* made conservative views about LGBTQ people seem respectable and civilized. It emboldened a whole generation of would-be "compassionate conservatives." These were people who still essentially felt that homosexuality was wrong but wanted

a nicer way to say that. After writing that book, my father consistently declined to speak publicly about the issue; nevertheless, it gave cover to others who wanted to "hold the line."

The longer I live, the more convinced I am that his earlier conclusion that LGBTQ people should abstain from living
out their sexual orientation is not a viable stance. Sexuality is a
fundamental part of our humanity, and while some people (of
all orientations) are called to celibacy, not all are. As for the rest
of us, when it comes to respecting other people, it's not plausi-
ble to hold our nose at something as important as whom people love most and still present ourselves as their friend, or their
"brother (or sister) in Christ." Most people are not interested
in that kind of grudging acceptance.

Fifteen years ago, I was hired by Fuller Theological Seminary, an institution largely governed by "compassionate conservatives." The faculty held diverse views, but I understood the
(conservative) institutional stance going in. I would have said that
I didn't think homosexuality was a pressing issue for the church
and that I wasn't a "culture warrior." Hindsight being 20-20, I
simply didn't care enough about it, or about the well-being of
LGBTQ people, to consider it a deal-breaker in taking my job.

My father's book shaped my thinking and underwrote exclusion at my institution and others. This is not speculation or
inference; numerous leaders at various Christian schools have
told me over the years that *Moral Vision* was a touchstone book
for them. Its chapter on homosexuality helped empower some
of them to see themselves as humbly and courageously standing up for the will of God while excluding and harming people
in their own communities. Given his work, I probably seemed
like a safe hire at Fuller. But I'm done being safe while many
others are not.

Having grown up in progressive mainline churches and
attended mainline and secular schools, there was a lot that

I didn't understand about evangelical culture. As I look back on it now, I did not yet understand how disregard for LGBTQ people was related to disregard for other humanistic values. What's happened over these fifteen years has made me realize that something much deeper is happening in Christian communities, and that my own experience is a window on that. The development of my thinking mirrors the changes in the Presbyterian Church (U.S.A.) that ordained me. In the course of my career, my church has embraced same-sex marriages, apologized for past harms, and sought to include LGBTQ Christians.[6] In the same period, my relationships with numerous LGBTQ friends and colleagues grew and deepened. Increasingly, I found anti-LGBTQ policies incomprehensible: What was the fear?

Some things have not changed. I remain committed to the unparalleled centrality of the Bible for Christian ethical discernment. The conclusions I have come to are not the result of a new revelation or some sudden, blinding vision along the road to Damascus, but rather the slow and logical outworking of years of reading the Bible. And it's not surprising to me that there is disagreement among people who also ground their arguments on the Bible. Even our best instincts—our desire to read texts closely and understand them—can mislead us if they cause us to overlook the main outlines of the biblical story. Exegetical debates can become red herrings and distract us from the character of God and the fact that in many cases clear biblical rulings and laws have been set aside by Christians—for example, laws allowing the ownership of slaves or instructions that women should wear head coverings. I would say plainly that whatever the contested biblical passages were envisioning, they were not envisioning LGBTQ Christians in the pews today who abundantly manifest the fruits of the spirit (Gal 5:22–23).[7] But in any case, our ways of living faithfully change—

and this is not an embarrassment. They *ought* to change, in accordance with our discernment of God's will in a changing world.

I've come to realize that the more basic issues at stake in the sexuality debates involve who God is, and who we're supposed to be in response to that. We noted above that this book is meant to serve as a fresh map, including territory in the Old Testament that many readers will be unfamiliar with—or at least unaccustomed to thinking about in relation to these issues. The book emerges partly from my experience of traversing this terrain regularly.[8]

A decade before I arrived at Fuller, its longtime theology professor Lew Smedes wrote an essay titled "Like the Wideness of the Sea?," advocating for the inclusion of same-sex couples in the church.[9] By the 2010s, a group called "One Table" had arisen to "advocate for the shared interests of the LGBTQ community on our campus" and serve as "a place for LGBTQ students to feel supported in their lives at Fuller." So I took it for granted that the institution would continue to evolve in its thinking about these issues. After all, that's what was happening to the whole culture, and to me personally.

But it didn't evolve. Instead, a series of institutional decisions ignored and disempowered contrary voices within. In 2015, New Testament professor Daniel Kirk was denied tenure, reportedly in part because of what he had written about sexuality issues.[10] In 2018 Fuller's leadership began expelling students on the grounds that same-sex marriage was against its community standards.[11] When that led to lawsuits, they used institutional resources to defend this decision in federal court. The students who brought the lawsuits in 2019 were Joanna Maxon and Nathan Brittsan, but many others have suffered less publicly.

Even as I grew more concerned about the school's direction over the years, I was too often silent. But a celebratory email sent to the faculty when the Maxon case was decided in Fuller's favor in 2021 turned my stomach and spurred me along toward writing this book.

Around the time of the lawsuits, a Fuller faculty committee that had been appointed to discuss revising the sexuality standards was shut down. Those close to the conversations have told me that they were moving toward revising the standards in a more progressive direction when they were disbanded. They were told by an administrator that any indication of differing views on these issues within the school was too risky, because its legal defense rested on the grounds that an institution "has the right to hold voluntary members of its faith community to agreed-upon religious and moral standards."[12]

The problem was that these standards were *not* agreed upon by everyone in the community. The school is based in an urban part of Southern California, and as such it has attracted many progressive people over the years, at all levels—faculty, staff, and students. Part of the argument in the Maxon lawsuit was that homosexual students had felt welcomed at Fuller. As a memorandum in the case stated, "Joanna's peers and professors respected her as a Christian woman who was married to another woman."[13]

Fuller was founded as "a Caltech for the evangelical world"[14]—a place where top-tier research and interchange of fresh ideas mattered—and once upon a time it was on a better course. Its faculty rejected biblical inerrancy in the so-called Battle for the Bible, and afterward it saw a boom in enrollment. It has repeatedly taken risks and strong positions on issues such as women in ministry and racial justice. As recently as 2003, it was touted in the *Los Angeles Times* as embodying "Jesus with a Genius Grant" in an article that portrayed the school as a primary representative of a postevangelical, post-conservative future for Christianity.[15] In light of all that, many people within the school were understandably shocked and dismayed by the expulsions and the legal defense; we thought we had signed on to an institution that at least had room for multiple views about sexuality.

As various progressive-minded faculty, staff, and students left Fuller over the years, the leadership seemed to simply pursue a narrower swath of Christians who were like-minded. But even after all that has happened, a 2023 survey found that 9 percent of the student body identified as LGBTQ, more than 50 percent had a family member or close friend who did, 40 percent did not want marriage defined as being "between one man and one woman," and less than half thought that the school should be in the business of enforcing sexual standards.[16] The faculty has not been formally polled, but there is a very significant progressive contingent within a broader diversity of views.

A year ago, a new round of "review and reflection" about sexuality was announced at Fuller. It has led to a draft statement that recognizes our denominational diversity by promising not to enforce community standards on students. It also cautiously affirms faculty academic freedom related to sexuality issues. It remains unclear how this will be implemented, and how it will apply to staff. Not long before the statement was drafted, Ruth Schmidt, a valued senior director of a Fuller center who had a long history as a student and staffer, was denied an exception to the community standard on sexuality and summarily terminated.[17] I hope against hope that she will be the last to suffer, and that this book will help establish a safe space for real conversations.

Some people seem to expect that biblical studies and theology, because they deal with ancient texts and history, will serve as conservative counterweights to all our experience of our LGBTQ colleagues, students, and friends and their gifts and graces in the church. Some people assume that "faithfulness to the Bible" inevitably leads to a traditionalist view of human sexuality. This book upends those expectations and offers a positive way forward.

Although my father and I have wanted to right some past wrongs, this book isn't just about us changing our minds, nor even is it just about changing other people's minds about sexuality. We hope that some people who are still conflicted in their own minds about this issue will be helped by the road map that this book lays out for understanding God, but the book is also for those who are already convinced that LGBTQ people are just as good as straight people *but who are unsure about God and Christianity*. Often, this means people who were raised within Christianity and were repulsed by some of its contemporary manifestations. We know many people in that company. To them—perhaps to you—we say: You're not crazy to think you and yours are created equal and loved equally by God.

It's not only in the interest of sexual minorities to recognize this. The future and flourishing of the church are also at stake. It would take a different book to argue it, but the church is not in decline because of its impurity; it is in decline because of its lack of curiosity and hardness of heart.[18]

Above all, these are family issues, for all of our families. In the early stages of my conversations with my father about his changing perceptions of these issues, after I suggested we write this book, he asked me, "Who is the intended audience?" And I said, "Maddie." That's my daughter, whom we have raised to appreciate the strength that comes from diversity and who can see very clearly that the future will have no patience with debates over human rights for those whose sexual orientation does not conform to "traditional" standards. This book is dedicated to her, and to all of my father's grandchildren, who will see and understand things that we do not.

Odds and Ends

It may be that most readers would be happy to get on to the biblical story without further ado, but we scholars are a harried and quarrelsome lot—we worry and argue a lot about details and word choices, because they matter. So for those of you who care as much as we do, here are some preliminary notes about those details.

"I" AND "WE": THE VOICES IN THIS BOOK

The chapters on the Old Testament that follow were written by Chris; the chapters on the New Testament were written by Richard. And so, although this was a shared labor and we have read and commented on each other's drafts repeatedly, we use the first-person singular at times to identify our own voices.

The first-person plural is used variously of the author and the audience ("We are meant to take seriously the assessment of God . . ."), of the author and other scholars ("As far as we can tell, however, the name Yahweh is derived from a verb"), and occasionally of both of us as authors ("Through most of this book we use 'the Lord' for the divine name in Hebrew"). The context should make this fairly clear.

A WORD ABOUT "APPLICATION"

Some readers may come to this book wanting answers to specific questions about sexuality: "Do they think bisexuality is okay?"; "What about transgender identities?"; "If I'm already married and realize I'm homosexual, what am I supposed to do?"; "Doesn't this reasoning lead to a slippery slope so that anything goes?" Et cetera. We do not extrapolate very much on the application of our biblical and theological analyses to specific cases. There are two primary reasons for this: The first is that we want to maintain a certain modesty about our work as biblical scholars. Others have more expertise in human sexuality, but we do think we know something about God that is relevant to the sexuality debates. Our task is to explore and expound what the biblical texts say, with a view toward their theological significance. Even though theology naturally extends to ethics and human practices, there is much that scientists and theorists of human sexuality will have to add to the conversation that we cannot do justice to. These topics are discussed in many other places. The second reason is that we are confident that these conversations will continue to unfold and change shape in the years to come, and it is likely that our own thinking will continue to evolve as well.

This is not to say that one cannot think theologically with the Bible about specific issues regarding sexuality. We would say that God wants humankind to flourish; this includes having healthy companionship with other humans—"it is not good for the human to be alone" (Gen 2:18).[19] Not every sexual practice encourages human flourishing; some are abusive or otherwise harmful. This is one lens that ought to be applied when specific questions come up, and we hope that the image of God that we discuss here is helpful in shaping the church's witness.

ON "MERCY" IN THE TITLE

For some readers, the term "mercy" in our title, and in the hymn on which it is based, may strike an unfamiliar note. It is a word with a rich history in the Christian tradition, describing God's grace, compassion, and favor, and this is the primary sense in which we use it. To speak of God's mercy is to point to God's overflowing love, God's propensity to embrace, heal, restore, and reconcile all of creation.

In common usage, the word has come to be associated most commonly with "clemency" shown to a guilty or unworthy party. In some ways we claim this tradition as well, knowing as we do that we—like other humans—are sinners in need of God's mercy (see the Epilogue). The belief in human sinfulness can become a weapon, however, when it is wielded by those who believe that other people's sins are more significant than their own. C. S. Lewis wrote, in *Mere Christianity:* "I want to make it as clear as I possibly can that the centre of Christian morality is not [sexual behavior]. If anyone thinks that Christians regard unchastity as the supreme vice, he is quite wrong. The sins of the flesh are bad, but they are the least bad of all sins. All the worst pleasures are purely spiritual: the pleasure of putting other people in the wrong, of bossing and patronising and spoiling sport, and back-biting, the pleasures of power, of hatred."[20]

Many people think of the "sexuality debates" as being about homosexuality and same-sex marriage. The set of issues has now become more complex, however, as diverse forms of gender identity and sexual attraction are widely discussed. In this book, Richard has used the term "gay and lesbian" when discussing past conversations about sexuality in which homosexuality was the primary issue. In more recent times, however, anyone thinking about these questions must take into account a range of nonheterosexual orientations and expressions, with a large and expanding literature around them. We do not mean to exclude bisexuality or other orientations.[21] There is of course a diversity of opinions about the best terminology. For example, some self-identify as "queer," while others find the term offensive. Nevertheless, we sometimes use the common acronym LGBTQ (lesbian, gay, bisexual, trans, queer) as a blanket, inclusive term. We trust that we will continue to understand better than we do now how to foster the flourishing of God's "fearfully and wonderfully made" creatures (Ps 139:14).

ON GENDER AND PRONOUNS FOR GOD

The choice of pronouns for God is a well-known problem for theologians, and it is sharpened in a book related to gender issues. There are certain relevant facts that we view as well-established:

1. God is not male; God is beyond human male and female identities.
2. The Bible predominantly uses masculine pronouns for God, and "Father" and "Son" are two of its primary images of God.
3. The Bible also contains feminine images of God—as a woman in labor (Isa 42:14), a nursing mother (Isa 49:14–15), and a mother hen (Matt 23:37, Luke 13:34). These have played a significant role in the Jewish and Christian traditions over centuries and theology in the present should embrace and affirm them.[22]
4. Even some of the biblical images of God that are understood to be masculine are more complex. For example, most would take the image of the Lord as a warrior who wades in gore (Isa 63:1–6) as obviously masculine, but its closest analogy in the ancient West Semitic world is a story about the warrior goddess Anat of Ugarit.[23] To some degree, modern readers impose their own notions of gender on the text.

It is possible to write theology while avoiding pronouns for God. But one of the central ideas of this book is that God is personal, and we want to emphasize this point by using personal pronouns. It is also possible to use new pronouns that avoid making gendered assumptions, such as "s/he" or "they." But we have decided to work within the frame and style of traditional theological discourse, for the sake of readability for a broad audience. We recognize that if styles of theological discourse change rapidly, this book might come to sound archaic, but we are writing it primarily for the audiences here and now who might benefit from it, and only secondarily for posterity.

Thus we have sometimes used traditional-sounding masculine pronouns for God, but we trust readers to recognize that God is not male. Our ideas of God should not be constrained by traditional ideas of masculinity, or else our ideas of God will be too limited.

ON TEXTS AND TRANSLATIONS

Any mainstream translation of the Bible inevitably compromises between readability and precise transparency to the text in its original languages. This volume generally hews to the New Revised Standard Version of the Bible (NRSV); but since the exegetical work depends very much on details that are perceptible in the original languages but obscured in translations, we sometimes offer our own translations for the sake of clarity. These are indicated in the notes. For the sake of nonspecialist readers, we have also cited the English chapter and verse numbers where they diverge from the Hebrew Masoretic Text and adopted an informal transliteration system.

ON HISTORY AND NARRATIVE

Some who read drafts of this book wanted more discussion of our interpretive assumptions, our methods, our (to use a fancy word) *hermeneutics*. We are setting aside theoretical and methodological reflections for another day, and we think the book is basically self-explanatory: It is written by and for people who think it matters what the Bible says, and who believe that the best way to do it justice is to read it carefully.

The book is essentially a literary and theological reading of a series of episodes in the story of God and humankind. These biblical narratives serve as the basis for the church's preaching and teaching; it is these narratives that have shaped the imagination of readers within the community of faith from antiquity to the present time. Accordingly, this book is an exercise in narrative interpretation; our goal is to demonstrate that the biblical story, taken as a whole, depicts the ever-widening path of God's mercy. We seek to commend that story as the truth by which Christians should shape our moral judgments and our own lives.

I

The Widening of God's Mercy in the Old Testament

1

Widening Through Creation

As you drive east toward Lake Tahoe through the pre-
dawn gray of the Sierra Foothills, the sky begins to
brighten, but you are all in shadow, until—if the tim-
ing is just right—you crest a summit and meet the morning
sun, and the forested basin spread out beneath you, and the
lake sparkling and unbelievably blue—and it's not the elevation
taking your breath away.

Even great writers like Mark Twain and John Muir have
struggled to do it justice. Muir wrote of the Sierras, "I never
beheld a place . . . where the tender fostering hand of the Great
Gardener was more directly visible"; and of Tahoe, "I am re-
minded of all the mountain lakes I ever knew, as if this were a
kind of water heaven to which they all had come."[1]

Some may better recognize this feeling of marvel in relation to the arrival of a new child or grandchild. Even at moments
like these, it's not often that we step back and ask: *Why? Why
should we be granted any of this?* Perhaps that's natural, when
we are enraptured. But it is one of the most basic questions.

Theism doesn't inherently solve this problem. That is,
even if you believe in a God who is good, why should anything

else exist? Isn't God enough? Pursing those questions leads to some starting points about what kind of God we're talking about.

If creation took place so that there could be wonderful things like playful dolphins and ice cream cones, then one would have to account for the horrors and terrors of the world as well, as if to sum it all up and argue for a net positive. If one is in an optimistic mood, this may seem possible. And probably every professor teaching theology and philosophy in recent years has taken note of the TV comedy *The Good Place* and its afterlife points system, in which everything every human on Earth does is recorded and assigned points based on the moral worth of each action. This point system is of course a caricature of popular conceptions of God's judgment and the afterlife. In the show, it's used to determine whether people go to the Good Place or the Bad Place, and so from an optimistic point of view, presumably the good would outweigh the bad if you summed everything up. But even in the show, the system is broken. This turns out not to be a feasible mode of argumentation; there's no way to keep score.

Why did creation happen at all? Why should the world exist, and why are we here in it? These sorts of basic questions, which have long motivated philosophers and theologians, are not discussed much in our culture. Even within the church, they're largely answered in the first breaths of catechesis and then set aside. A whole genre of sermons about creation does little more than repeat the answer to the Westminster Catechism's first question:

Q. What is the chief end of man?
A. Man's chief end is to glorify God, and to enjoy
    him forever.

This is a pleasingly simple answer, and it keeps the focus on God. But perhaps the reason it's repeated so often, when other points of Reformation theology are not, is that it is a useful answer for pastors, in that churches are the places where Christians most commonly go to glorify and enjoy God. This is an answer that drives church attendance, engagement, investment, etc. But in its *what-ness,* it skirts the holy mystery of *why* anything other than God exists, if the whole point is God.

The catechism never dares to ask a "why" question, but an answer is implied: We're here because God wanted to be glorified, and because he wants us to enjoy . . . something. But the biblical prooftexts supplied for this have little to do with creation.[2]

Psalm 8 steps outside the sanctuary and edges closer to the mystery:

When I look at your heavens, the work of your fingers,
     the moon and the stars that you have established;
what are human beings that you are mindful of them,
     mortals that you care for them?

Yet you have made them a little lower than God,
     and crowned them with glory and honor.
You have given them dominion over the works of your hands
     . . . (Ps 8:3–6)

The psalm connects the mystery of God's grace with creation, and humankind's divinely granted authority over it. We can hear echoes to the early chapters of Genesis here in the creation of the heavens and humankind and the granting of dominion.[3] But the psalm doesn't explain the mystery.

Surely somewhere in Genesis we should find the answer to why anything came to exist. But we don't find it in the very beginning of the book. It doesn't matter whether you think that Genesis 1:1 points to creation from nothing or creation from preexisting matter; in neither case does the author give any reason why.

Perhaps the Bible's interaction with its context sheds some light? After all, the world was already old when the Old Testament began to be written around the beginning of the first millennium BCE. Humankind had been around for more than two hundred thousand years, and writing had been in use for two thousand of those. So we know something about the ideas that were already in circulation. The most prominent reason given outside the Old Testament for the existence of humans was that the gods needed us to work the land.[4] The Bible preserves an echo of that explanation in the older of its two primary creation stories: "The LORD God took the man and put him in the garden of Eden to till it and keep it" (Gen 2:15).

In the final shape of things, however, the Old Testament "primeval history" offers another answer. In Genesis 1:26–31, God creates humanity in his own image and likeness, to rule creation with him. We are therefore not merely vicars or proxies, but also partners with God in the project of creation. So we might expect some of the contours of God's purposes to begin to become visible in the dark mirror of humanity. But like the Genesis 2 account, this one does not explain the existence of the natural world. Both of them push the larger question back only a step: Why do the earth and its vegetation and creatures exist?

Because scripture doesn't really answer the question, past theologians have been pushed toward more philosophical forms of reasoning. Although most of the present book is about the interpretation of the Bible, I indulge in a bit of speculation here because it may be borne out by the rest of the book.

When I was a student, I was handed what seemed like a winsome answer to the present question. It came from Jonathan Edwards's treatise "The End for Which God Created the World," which has continued to be one of the most influential discussions of the topic in the history of Christian thought.[5]

Edwards said that God's perfections include "a propensity of nature to diffuse of his own fullness" and that God cannot "be hindered in the exercise of his goodness and his other perfections."[6] In other words, God will tend to expand on what God already is, and nothing can stop God from doing so. God's glory and love are increased and diffused by having a creation to love and be loved by, and thus (although God is free) it is *logically* necessary for God to create.

This has always struck me as a wonderful point: The fact that we exist at all is an effect of the initial expansion of God's grace and love to include things other than himself, and that expansion of grace and love is consistent with who God is.

When I returned to read Edwards's "dissertation" in more detail, though, I was somewhat disappointed by it. Rather than marveling, like the psalmist, at God's grace toward humankind as expressed in creation, Edwards was actually much more concerned about protecting God from any dependence on humankind. This densely argued, forty-thousand-word treatise ceaselessly revolves around God's love of God, rather than of humanity. Because God is the epitome of goodness, Edwards says, "God's own holiness must primarily consist in the love of himself."

Edwards's god is a philosopher's god: His god creates out of logical necessity. There is no hint of a *decision* to create. There is no personality reaching out toward the creation in love.

Edwards incorporates scriptural proofs, to be sure—for example, to assert that God is the first and last, the Alpha and

Omega of all creation (Rev 1:8, etc.). He also repeatedly uses solar imagery; for example:

> The glory of God . . . is fitly compared to an efful-
> gence or emanation of light from a luminary. Light
> is the external expression, exhibition, and manifes-
> tation of the excellency of the luminary, of the sun
> for instance: It is the abundant, extensive emana-
> tion and communication of the fullness of the sun
> to innumerable beings that partake of it. It is by this
> that the sun itself is seen, and his glory beheld, and
> all other things are discovered: it is by a participa-
> tion of this communication from the sun, that sur-
> rounding objects receive all their lustre, beauty, and
> brightness. It is by this that all nature is quickened
> and receives life, comfort and joy.

This solar-deity tradition certainly has a deep scriptural heritage (e.g., Ps 104:1–2: "You are . . . wrapped in light as with a
garment," etc.)—but when taken to this philosophical limit, it
leaves humans huddling off to the side, as if seeking the warmth
of a cold Antarctic sun. Edwards's image of a burning orb em-
anating its blessings omits the even more pervasive biblical
image of God as personal, as three persons making decisions
in relationship with humankind: a God who speaks to his people, shepherds them, wrestles with them; a God who suffers
with them and lays down his life for them in love.

It is remarkable, in an essay that uses the word "love" a
lot, how little is said about God's love for creation and humanity. Rather, Edwards's discussion circles around God's self-love
and desire to be loved by his creatures: "the communication of
God's virtue or holiness is principally in communicating the
love of himself." For Edwards, God loves human *virtue,* because

it is love of God himself. But humans *as such,* in our sinful state? This is not said. It is true, of course, that this first expansion of divine love was toward a world that had done nothing to deserve it—because it did not exist! But Edwards seems to me not to have rightly captured God's character.

Although Edwards was the most prominent progenitor of the Calvinist intellectual movement that eventually underwrote the American Revolution (to the point that it is often called the "Presbyterian Rebellion"),[7] he himself was a Tory, a royalist.[8] This comes across in his image of God: He portrays God as a Sun King, resplendent in glory and wielding sole power, without need of any of his dependent subjects.

As I read Edwards more deeply, I realized that I should not have been surprised that he wasn't particularly rapturous about God's love and grace. Probably every pastor and theologian has, at some point in their education, encountered his stinging sermon "Sinners in the Hands of an Angry God":

> The God that holds you over the pit of hell, much as one holds a spider, or some loathsome insect, over the fire, abhors you, and is dreadfully provoked; his wrath towards you burns like fire; he looks upon you as worthy of nothing else, but to be cast into the fire; he is of purer eyes than to bear to have you in his sight; you are ten thousand times more abominable in his eyes than the most hateful venomous serpent is in ours. You have offended him infinitely more than ever a stubborn rebel did his prince: and yet 'tis nothing but his hand that holds you from falling into the fire every moment: 'tis to be ascribed to nothing else, that you did not go to hell the last night; that you were suffer'd to awake again in this world, after you closed your eyes to sleep.[9]

This sermon is still famous as an example of the "revival preaching" of the First Great Awakening. Notably, Edwards preached it in 1741, half a decade after his preaching sparked a rash of suicides and suicidal ideations among his congregation in Northampton, Massachusetts. One of the suicides was Edwards's own uncle, Joseph Hawley II, and this did give Edwards pause. He reflected in his "A Faithful Narrative of the Surprising Work of God" (1736) that Hawley had been "a gentleman of more than common understanding, of strict morals, religious in his behavior, and a useful and honorable person."[10] Edwards goes on to explain that Hawley, whose family was prone to depression, was for some reason discouraged and "exceedingly concerned about the state of his soul. . . . The devil took the advantage, and drove him into despairing thoughts," until he could not sleep and finally slit his own throat. Edwards marvels at this phenomenon:

> The news of this extraordinarily affected the minds of people here, and struck them as it were with astonishment. After this, multitudes in this and other towns seemed to have it strongly suggested to them, and pressed upon them, to do as this person had done. And many who seemed to be under no melancholy, some pious persons who had no special darkness or doubts about the goodness of their state—nor were under any special trouble or concern of mind about any thing spiritual or temporal— had it urged upon them as if somebody had spoke to them, *Cut your throat, now is a good opportunity. Now! now!* So that they were obliged to fight with all their might to resist it, and yet no reason suggested to them why they should do it.

No reason suggested it to these pious people, except perhaps the persistent message that they were loathsome to God, and also unnecessary, and that they were somehow falling short of glorifying and enjoying him. This is Edwards's ministry in his own words.

Edwards was also an enslaver of human beings; and despite his genius and renown, he was fired from his longtime pulpit (by a 90 percent vote of the congregation) for being too rigid and exclusionary about membership and sacraments. The controversy was fueled by his efforts to control which books his parishioners read. Lest this seem *ad hominem*—we are interested in the man, because we are interested in the ways that people see God.

I have not dug up Edwards in order to bury him. I think he was on to something. The tension between his royalist rhetoric and the fact that he helped to inspire the American Revolution may offer a parallel to what's happening here: He would have despised the present book, but he also helped to inspire it.

Edwards ends up being a microcosm of much biblical interpretation since: He channeled the incredible power of the Bible, but because his understanding of divine love was skewed, the trajectory of his theology and ministry now looks far off target.

What if Edwards had taken his own idea more seriously, that everything exists because it was in God's nature to create more life and love? What if we described such a God in personal rather than impersonal terms? After all, despite all of his proof-texting, Edwards in this case overlooked the central, confessional fact that God is consistently portrayed in personal terms in the Bible—as a loving Father, and as a Son who wept and died for humankind. In light of this, we should ask: What kind of *person* would be experienced as a radiating sun—not in their outward garb like a gilded Sun King, but in their actual personhood?

Here, in fact—finally—we seem to learn something from the early chapters of Genesis about the reason for creation, because we are told what God thought of the development: He was delighted. All of the creation is good, in God's sight: The light is good (Gen 1:4); the land and water are good (1:10); the heavenly lights are good (1:18); the sea creatures are good (1:21); and the land animals are good (1:25). And finally, after creating humans as a kind of capstone, "God saw *everything* that he had made, and—*hinneh!*—it was *very good*" (1:31).[11]

A brief aside about that Hebrew word *hinneh,* which I have left untranslated: In the old King James English, it is typically rendered "Behold!" And that's actually closer to the sense of it than the NRSV's "indeed." It is an exclamation, like *hey!,* that serves to call attention to something. And so it expresses a bit of God's enthusiasm, and also invites the reader, who is still living in the midst of this creation, to look around and join God in appreciating its wonders.

No reader will miss the symphony of goodness in Genesis 1, but the last statement ("very good") is even stronger and more effusive than I had realized until recently. This is one of the only cases in the Bible where anything is called "*very* good" (in Hebrew, *tov me'od*).[12] It was surprising to me, as a longtime teacher of Hebrew who frequently calls student work *tov me'od,* that the phrase is not more common. It stands out.

The storytelling of the book of Genesis is notoriously understated, to the point of being reticent. Much is left unsaid, and what is said is often sketched with just a few words. The fact that we meet God for the first time in this wave of appreciation and pleasure in creation speaks loudly about God's character. There might have been nothing, but instead there was something—more life, more to love—and he reacts to it with extraordinary joy.

At each step of the creation in Genesis 1, God speaks things into existence. But when he sees that each thing is good, or very good, he does not say so out loud. We might imagine him as an elder figure surveying the world with a gleam in his eye. (Presumably he had already been around for what would seem to us an eternity, before anything else existed; he is elsewhere called the "Ancient of days" [Dan 7:9].[13])

Instead of Edwards's solitary Sun King, the figures whom this picture of God reminds me of are Sarah and Abraham. They were the progenitors of the entire family of Israel, the ones from whom life and the divine plan proceeded. And their reaction to this news, in both cases, was to laugh (Gen 17:17, 18:12)—in disbelief of their own fertility and blessedness, yes, but seemingly also out of simple joy.

The same joy is on display in another biblical account of parenthood, when Isaiah imagines Jerusalem restored after the exile as a mother surprised by new life. The restored children are imagined jostling for space in the land:

> Then you [Jerusalem] will say in your heart,
>   "Who has borne me these?
> I was bereaved and barren,
>   exiled and put away—
>   so who has reared these?
> I was left all alone!—
>   where then have these come from?" (Isa 49:21)

Abraham and Sarah didn't need to have a child, except that it was God's plan. Why was it God's plan? Because that's who God is. In the same way, creation seems a bit unnecessary, except that it's who God is. This widening of God's sphere of grace is not only demonstrated by the otherwise inexplicable selection of this random Mesopotamian guy Abram; it is also encoded in the invisible DNA of God's universe in ways that scripture itself can only hint at.

The authors of the Bible sense God's joy at creation but exercise appropriate restraint in the presence of this holy mystery. Some things that one cannot speak are best approached as suggestive questions: "what are human beings that you are mindful of them, / mortals that you care for them?" (Ps 8:4). What did we do to deserve the glories of the natural world or the pleasure of a baby's smile? Not a thing. Not a thing.

The widening of God's love and mercy is arguably the reason that anything exists at all. But "logical necessity" is a cold way to calculate it. The rest of this book surveys the rest of the Bible to see whether it tells the story of a God who would laugh with pleasure at the extension of his love to new things. Because worshipers are prone to imitate their image of God as an almost subconscious reflex, this will have implications for the way that we, too, meet creation, including humankind.

A gay acquaintance tells the story of when he was first coming to grips with his sexuality as a grade-schooler, and his Sunday school teacher gave the class a coloring sheet with a little messy kid on it and the words, "God don't make no junk." Most of the sheets probably wound up in the trash fairly soon, but he hid his under his bed. He would take it out occasionally, when he needed a reminder that he had been created as he was, and he's never forgotten it. No one forgets when the church manifests the love and joy that God feels toward creation; nor do they forget when it doesn't.

2

Mercy for God's People

Almost immediately after the divine explosion of joy in creation, the story takes a series of darker turns. Eve and Adam are caught in the tension between being made in the image of God and being subject to him. Tempted by one of the other creatures God created, they eat from the tree of knowledge. God expels them from Eden and blocks the way back with supernatural guardians and a flaming sword.

Yet we see here the emergence of a God who is already changing his mind in response to the reality of the world he has created, and especially to humankind.

The first indications of this are very subtle, and are easily overlooked; they seem to fall into unspoken seams in the story. In Genesis 2:17, God warns the humans: "You shall not eat from the tree of the knowledge of good and evil, for in the day that you eat of it you shall die."[1] Of course, they go on to do just that. And yet, they do not die on that day.

Interpreters have long struggled with this problem of the contrast between God's warning—which Eve repeats in Genesis 3:3—and the outcome. Some interpreters argue that "day" meant something different in this primeval period, as attested by the seven "days" of creation. Many earlier interpreters alluded to Psalm 90:4 ("For a thousand years in your sight / are like yesterday") to argue that Adam's death at 930 years of age (Gen 5:5) was in fact only a day from God's perspective.[2]

Others say that what God meant was, "On that day you will *begin* to die." In their view, humankind would have been immortal but at this point became subject to death. But in that case, is God concerned about a *restoration* of immortality when he worries that humankind "might reach out its hand and take also from the tree of life, and eat, and live forever" (Gen 3:22)?[3] The text does not say so.

No definitive answer is forthcoming from the text. It is characteristic of archetypal tales to invite conversation about what they mean, and to mean more than they say. In light of who God actually seems to be in these stories of primeval times, the efforts of interpreters to make God's response consistent with his warning may be special pleading. Perhaps God has simply changed his mind and shown mercy to Adam and Eve.

God's final action toward them before sending them out from Eden hints in this direction; it is surprisingly tender and poignant: "the Lord God made garments of skins for the man and for his wife, and clothed them" (Gen 3:21). God is not above acting as a seamstress for these humans who have just ignored his command. Like a parent sending his growing children off to their first day of school, he wants to help them be prepared.

The story of the garden of Eden is only the first in a sequence of episodes in which God's judgment on humans is softened by mercy. The next one comes right on its heels, in the story of Cain and Abel. Cain, seemingly provoked by God's preference for his brother, kills him—and he too is driven away from the arable land to wander the earth: God tells Cain that the ground "will no longer yield to you its strength," and so he "will be a fugitive and a wanderer on the earth" (Gen 4:12).

This time the psychological shadings of the divine-human interaction are filled in slightly more: God perceives Cain's anger and warns him, "sin is lurking at the door; its desire is for you, but you must master it" (Gen 4:7). And then when Cain commits murder anyway, God seems genuinely dismayed: "now you are cursed from the ground, which has opened its mouth to receive your brother's blood from your hand" (4:11). This phrasing, "cursed *from the ground*" is unique in Biblical Hebrew. In conjunction with the parallel phrase "blood *from your hand,*" it seems to emphasize that the curse is less something issued by God and more of a natural process of cause and effect—like being unable to drink from a well that one has polluted.

A principle is enunciated about divine justice in cases of bloodshed just a few chapters later, in Genesis 9:6:

> Whoever sheds the blood of a human,
> by a human shall that person's blood be shed;
> for in his own image
> God made humankind.

This principle is later fleshed out more fully in the Torah as talionic (i.e., retributive) justice: As Exodus 21:23–25 says, "If any harm follows, then you shall give life for life, eye for eye, tooth for tooth, hand for hand, foot for foot, burn for burn, wound for wound, stripe for stripe." Deuteronomy 19:21 prefaces this same list with the exhortation, "Show no pity."

At many levels of society, from capital punishment to gang warfare, this logic has consistently seemed intuitive to humankind. Furthermore, God has every reason to enact this sort of justice against Cain in Genesis 4: Cain has been specifically admonished to show self-control, and has not done so. He laments: "I shall be a fugitive and a wanderer on the earth, and anyone who meets me may kill me" (Gen 4:14). It is a stunning bit of hypocrisy from a murderer, and yet God again is willing to soften the blow of judgment. In contrast to Deuteronomy's admonition, he *does* show pity. Cain cries out: "My punishment is greater than I can bear!" (4:13). God doesn't completely reverse himself, but he does address Cain's fears. He puts a mark on Cain, "so that no one who came upon him would kill him" (4:15). Here again, God seems willing to change his mind and reconsider his judgments, out of mercy.

This trend continues with the account of the flood—but before we come to that, we might note that the flood itself is the result of a different sort of change of mind.

We met the Hebrew verb *nacham* in the Introduction, in the story of God changing his mind about Saul's kingship. The first time that verb appears is in Genesis 6:6–7: "And *the LORD was sorry* that he had made humankind on the earth, and it grieved him to his heart. So the LORD said, 'I will blot out from the earth the human beings I have created—people together with animals and creeping things and birds of the air, *for I am sorry that I have made them.*"[4] *Nacham* has two primary meanings: It can refer to a change of mind and to a feeling of regret. Both of those are implied here: God not only regrets creating humankind, but he has also had a change of mind and decided to wipe them out. After the auspicious start to creation, things have not worked out the way they were supposed to. The whole thing has been a mistake.

We are meant to take seriously the assessment of God that precedes this judgment: "The LORD saw that the wickedness of humankind was great in the earth, and that every inclination of the thoughts of their hearts was only evil continually" (Gen 6:5). The good that he intended has led instead to evil.

It is significant that God destroys by undoing the divisions between dry and wet that he had made in creation. In Genesis 1:7–10, before there could be vegetation and animal life, it was necessary for God to set limits on the watery chaos of the uncreated world:

> So God made the dome and separated the waters that were under the dome from the waters that were above the dome. And it was so. God called the dome Sky. And there was evening and there was morning, the second day.
>
> And God said, "Let the waters under the sky be gathered together into one place, and let the dry land appear." And it was so. God called the dry land Earth, and the waters that were gathered together he called Seas. And God saw that it was good.

The flood, then, is the retraction of these barriers that had made life possible: "the fountains of the great deep burst forth, and the windows of the heavens were opened" (Gen 7:11).

There is no reason anything had to exist in the first place, and so God destroys not as a new act, but simply by taking away the gifts of creation that he had previously given. This time, instead of a joyful matriarch, God is like an angry mother who says to her children, "I made you, and I can unmake you."

Of course, the story does not end with this change of mind, or with the uncreation of the divine order. After flooding the earth, God has yet another change of mind, though this one is not marked by the same verb. He smells the "pleasing odor" of Noah's sacrifices. Therefore, "the LORD said in his heart, 'I will never again curse the ground because of humankind, for the inclination of the human heart is evil from youth;

nor will I ever again destroy every living creature as I have done'" (Gen 8:21). The cries of all the living things that died in the flood are omitted from the story, but presumably God decides it was too much.

This is a story about the hearts of people and the heart of God: The hearts of humans are wicked (Gen 6:5), which grieves the Lord to his heart (6:6), and he declares his intention to blot them out; but in the end the heart of God is changed from grief to mercy. Although it is Noah's sacrifice that sparks the change, the reason given is a surprising one: "I will never again curse the ground because of humankind, because the inclination of the human heart is evil from youth" (8:21). Life, God decides, has to go on:

> As long as the earth endures,
> > seedtime and harvest, cold and heat,
> summer and winter, day and night
> > shall not cease. (8:22)

God's purposed flourishing for the world will not be stopped by the simple fact that people are as they are. God again relents from righteous wrath and shows mercy.

The story of the creation of the world and its people in the beginning of Genesis is followed by the story of the creation of the people of Israel in the rest of the book. Abraham is called from Ur—and as was the case in the creation account of Genesis 1, no reason is given. Abraham later shows faith and merit, but he is chosen by grace.

In Genesis, the creation of the people Israel is similar to the creation of the world and the creation of humanity. The chosen people faces uncreation while wandering in the wilderness just as the world is threatened with uncreation in the flood account and Adam and Eve face uncreation in the garden ("out of [the ground] you were taken; / . . . and to dust you shall return" [Gen 3:19]).

The family (if we can still speak of it that way) goes through a lot before they ever reach the wilderness. Abraham encounters God's wrath in the destruction of Sodom and Gomorrah, and he avoids being swept away with it, but it worries him. In their exchange in Genesis 18:22–33, both Abraham and God come out looking just; God grants Abraham that even ten righteous souls would be enough to spare the whole city. The answer to Abraham's question, "Shall not the Judge of all the earth do what is just?" (Gen 18:25), appears to be *yes*.

As Genesis goes on, Abraham's grandchildren and great-grandchildren are driven by a Canaanite famine to Egypt, where they find that they are not the first foreigners to immigrate there for better opportunities. With some support from friendly politicians, they seem to flourish quite nicely.

After some time, though, Egyptian labor policy shifts, and the situation becomes untenable. With the bicultural Moses as a consultant, the Israelites decide to leave—but they find that it is difficult to go home again. The descendants of Abraham, Isaac, and Jacob remember Canaan as home, and it is advertised as "promised," but it's also full of imposing people who take up a lot of space and seem unlikely to make room for the returnees (Num 13:31–33).

The events that surrounded their departure (Exod 12–15) make it difficult to imagine patching things up with the Egyptian authorities, but conditions in the desert are difficult enough to prompt an overwhelming outcry against Moses and his chief of staff, Aaron: "Would that we had died in the land of Egypt! Or would that we had died in this wilderness!" (Num 14:2). The people accuse God of bringing them out of slavery only in order to be raped and killed, and they immediately form an

Executive Subcommittee on Returning to Egypt (14:3–4). When Joshua and Caleb, leaders of the delegation who had gone to see the land, try to emphasize that *really it's very nice*, the rest of the people threaten to stone them (14:7–10).

Moses hurriedly goes to consult in private with God, who has *just about had it up to here*. God says, *I can't even . . . I'm going to kill them all and start over*. His actual words again point to a kind of poetic justice: "I will strike them with pestilence and disinherit them" (Num 14:12). This is exactly what he had done to free them (strike Egypt with plagues; Exod 5:3, 9:3) and what he had promised to do in order to make room in the land (disinherit the Canaanites; Exod 34:24, etc.). Now these punishments could be turned against God's own people.

God has thought this through, however, and has concluded that it would be helpful to have Moses on board with this plan. No doubt God could start completely from scratch, but he alone knows exactly how time-consuming it is to do so. And who knows whether things would go any better if he started over? So he says to Moses, "I will make of you a nation greater and mightier than they" (Num 14:12).

Many corporate executives have been won over by this same kind of offer of security and glory and have sold out the people who work for them, so it's to Moses's credit that he says no. Instead, like Abraham before him, he acts as a kind of conscience for God himself: He reminds God of who he is supposed to be:

> "If you kill this people all at one time, then the nations who have heard about you will say, 'It is because Yahweh was not able to bring this people into the land he swore to give them that he has slaughtered them in the wilderness.' And now, therefore,

let the power of Yahweh be great in the way that you
promised when you spoke, saying,

> 'Yahweh is slow to anger,
> and abounding in steadfast love,
> forgiving iniquity and transgression,
> but by no means clearing the guilty,
> visiting the iniquity of the parents
> upon the children
> to the third and the fourth generation.'

"Forgive the iniquity of this people according to
the greatness of your steadfast love, just as you have
pardoned this people, from Egypt even until now."
(Num 14:15–19)

Through most of this book we use "the LORD" for the divine
name (Hebrew *Yhwh*).[5] I break with that style (and the NRSV)
here partly because this story is *about God's name,* in the sense
of God's reputation. And as noted in the previous chapter, the
image of God as a "lord" or king brings with it cultural and
emotional baggage. Sometimes the connotations of "LORD" fit
the context very well, but here the text paints a different portrait of God.

This is in fact the second time that God has intended to
kill the people and offered to start over with Moses. The first
was in Exodus 32, in the episode of the golden calf; that first
time, Moses did not appeal to the "slow to anger" formula. Now,
in Numbers 14, he seems to be catching on about who God is.
Indeed, Moses is quoting God's own words back to him here.
God declared these same words to Moses in Exodus 34:5–7, and
the theological affirmation is somehow part and parcel of God's
declaration of his own name. At that point, Moses has just taken

up the new stone tablets, replacing the ones he had broken in frustration, and he says to God: "O LORD, I pray . . . go with us. Although this is a stiff-necked people, pardon our iniquity and our sin, and take us for your inheritance" (Exod 34:9). And God does—he shows mercy and reaffirms the covenant.

And now, in the wake of this latest example of stiff-necked-ness in Numbers 14, Moses reminds God of who he has declared himself to be and asks him to do it again.

And God does forgive (Num 14:20–21). Or, better to say: He compromises, yet again (14:22–25). As in the other stories we've looked at so far, God's heart is softened, and he doesn't follow through on his own plans.

As with Adam and Eve and the garden, and Cain and the fertile land, there is still a cost to the people: The entire older generation will not enter the promised land (Num 14:22–23), not even Moses himself (Deut 1:34–37). In fact, Moses has essentially invited this outcome. The opening sentence of his plea is specific: "If you kill this people *all at one time* . . ." (Num 14:15). So instead of smiting them in a single stroke, God lets them die off slowly, naturally, in the wilderness. As with a genie in a lamp, be careful what you ask for.

For all the talk of sin and destruction, there is a touch of dark humor in these stories about God trying to come to terms with the people he has created. Interpreters sometimes speak of the portrait of God in certain strands of the Torah as a naïve phase of religion that soon passed away, as monotheism developed. In these early chapters, God is anthropomorphic. He walks around in the garden, sews animal skins to make clothing, and has to come down from the heavens to see what the humans are getting up to (Gen 11:5, 18:21). He argues with his middle managers such as Abraham and Moses. And he seems to keep making blunders: Where did that serpent come from? Why couldn't God just have smiled and enjoyed Cain's vegan cuisine? The portrait is quite a distance from that of the transcendent emperor in Isaiah 66:1 ("Heaven is my throne / and the earth is my footstool") or Daniel 7:9–10 (where fire streams from his throne and multitudes attend him).

Upon rereading these stories, I find myself less interested in their place in the history of religion and more interested in the perspective of their authors. These stories are, at bottom, characterized by a good-natured, if weary, sense of humor about humanity, and about God's relationship to us. *We are nothing but trouble,* say the authors, *but God learns this and decides to stick with us anyway.*

A couple of basic themes emerge from the stories. The first is that God's presence is meant to be a blessing for humans. The earth was created good; Adam and Eve—and by extension all of us—were meant to live in the garden; Cain was meant to cultivate the land; and the people were meant to enter the promised land. So there is a tragedy in God's sending humanity from the garden and denying most of the people entry into the land. In Cain's case, the blessing of the divine presence is made explicit: He is not merely sent away from the arable land; he also goes "away from the presence of the LORD" (Gen 4:16).

In these early stories, God's blessing may appear localized— to the garden, to the land, and so forth—so that it seems possible to be pushed from the regions of blessedness into outer orbits where the divine presence is attenuated. But even those pushed away go out protected, with a mark or a garment. Even a murderer is not entirely abandoned. The earth sits under a rainbow, as a sign of peace (Gen 9:8–17). Hagar is sent away by Abraham even after bearing him his first child, but God never loses sight of her; and her son Ishmael is excluded from the covenant, but "God was with the boy," and makes of him, too, a great nation (Gen 17:20; 21:17–20).[6] As for the chosen people, their story goes on despite their stubbornness.

The second theme is God's propensity to relent from punishment, to show mercy even at the cost of changing his mind and bending his principles of justice. Although these stories are told as if God is "learning on the job," the portrait they create is consistent with a recurring image of God throughout the Bible. Even where judgment seems to narrow the scope of blessing, there are signs of the wideness of God's mercy. God's plan for the world is broader than some think.

3

Widening Justice

The story of Zelophehad's daughters begins with counting people and ends by rethinking which people count. It reveals that God responds to the agency of humans, and also that biblical laws and customs change.

In the background of the story is a census taken by Moses in Numbers 26. The occasion for counting the people was the passing of the generation of Moses and Aaron, which had been forbidden to enter the land. Like a modern census, this one had practical repercussions. The Lord lays these out for Moses: "To these the land shall be apportioned for inheritance according to the number of names. To a large tribe you shall give a large inheritance, and to a small tribe you shall give a small inheritance; every tribe shall be given its inheritance according to its enrollment" (Num 26:53–54).

The text tells us how many people were counted in each of the twelve tribes; their numbers add up to 601,730 Israelites. And for each of the twelve tribes it lists two or three descendants as leaders of clans—with one exception: For the tribe of Manasseh, the genealogy goes *seven* generations deep, just to get to this point: "Now Zelophehad son of Hepher had no sons, only daughters, and the names of the daughters of Zelophehad were Mahlah, Noah, Hoglah, Milcah, and Tirzah" (Num 26:33).

Not a lot of people read the Bible's genealogies, but if you're reading this whole passage, this stands out as unusual. The authors of the Bible did not tend to relate extra details for no reason. In the next chapter, we find out the reason. After Moses finishes the census,

> the daughters of Zelophehad came forward. Zelo-
> phehad was son of Hepher son of Gilead son of
> Machir son of Manasseh son of Joseph, a member
> of the Manassite clans. The names of his daughters
> were Mahlah, Noah, Hoglah, Milcah, and Tirzah.
> They stood before Moses, Eleazar the priest, the
> leaders, and all the congregation, at the entrance of
> the tent of meeting . . . (Num 27:1–3)

They haven't even started talking yet, but the story already tells us a lot about them. First of all, they have names, which have already been mentioned twice in just a few verses. When you think of all the significant women in the Bible who are not given names (the wise woman of Abel-Beth-Maacah in 2 Sam 20, the prophetess of Isa 8:3, the Samaritan woman at the well in John 4, or the woman at Bethany who anointed Jesus "for burial" in Mark 14:3–9) and/or are identified only in terms of male characters (like Jephthah's daughter in Judg 11), that's something. Naming is a powerful thing in the Old Testament; it carries the senses of reputation and ownership, and Hebrew names carry messages. The names of Zelophehad's daughters suggest vigor and joy: Milcah, "Queen"; Mahlah, "Dancer"; Hoglah, "Partridge"; Tirzah, "She is pleasant." It's worth saying their names, and the Bible does so repeatedly (they are given again in Num 36:11 and Josh 17:3).

Second, the daughters "came forward," or as some trans-lations have it, "drew near." Today, a business executive might say they *leaned in*—and not in any ordinary way. They stood up before Moses and the high priest and the entire people. You have to imagine that the census was a laborious process, count-ing hundreds of thousands of people, and surely Moses and Eleazar were heading for the exit of the tent of meeting and looking forward to a break.

Now, there were supposed to be processes for these sorts of things. In the early days of the people, Moses was wearing himself out hearing people's concerns all day, until his father-in-law, Jethro, scolded him and told him to appoint judges, who would bring only the difficult and important cases to him (Exod 18:13–23). One did not just knock on Moses's tent flap.

Yet the daughters have created a very public scene. The author tells the reader vanishingly little about the details—which, as Katharine Sakenfeld has pointed out, invites readers to use their imaginations:

> [O]ne may imagine the responses of the onlookers (shock, amazement, incredulity) and play with the adjectives they may have whispered to one another concerning these women—foolhardy, daring, asser-tive (aggressive), uppity. . . . Did someone perhaps whisper more softly "justified," even before Moses' response? The text is equally silent concerning the women's own feelings as they came to stand before Moses. Were they frightened or self-confident, clear or tentative about their decision to speak?[1]

However we imagine the scene, there must have been tension in the air.

※

The women have a request—but before we come to it, notice that there is never a moment in any of the stories about them when one of them acts apart from the others. This makes them less colorful characters than, say, Moses, Aaron, and Miriam, who are supposed to be on the same team but often were not on the same page (Num 12). But it does portray them as united in a sisterhood seeking justice. They have each other's backs.

They say: "Our father died in the wilderness; he was not among the company of those who gathered themselves together against the LORD in the company of Korah, but died for his own sin" (Num 27:3).

This probably doesn't sound like a great way to begin a request, so we should pause here briefly to review the fact that Numbers is a bit of a disaster for the people. One reason they keep having to count the people in the book is that God keeps killing them off by the hundreds and thousands. Mahlah, Noah, Hoglah, Milcah, and Tirzah are saying that their dad was just another regular whiner who was cursed by God to die in the wilderness (Num 14:26–33). He paid the price, and he could have done worse: In Numbers 16, a man named Korah leads a populist uprising against Moses and Aaron, and the underworld literally swallows him up along with his followers (16:31–35). So, at least Zelophehad wasn't with him.

The sisters go on about their father: "and he had no sons. Why should the name of our father be taken away from his clan because he had no son? Give to us a possession among our father's brothers" (Num 27:3–4).

Now we come to the problem: Zelophehad had no male heir. In ancient Israel, inheritance worked on a patrilineal system: Property was passed from father to son. This was meant to keep the land within the family and within the tribe, and so its goals were practical, even noble: In an agrarian economy, this system was meant to ensure that everyone had enough land to support them. But now Zelophehad's daughters have to ask that their family land not be taken from them just because they're women.

The importance of the inheritance of the firstborn is emphasized in Deuteronomy 21:15–17, which says that a father must give his firstborn son a double share of his estate, even if he dislikes that son and favors another one. The rule that it has to be a son rather than a daughter is not recorded in the biblical law as it has come down to us. That's probably because it was taken for granted. There are numerous examples of laws and customs that the Old Testament takes for granted that are not preserved in the Mosaic law.[2]

There is an interesting discrepancy in ancient versions of the Bible: Some say that the daughters used a plural imperative verb when they said, "*Give* to us a possession." This is what we would expect since they're speaking to at least Moses and Eleazar, and perhaps to the whole assembly. But the most authoritative Hebrew text presents it as a singular imperative verb, as if they were speaking directly to Moses . . . or even to God, as if in prayer?

The most important part of the sisters' story, to me, is what Moses says: nothing. We are prone to miss his silence, because it's in the gap between verses 4 and 5. A bit like Abraham, who says nothing when told to leave his homeland (Gen 12) or to sacrifice his son (Gen 22), Moses just listens—first to the sisters, and then to God: "Moses brought their case before the LORD" (Num 27:5).

There is no hemming and hawing. He does not say, "That's not the way we do things." He goes directly to the Lord.

We are told in Exodus that "the LORD used to speak to

Moses face to face, as one speaks to a friend" (Exod 33:11), and Numbers reminds us of that tradition (Num 12:8, 14:14). There is also a contrasting tradition that Moses was *not* allowed to see God's face (Exod 33:20–23). These traditions might be harmonized, however. Arguably, knowing God face-to-face doesn't mean seeing God's face, but rather being willing and able to bear the encounter with the living God, even and especially in uncertain situations.

God's response to Moses doesn't mince words: "The daughters of Zelophehad are right in what they are saying; you shall certainly give them land as an inheritance among their father's brothers! You shall pass their father's inheritance on to them" (Num 27:7).[3]

The only characters in this story who speak are the daughters and God. And when God speaks, he doesn't just render a decision in their favor: He does so emphatically, and he affirms their righteousness in raising the issue.

What if powerful people more often affirmed their subordinates when they challenged unrighteous aspects of systems? This scene has a parallel in the last chapter of the book of Job. After Job's long-winded friends have spent many chapters haranguing him with pious-sounding speeches that blame him and try to explain away his suffering, God finally weighs in, and he says to the friends: "My wrath is kindled against you . . . for you have not spoken of me what is right, as my servant Job has done" (Job 42:7, 8). And this after Job has spent most of the book challenging God and his friends' seemingly traditional ideas.

God can handle being challenged. Both of these stories reflect that challenging God and tradition can be one of the most profound forms of piety. A God who cannot be challenged is too small to be the God described in the Bible.

Humans, however, really like to put God in a box.[4] We

have already seen how Samuel, in his frustration at the failure
of the king he anointed, misrepresents God by saying that God
does not change his mind. Thankfully, Moses is not as presumptuous as Job's friends or Samuel. He seems to sense that God
might have something new to say.

The Lord is not done after having ruled in favor of the
daughters. He goes on to codify the new judgment as law:

> "You shall also say to the Israelites, 'If a man dies,
> and has no son, then you shall pass his inheritance
> on to his daughter. If he has no daughter, then you
> shall give his inheritance to his brothers. If he has
> no brothers, then you shall give his inheritance to
> his father's brothers. And if his father has no broth-
> ers, then you shall give his inheritance to the near-
> est kinsman of his clan, and he shall possess it. It
> shall be for the Israelites a statute and ordinance.'"
> (Num 27:8–11)

Again, not only does God respond to the agency of humankind, but we can see that *biblical laws and customs change.*

This is not news, of course. The story of Zelophehad's
daughters is only one example of changes in laws within the Old
Testament. There are three major collections of laws in the Torah:
the Book of the Covenant (Exod 20:22–23:33), the Priestly Code
(Lev 1–26), and the Deuteronomic Code (Deut 4:44–28:68).
Not only do these cover different topics, but they also differ
significantly from each other when discussing the same topics.
For example, Exodus 20:24 allows sacrifice on any altar where
the Lord's name is remembered, but Deuteronomy 12:13–14 warns
against sacrificing just anywhere and specifies that it must happen only at one location.[5]

These are not special cases! There are many, many places where Old Testament laws on the same topic in different collections disagree with each other. These differences are one of the main reasons that the traditional Jewish Oral Torah exists: The Mishnah and Talmud are largely discussions about and around different ways to interpret disagreements and omissions in the Torah. And among these Jewish sages, who knew the Hebrew Bible better than anyone, multiple opinions are preserved. Today, these conversations go on, and a modern scholarly subfield ("inner-biblical legal exegesis") analyzes the differences from an historical standpoint.

All this is to say, in a different way, that biblical laws were not unchanging, nor can they easily resolve ethical questions. They present us with complex interpretive dilemmas for real life and invite us to wrestle with the meaning of the laws and stories of the Torah (what the Jewish sages would call *halakhah*).

The story of Zelophehad's daughters suggests that the diversity and disagreements within the biblical laws are not an accident or an embarrassing error caught by pesky scholars. This story shows God himself taking part in reinterpreting and outright revising existing practices. In the Bible, God seems less troubled by change than his spokesmen are. This should not be surprising, since God, incarnate in Jesus, continued to reinterpret the law in the New Testament. (More on that later.)

This story is about the system when it works right: People bring real concerns for theological considerations, and they discern the will of God. When justice systems work, those who are unfairly disadvantaged are able to speak up. When justice systems work, the people in positions of authority listen.

The ability to hear the cries of the oppressed is a quintessential attribute of the God of Israel, who from the beginning of the nation's story heard his people crying out under oppression (Exod 2:24, etc.) and took notice of them (2:25). It's also one of the most straightforward opportunities for humans to imitate God, as Moses did. When God first appears to Moses, in the burning bush, Moses's behavior suggests his aptitude for the mission. He notices it and says, "I must turn aside" (3:3). He notices things, much as God does. He goes out of his way.

When people stand up today to challenge biblical statutes and ordinances, the best biblical response is to ask whether they are correct. That was the way of Moses with the daughters of Zelophehad, and the principle that Jesus applied to the law: "The Sabbath was made for humankind and not humankind for the Sabbath" (Mark 2:27). This is what it means, quite literally, to be *humanitarian*. God is more humanitarian than some people give him credit for being.

There is a tension in the story between the daughters' own interests and the *reasons* that they get what they want. This is often the case in legal proceedings, but some readers have argued that this story is not really liberating. They point out that the women make their case in terms of their father's name. They point out that it is decided not because of any sense of justice for women, but because of the overriding concern for preserving each tribe's land. (The extended law that is given in Num 27:9–11 shows that those concerns are important.) Although the protagonists are women, some readers object that the underlying interests are all about men and their land. These are not the arguments of conservatives, but of progressives for whom the Bible is not progressive enough.[6]

It is good to notice these things, and to express these reservations. Justice is not fully achieved within the scope of the story, and it is appropriate that the dissatisfactions that impelled the daughters still press us further today. But it is important for both traditionalists and progressives to appreciate the work of these women. As Dennis Olson has written:

> They seek change by appealing to the basic values of the tradition that may override other less important customs of that same tradition. . . . They may provide encouragement and direction for those in our own time concerned about issues of justice and gender. These five women teach us to dig deeply and argue persuasively from within a shared biblical tradition if we would overturn old customs and create new possibilities in the social and economic relationships between women and men. These women are models of boldness fueled by hope, models of advocacy fueled by a concern for the larger community, and models of faithfulness fueled by a dynamic relationship with their tradition and with their God.[7]

History continues to teach us that the work is ongoing. Under the pressures of history, justice does not always come naturally to the human heart, and so one generation forgets what the previous one learned. As Sakenfeld notes, those who are engaged in struggle all too often experience "'two steps forward, one step back,' with those in authority counting the step back as a step ahead."[8]

The Bible even portrays this challenge: Later in the story, after the conquest of the land under Joshua, the land is apportioned, and Mahlah, Noah, Hoglah, Milcah, and Tirzah come before Eleazar and Joshua, and they remind them, "The LORD commanded Moses to give us an inheritance along with our male kin" (Josh 17:4). And so it is done for them. Eleazar and

Joshua raise no more objection than Moses did, but apparently
the women did have to insist *again*. They had to remind the
male leadership of God's promise.

This process of simply holding onto the promises is surely
exhausting, and could even try one's faith. Where did Mahlah,
Noah, Hoglah, Milcah, and Tirzah get the strength? That's a
question that even ancient Jewish interpreters asked themselves.
It may surprise some readers that talmudic literature was even
more interested in the gender aspects of this story than the
biblical author, and more lavish in its praise of the women. In
one exchange, Rabbi Nathan says (probably with a smirk): "The
power of women is greater than the power of men. Men say,
'Let us appoint a head and return to Egypt' (Num 14:4), but
women say, 'Give us a portion among our father's brothers.'"[9]

The passage continues with a midrash on the women and
their extraordinary faith: "They said, 'God's mercy is not like
that of flesh and blood. The latter's mercy is for the males more
than for the females, but He who spoke and the world came
into being is not that way. His mercy is for males and females.'"
Paul seems also to have understood this when he wrote, "there
is no longer male and female; for all of you are one in Christ
Jesus" (Gal 3:28), but clearly he still had to make the case in his
time. In our time, new groups are asking for God's mercy and
asking to be accepted.

There are many ways to be faithful, but this is one of the
most important: to know that God listens, cares, and responds;
to know that God is just and is open to widening his justice
and mercy; and to act on that knowledge despite the resistance
that the world can throw up. When those who speak for God do
not understand God clearly—like Job's friends—it is an act of
faith to persist in questioning and challenging. Although conservative religious leaders today may act as if challenges are
threats to the community, to its faith, and even to God Himself,

ironically it is just such challenges that enable the church to
endure. It is a prophetic role to hear when God says:

Do not remember the former things,
        or consider the things of old.
Look! I'm doing a new thing;
        now it springs forth; do you not perceive it? (Isa 43:18–19)[10]

4

"I Gave Them Statutes That Were Not Good"

The last chapter looked at ways in which God's laws might change and customs might be reconsidered. Perhaps the most challenging example of divine mutability occurs in the book of Ezekiel. It's a difficult one to discount, because it's described in God's own words by the prophet—and, as we saw in the case of Saul and Samuel, God's voice can carry more weight in the text than others.

Ezekiel issues a lengthy divine speech (Ezek 20:1–44) that recounts the people's history. He is writing from exile in Babylonia, having been taken away there with the first group of exiles in 597 BCE. Although the destruction of Jerusalem was still a few years away, many people were already suffering greatly, and the forces that eventually ended the Davidic monarchy and the status of Judah as an independent nation were already clear. So the divine speech is meant to recount the many problems and wrong turns that had led the people there.

In the midst of this speech, God says that because of the people's disobedience, "I gave them statutes that were not good and ordinances by which they could not live. I defiled them through their very gifts, in their offering up all their firstborn, in order that I might horrify them, so that they might know that I am the LORD" (Ezek 20:25–26).

The implication probably isn't immediately clear to those who don't live by the Mosaic law, but God's comment refers clearly to Exod 22:29b–30: "The firstborn of your sons you shall give to me. You shall do the same with your oxen and with your sheep: seven days it shall remain with its mother; on the eighth day you shall give it to me." And how did they give oxen and sheep to God? By blood sacrifice—as Exodus 22:31 makes clear with its reference to eating meat.

It is no less horrifying today than it was in Ezekiel's time to contemplate that child sacrifice was commanded or carried out, but there is ample evidence that it was. In Genesis, God tells Abraham, "Take your son, your only son Isaac, whom you love, and go to the land of Moriah, and offer him there as a burnt offering on one of the mountains that I shall show you" (Gen 22:2). And in Judges, Jephthah, having been inspired by the spirit of the Lord, vows to sacrifice the first living thing he meets upon his successful return home from battle (Judg 11:29–31), which turns out to be his daughter (11:34–40).

As the Jephthah story reflects, child sacrifice is said to have been practiced in moments of extreme crisis, like Agamemnon's sacrifice of Iphigenia during the Trojan War.[1] The clearest biblical example of this is King Mesha of Moab's sacrifice in 2 Kings 3:26–27: "When the king of Moab saw that the battle was going against him . . . he took his firstborn son who was to succeed him, and offered him as a burnt offering on the wall. And great wrath came upon Israel, so they withdrew from him and returned to their own land." This act may not have been viewed positively by the historian, but it was viewed as effective. Similarly, Micah 6:7 suggests that human sacrifice might be entertained in a case where even "thousands of rams" were not enough: "Shall I give my firstborn for my transgression, / the fruit of my body for the sin of my soul?"

In Ezekiel 20, God returns to the topic of child sacrifice later in the speech, using the same keyword, "gifts," for sacrifices, as in v. 26:

> Therefore say to the house of Israel, Thus says the Lord GOD: Will you defile yourselves after the manner of your ancestors and go astray after their detestable things? When you offer your gifts and make your children pass through the fire, you defile yourselves with all your idols to this day. And shall I be consulted by you, O house of Israel? As I live, says the Lord GOD, I will not be consulted by you. (Ezek 20:30–31)

We are meant to imagine Jerusalem in the midst of the series of international political crises that led to its destruction, grasping for any emergency measure that might be thought to help—child sacrifice included.

Ezekiel's reference to child sacrifice as "making children pass through fire" opens up a wider set of allusions to the practice. Various Israelite and Judahite kings are accused of making their children pass through fire (Ahaz in 2 Kgs 16:3; the rulers of Israel in 17:17; Manasseh in 21:6). Child sacrifice was closely associated with the (Ben-)Hinnom Valley, and specifically a cult site called Topheth, meaning "stove, oven."

Child sacrifice was portrayed by other biblical authors as originally a Canaanite practice associated with a deity called Molech (Lev 18:21–27; Deut 12:31; 2 Kgs 16:3, 21:2). There is indeed evidence for child sacrifice among ancient Syro-Palestinian peoples, most notably from the Phoenician colony in Carthage, where a large cemetery of children's remains has been excavated.[2] Such a large concentration of children's remains is exceedingly rare, however, so if child sacrifice were occasionally practiced elsewhere, such as in Israel and Judah, we would almost certainly not be able to tell from the archaeological record.

We have dwelt on the evidence for child sacrifice in the biblical world precisely because it is awful; because it is awful, we are prone to turn away from it and deny it, even when God Himself testifies to it.

We can also be clear that, in the end, the Bible bans child sacrifice. The prophets repeatedly condemned it (Jer 7:31–32; 19:5–6, 11; cf. 2:23, 3:24; Ezek 16:20–21; 20:25–26, 30–31; 23:36–39; and the aforementioned Mic 6:7–8 immediately advises against it). It is banned in the law codes as well (Lev 18:21, 20:3; Deut 12:30–31).

This took time, however. The commandment to sacrifice the firstborn sons in Exodus occurs in the Book of the Covenant, just after the revelation of the Decalogue to Moses on Mount Sinai. This section of Exodus is generally taken to be the oldest legal collection in the Bible. It has later been bracketed on both sides by laws clarifying that one should redeem (and not sacrifice) firstborn sons, as well as donkeys: "All that first opens the womb is mine, all your male livestock, the firstborn of cow and sheep. *But* the firstborn of a donkey you shall redeem with a lamb, or if you will not redeem it you shall break its neck. All the firstborn of your sons you shall redeem. *But* no one shall appear before me empty-handed" (Exod 34:19–20; cf. 13:12–13).[3] The passage starts with a restatement of the principle from Exod 22:29b–30, and the "but's" (which are often omitted in translations) are meaningful: The first one tells us that the old law is being augmented, and the second emphasizes yet again that everyone must offer sacrifice.

The end of the story of Abraham's binding and near-sacrifice of Isaac in Genesis 22 makes a very similar point. Abraham comes to the point of drawing his knife to slaughter his son, when suddenly an angel appears to stop him; he sees a ram caught in a thicket by its horns, which he is to sacrifice in Isaac's place. According to this story, the Lord does not actually want children sacrificed, but he does want worshipers who are *willing* to kill their children for him; the angel appears a second time and delivers this word: "By myself I have sworn, says the LORD: Because you have done this, and have not withheld your son, your only son, I will indeed bless you" (Gen 22:16–17).

This may not have been enough to discourage the practice of child sacrifice, in that other condemnations follow. It is also forbidden, along with various heterodox religious practices, in Deuteronomy 18:10: "No one shall be found among you who makes a son or daughter pass through fire, or who practices divination, or is a soothsayer, or an augur, or a sorcerer," etc. This is a passage universally taken to be much later than Exodus 22; it is part of the correction to the earlier practice, along with Ezekiel 20.

The propagation of these Deuteronomic laws is generally associated with the reign of Josiah in the late seventh century BCE, which was also the time of the prophet Jeremiah. Jeremiah goes farther than the other texts; in one of the book's divine speeches, God similarly recounts "all the evil of the people of Israel and the people of Judah that they did to provoke me to anger" (Jer 32:32), including, "They built the high places of Baal in the valley of the son of Hinnom, to offer up their sons and daughters to Molech, *though I did not command them, nor did it enter my mind that they should do this abomination,* causing Judah to sin" (32:35). He doesn't simply forbid the practice; he denies that God ever commanded it. This is irreconcilable with Ezekiel 20:25, which says God did command it. It's possible that Jeremiah hoped Deuteronomy would replace the earlier law codes and settle some of the internal scriptural debates. But it did not.

What both prophets agree on is that child sacrifice was practiced in Israel and Judah in the past. Some interpreters have argued, in spite of the explicit divine statement in Ezekiel, that child sacrifice results from a misunderstanding of the law. But as Jon D. Levenson remarked, "If it is, in fact, a mistake for us to read the requirement to sacrifice the first-born son in Exod 22:28–29 independently of the provisions for redemption that appear in other texts, it is a mistake of a sort that numerous Israelites seem to have made."[4]

We cannot settle this dispute between Ezekiel and Jeremiah, nor the one between the Book of the Covenant and the other legal texts, but it invites us to reflect on the law and our role as readers and interpreters. Early in Israel's history a law was given that had potentially tragic consequences. Someone had to step up and recast it.

Perhaps there were always guardrails, in practice, on the way the text was applied. There is no evidence, in the text or in archaeology, that children were *regularly* sacrificed in ancient Israel. As we have seen, many laws went unspoken, and it is entirely possible that the redemption of the firstborn was the unwritten norm early on and only later did child sacrifice need to be explicitly prohibited. If so, this probably took place in the reign of Josiah, who "defiled Topheth, which is in the valley of Ben-hinnom, so that no one would make a son or a daughter pass through fire as an offering to Molech" (2 Kgs 23:10). The sacrifice of male children on the eighth day may later have been sublimated in the practice of circumcising them on the same day (Lev 12:3).

In spite of this, and in spite of the real clarity in the canon that such sacrifice is not wanted, it seems to me that many continue to admire the kind of steely "faith" demonstrated by these characters, and by Mesha and Agamemnon. These are "real men of faith" who do not doubt God but "do what they have to do." Jephthah is mentioned in the pantheon of the faithful in Hebrews 11:32. Even the theologian and philosopher Søren Kierkegaard, who professed himself "shattered" by imagining what was asked of Abraham, nevertheless held up his act as a paradigmatic instance of faith surpassing ethics.[5]

"Offering children to Molech" is a powerful metaphor for interpreting laws in a way that we know to be harmful to children. Author and historian Garry Wills has tried to raise Americans' consciousness about the deaths of children by gun violence due to the failure in the United States to enact gun control. These deaths, he says, are an "offering, out of devotion to our Moloch, our god. The gun is our Moloch. We sacrifice children to him daily."[6] Most people are capable of understanding the statistics about gun deaths, and the many things we could do to reduce them, but alas, they are sure that the Second Amendment means free access to all sorts of firearms. When we grit our teeth in the face of the death of children, we sacrifice them to false gods.

Many in the church treat sexuality in a similar way: They understand that traditional church teaching about sexuality can be harmful, and they often have people in their families and networks whom they know are affected, but because of their faith and their reverence for God and tradition, they feel unable to support a systematic rethinking of the questions. The situation is especially excruciating for parents of LGBTQ teens who feel pressure to choose between the teaching of their church communities and support for their own children.

The harmful effects of social pressures on LGBTQ youth can be measured in various ways, but one of the most stark, tragic, and comparable is their rate of suicides and suicide attempts. A recent study endorsed by the American Academy of Pediatrics and the American Psychological Association reported that 20.1 percent of sexual minority teens reported attempting suicide in 2017—3.8 times the rate of heterosexual teens.[7]

This rate is down from 26.7 percent in 2009, reflecting the effects of changing views in the wider society. (Suicide attempts among heterosexual teens remained the same over that time, at 6 percent.) But in Christian churches, especially evangelical ones, the culture has not changed so much. If we look at the whole population, religious adherence generally correlates with reduced suicidal thoughts and behaviors—but for both LGBTQ youth and adults it does not do this, and it can increase such thoughts and behaviors if they receive negative messages about their sexuality from people in their environments. Similar data have been compiled from other conservative Jewish, Muslim, and Mormon communities.

I do not know a single pastor or theologian who would cheer for the high rate of suicide attempts among LGBTQ youth. But I do think conservatives would be inclined to say, "I did not command them to attempt suicide, nor did it enter my mind!" It's what my father would have said when he wrote his chapter on homosexuality in *The Moral Vision of the New Testament*. It's what I would have said when I accepted a job at a school that went on to expel gay and lesbian students. And it would have been true. And yet.

Rather than denying we mean harm and continuing to do harm, it may be better to say that we have been following statutes that are not good. As with the law of the sacrifice of the firstborn, the laws about sexuality in the Torah have done harm to children. I and many other biblical scholars are in a camp analogous to Jeremiah's, believing that the laws have been misunderstood and misapplied.[8] Others may prefer to take a stance like Ezekiel's and simply say that the laws given were not good.

But hopefully like the two prophets we can agree that they should not hold today. We consider these laws, with their conflicted interpretations, to be superseded by the overwhelming divine command to love, and by the expansion of God's grace.

We have seen that even where the will of God is stated and clear, the faithful are empowered to argue. We have seen it with Moses, Job, the daughters of Zelophehad, and even Abraham himself.

With that in mind, it is curious that Abraham does not find the will to argue with God on behalf of his son in Genesis 22, as he did on behalf of Sodom in Genesis 18. This seems to have troubled the rabbis as well. In a midrash, they reimagined—or rather, fleshed out—the divine order to sacrifice Isaac. In the Hebrew text, it simply reads: "Take your son, your only one, whom you love: Isaac." Why, the rabbis asked, did the Lord have to use so many words? And so they proposed that it was a dialogue rather than a monologue:

> He said to him: "Take, I beg you—please—your son."
>
> "Which son? I have two sons," he said [i.e., referring to Ishmael].
>
> "Your only son," He replied.
>
> "This one is the only one of his mother, and this one is the only one of his mother."
>
> "The one whom you love."
>
> "Are there boundaries to the affections?" [i.e., "I love them both"].
>
> "Isaac," He said.[9]

I can't imagine what I would do if the God around whom I had built my life appeared to me and gave me a direct order to harm my child. As Kierkegaard said, it's unthinkable. It is sometimes observed that Abraham is a changed man after this "near-death experience"—it is perhaps not an accident that he never speaks to God again in the Bible.

If harming human beings can ever be justified, it is only in the interest of avoiding greater harm—and then only in clear circumstances, such as defending the innocent from genocide.[10] Stopping two consenting adults from sexual partnership is not.

Clergy would do well to embrace the spirit of the Hippocratic oath—*First, do no harm*—as a bare minimum ethical standard. Claiming that we harm other humans in the name of God takes his name in vain. We dare not. We can act only in the humility of the limits of human perception. In a world with evil in it, intervention will sometimes be needed to minimize harm, but ultimately judgment belongs to God.

And so, because of my faith in the God who is the judge of all the earth and will do what is just, I argue with God—or rather, with fatally harmful interpretations of God's law. Because "the letter kills, but the Spirit gives life" (2 Cor 3:6). Sometimes the widening of God's mercy depends on our willingness to insist upon it; and sometimes in our faithful perseverance we find that we were wrong about the things we once believed that God wanted.

5

Widening the Borders

There is no better example of God changing his mind and doing new things in the course of the Bible than warfare.

One of the most troubling and frequently mentioned ethical criticisms of the Old Testament is its tribalism, nationalism, and violence. God chooses one people—the family of Abraham, the tribes of Jacob—and promises to make them great. He crushes Egypt to set them free (Exod 6:6) and then drives out the peoples of the land that they are to inhabit (Exod 33:2, 34:11; Deut 11:23). Deuteronomy 7:1–4 presents one version of that story:

> "When the LORD your God brings you into the land that you are about to enter and occupy, and he clears away many nations before you—the Hittites, the Girgashites, the Amorites, the Canaanites, the Perizzites, the Hivites, and the Jebusites, seven nations mightier and more numerous than you—and when the LORD your God gives them over to you and you defeat them, then you must utterly destroy them. Make no covenant with them and show them

no mercy. Do not intermarry with them, giving your daughters to their sons or taking their daughters for your sons, for that would turn away your children from following me, to serve other gods. Then the anger of the LORD would be kindled against you, and he would destroy you quickly."

And indeed those among the Israelites who fail to carry out this genocidal order are judged exceedingly harshly: For withholding from the Lord, Achan is stoned and burned (Josh 7), and Saul is rejected by God, driven mad, and ultimately killed in battle (1 Sam 15–31).

Were it not for the formation and survival of ancient Israel, there would be no Bible witnessing to God; it depends on the existence of ancient scribes and the powers that supported them. The preservation of texts depended on states in this period—and states, almost by definition, depended on controlled violence. But a reader who took these violent texts as reflective of the will of God today would be making a grave error, and in danger of doing worse. The story goes in a different direction.[1] Still, faced with the reality of divinely commanded violence in the Old Testament, Christians should not make excuses or practice apologetics. We know that this is not now the plan of God, but we cannot deny that it is part of the account that our own Bible gives of our "family story." Like Job's friends, the best way to show our wisdom is by sitting in silence (Job 13:5), in mourning for the destruction that our ancestors in faith carried out, lest we speak falsely (42:7–8). This is all the more true for teachers (James 3:1).

We can, however, ask: How was it possible to get from there to Paul's speech on the Areopagus in Athens, in which he says to a diverse, multiethnic group in that cosmopolitan city: "We are God's family" (Acts 17:29)?[2] It is one of the most strik-

ing examples of God's widening mercy, and it has deep roots in
the Old Testament itself.

There are strong indications from the very beginning of the
Old Testament story that God's plan for the other nations was
much broader and more inclusive than it sometimes appears.
It's often said that the Hebrew Bible is the story of the "chosen
people," but the Bible itself says that God's story with this people is only a microcosm of his purposes for the whole creation.
As God says in Exodus 19:5–6: "*the whole earth is mine,* but you
shall be for me a priestly kingdom and a holy nation."

Indeed, when Abram is first called, this is the first thing
God says about the purpose of this calling: "I will make of you
a great nation, and I will bless you, and make your name great,
so that you will be a blessing" (Gen 12:2). And God repeats this
with a specification: "by you *all the families of the earth* shall be
blessed" (12:3).[3]

This goal took a long time to be achieved. In fact, some
would say it never has been.

Perhaps just as significantly, this call begins with the command to "go from your country and your kindred and your
father's house" (Gen 12:1). Abram is a man of few words, so we
don't know what he makes of this; he just goes. But it would
seem that to answer the most difficult calls of God often means
breaking one's ties with the families and culture one is accus-
tomed to. In much the same way, Moses had to break his ties
with Egypt and leave the comfortable palace of Pharaoh (Exod
2:11–15). This is true in the New Testament as well. Jesus tells
prospective disciples to leave their families (Luke 9:57–62), and
does so himself (Matt 12:46–50; Mark 3:31–35; Luke 8:19–21,
14:26). In some of the most significant cases, following the God
of Israel does not align with our preexisting identities.

In truth, the tribalism of the Old Testament also sits very

uneasily with the actual stories of the people's origins, which are repeatedly said to be highly diverse. In Israel's very beginnings as a "nation," when the people go out from Egypt (Exod 12:38), it is said that "a mixed multitude went up with them."[4] These people aren't "Israelites," but there they are anyway, inspired to stand up with God's people and walk alongside them.

Something similar happens at the roots of the monarchy. Not only do the people continue to incorporate foreigners, but David is also said to have chosen many of them for top leadership roles. For example, Ittai the Gittite (i.e., man of Gath) is one of his generals (2 Sam 18:2). Gath was a Philistine city; David had collaborated with its ruler after he came into conflict with Saul (1 Sam 27), and it is clear that some of the Philistine soldiers eventually returned to Jerusalem with David. Before the ark of the Lord—the most sacred item in the later temple—made it to Jerusalem, David stored it for a time in the house of Obed-edom the Gittite, and the Lord blessed all his household (2 Sam 6:10–11).

David also had Hittites—a term that in this period would have referred to Arameans—in the highest levels of his military. He is accompanied by Ahimelech the Hittite (1 Sam 26:6), and Uriah the Hittite is one of his elite soldiers (2 Sam 23:39). In this same list is Zelek the Ammonite. The story of Uriah ends badly, but not because he was a Hittite; in fact, the storyteller makes a point of Uriah's rectitude and faithfulness to David and his fellow soldiers. Another important role in the story is played by Hushai the Archite, whom David sent as a spy into the court of Absalom (2 Sam 15:32–17:16); the Archites were a Canaanite group (Josh 16:2). Sometimes names indicate foreign ethnicity, as in the case of Adoram, whom David put in charge of forced labor (2 Sam 20:24); his name means "[the god] Hadad is exalted," and thus also suggests foreign birth. This list is only partial, but it is clear that some of the most trusted people in David's administration were foreigners.

Given these indications of internationalism in Israel, marriages with other nations would have been common. This is, paradoxically, reflected by the repeated prohibitions of this very thing, both early (Deut 7:3, Josh 23:12) and late (Ezra 9–10, Neh 13). But intermingled with these prohibitions are affirmations of foreign wives. The story of Ruth is one; the great-grandmother of David (and foremother of Jesus) is a Moabite. With apologies for the anachronism, we can say that Ruth clearly "converts" (Ruth 1:16: "your people shall be my people / and your God my God"), such that she is not a religious threat to Israel but a "model immigrant."[5] Still, we again see that the origins of the Davidic monarchy are more diverse than one might expect.

Even more striking is God's judgment of Miriam and Aaron when they "spoke against Moses because of the Cushite [i.e., Nubian][6] woman whom he had married" (Num 12:1). In this case, there is no hint to the readers that we should be concerned about this woman, but also no mention of her faithfulness to the God of Israel. Miriam and Aaron are trying to use Moses's marriage to a foreign, dark-skinned woman to undermine his prophetic authority: "Has the LORD spoken only through Moses? Has he not spoken through us also?" (12:2). God is not happy about this: He confirms that Moses has a unique relationship with him, unlike other prophets, and adds, "Why then were you not afraid to speak against my servant Moses?" (12:7–8). We are left with the impression that Miriam and Aaron were simply trying to capitalize on popular bigotry, and that this is condemned.[7]

All this is to say: From the beginning of the Old Testament and throughout the story run a vision and a theology that relativize the familial and national ties that bound people

together, then as now. It doesn't abolish those natural ties, but
it makes room for others to be included, even in the most important roles. The people are called instead to be a community
formed around the service of the Lord.

This broader divine vision for the whole world is named at the
people's origins, and it continues to play a role in the stories
about its exodus and state formation. It was always God's will.
But it is probably fair to say that as Israel's and Judah's international horizons were stretched by their encounters with Mesopotamian empires, it prompted the Hebrew prophets to state
that vision in new and more provocative ways.

These prophecies indicate that God is working equally
through other nations' histories, challenging the very idea that
there was a single chosen people. For that reason they are less
talked about. Some of the nations most invested in biblical interpretation—the United States, England, Germany, and Israel—
are also historically some of the most invested in the idea of
their own exceptionalism and chosenness. On the whole, we
would prefer not to hear these texts.

Former Secretary of Defense Donald Rumsfeld (who would
have benefited from reading this chapter) famously said: "There
are known knowns; there are things we know we know. We also
know there are known unknowns; that is to say we know there
are some things we do not know. But there are also unknown
unknowns—the ones we don't know we don't know."[8] Rumsfeld went on to say that the things in the last category "tend to
be the difficult ones."

What is true for politics is also true for theology: The most
difficult things to teach are those that people don't know they
don't know. So let's look at an example.

Amos 9:1–10 is a pointed indictment of those in Israel
who sin blithely, who refuse to countenance the prospect of

disaster. It is an impressive declaration, asserting the Lord's power to track the sinners down even if they flee to the under-world or to a mountain peak (Amos 9:2–3). In the midst of this is a statement about the Lord's power over even the Nile, which was the source of life for all Egypt: He controls the annual Nile flood, on which all farming depended (9:5–6). Then Amos goes on: "Are you not like the Cushites to me, / O people of Israel? says the LORD" (9:7). The connection between the Nile passage and this question is probably lost on readers today, but it would have been clear to Amos's audience. Amos prophesied in the middle of the eighth century BCE. That was a time when the traditional pharaonic dynasties were weak; Egypt was frag-mented, and it had lost control of its former imperial territo-ries. This was true of the north, in Israel and Judah, and it was also true of the south, in the land of Cush. Egypt had domi-nated and enslaved Cush within memory. But by the middle of the eighth century, not only was Cush liberated, but it was rising in power and was about to conquer all of Egypt and become the Twenty-Fifth Dynasty.

What Amos is saying here is that God has also been working to liberate and establish the Cushites, just as he did the Israelites. This is the same Cush from which Moses's wife came; we might imagine that the prophet was playing with the shock value created by the announcement that, as far as God was concerned, Cush was like Israel.

In case there was anyone in the audience not yet surprised, Amos goes on: "Did I not bring Israel up from the land of Egypt, / and the Philistines from Caphtor and the Arameans from Kir?" (Amos 9:7). The allusion here is unmistakable: The confession that the Lord "brought Israel up from the land of Egypt" was an essential credo of the people's faith (Lev 11:45, Deut 20:1, Judg 6:13, Mic 6:4). Amos says that Israel's proud tradition of the exodus was not unique: The Lord had been at

work in the same way in the histories of other nations—even
Israel's enemies. The Philistines in this period remained one
of Israel's rivals and competitors to the south (2 Kgs 18:8); the
Arameans played this same role in the north (13:22, 15:37, 16:5).
Caphtor and Kir are known from other sources as the places
where these nations originated; Amos says that the Lord has
brought them all to the Levant.

Unfortunately, these stories to which Amos alludes are
lost to us today; the nature of writing technology at the time
means that very few Aramean or Philistine texts have survived.
But because they are "known unknowns," we can use our imaginations to perceive God's work in the piecemeal histories of
those other nations. These stories point to a surprising broad-
ness in God's grace toward the world, throughout its whole history. In much the same way, we can use our theological imaginations to perceive where God is at work today in the lives of
people who are not like us.

Amos's claim would have been very frustrating for those
who felt they had a stake in the superiority of their own nation. Presumably that's the sort of reason why King Jeroboam
of Israel and his high priest Amaziah told Amos to go home
to Judah and prophesy there instead—and especially to stay
out of the king's sanctuary at Bethel (Amos 7:12–13). It's the
sort of reason why King Ahaz of Judah refused to seek a sign
from Isaiah (Isa 7:12) and Zedekiah threw Jeremiah into a cis-
tern (Jer 38:1–6). Where national interests were at stake, you
just couldn't trust some prophets.

Isaiah was definitely a problem for nationalistic zealots (and still
is). Like Amos, he took up Israel's foundational exodus story in
challenging and surprising ways. In Isaiah 19, that story is turned
upside down: Isaiah imagines that the Egyptians—the great
enemy of God's people, who had oppressed them as slaves—

would come to know and embrace the Lord alongside Israel. Yes, the Lord would discipline them, but only in the way that he also had done to Israel; he would strike them, but also heal them: "when they [the Egyptians] cry to the LORD because of oppressors, he will send them a savior, and will defend and deliver them. The LORD will make himself known to the Egyptians; and the Egyptians will know the LORD on that day" (Isa 19:20–21).

This cycle is strikingly similar to Israel's own pattern with God, recounted in Judges 2—they would forget the Lord and suffer for it, only to be delivered again by him after a time. It says that when the people worshiped other gods, "the anger of the LORD was kindled against Israel, and he gave them over to plunderers" (Judg 2:14); but then "the LORD raised up judges who delivered them out of the power of those who plundered them" (2:16).

Isaiah says that God will save Egypt, much as he had Israel. That's surprising in itself, especially coming from a prophet who was still living in the shadow of Egyptian power and who elsewhere advises against making political alliances with Egypt (Isa 20:1–6, 28:15, 30:1–5).

But Isaiah goes even farther. Having incorporated Egypt into the story of God's grace, he also includes the terrifying military superpower Assyria. The prophet says that the Assyrians will worship the Lord with the rest of the world: "there will be a highway from Egypt to Assyria, and the Assyrian will come into Egypt, and the Egyptian into Assyria, and the Egyptians will worship with the Assyrians" (Isa 19:23). These are the same people who had come to crush Israel and Judah, to "tread them down like the mire of the streets" (10:6). Now, instead of being roadkill, they are going to be one of the hubs in a network of peace.

The passage reaches its pinnacle in Isaiah 19:24: "On that day Israel will be the third with Egypt and Assyria, a blessing in the midst of the earth." Then the Lord says to the assembled nations, "Blessed be Egypt my people, and Assyria the work of my hands, and Israel my heritage" (Isa 19:25). In the world the prophet envisions, it will not be "Israel First!" Instead, Israel will be third, behind two of its historic enemies. Israel "will be a blessing," just as Genesis 12:2 said, so Isaiah reaffirms God's original plan for the people. But in other respects the vision is much broader and more inclusive: Egypt (to the southwest) and Assyria (to the northeast) were essentially the extremities of the known world.

So the chosen people are told that others were chosen and beloved by God as well. In fact, given that these texts from Amos and Isaiah include a Hall of Fame of Israel's enemies, it seems speculative to imagine that *any* nation was excluded. It makes sense that Amos 9 becomes part of James's argument for the inclusion of the nations in Acts 15 (see the discussion of this passage in Chapter 16, below).

From start to finish, Isaiah's vision of God is expansive, in ways that would have been uncomfortable for the book's original readers. But Isaiah's prophecies also crystallized the image of a universal God that we still hold today.

In the book's earliest layers, it declared that the Lord would use Assyria to punish his own people: He calls it "the rod of my anger" (Isa 10:5) with which he plans to punish Judah. Judah had by this time lived in an uneasy symbiotic relationship with Assyria for decades as a "client state"—a vassal taxed heavily for the empire's benefit—so the idea that Assyria was doing God's will by destroying much of Judah (as it did in 701 BCE) would not have been popular.

Isaiah must always have attracted followers and readers who were willing to think outside the nationalistic box. When the book was expanded around the end of the Babylonian exile, more than a century later, one of the goals of the new edition was to argue that Cyrus, the Persian king who conquered Babylon, was the rightful king of Judah as well:

> Thus says the LORD to his anointed, to Cyrus,
>   whose right hand I have grasped
> to subdue nations before him
>   and strip kings of their robes . . . (Isa 45:1)

The key word in this is the identification of Cyrus as the anointed one: in Hebrew *mashiach,* the messiah. Isaiah says that Cyrus is to take on prerogatives of the Davidic kings, such as building Jerusalem (45:13).

In the Old Testament, various figures, including priests and prophets, are anointed—but the possessive form, the *Lord's* anointed, is a technical term for the rightful king. If we look at the use of that phrase, it appears mainly in the context of David's refusal to kill Saul (1 Sam 26:9, 11, 16, 23; 2 Sam 1:14, 16), and then again when Abishai suggests that Shimei should be killed merely for speaking against David (2 Sam 19:21). Acting against the Lord's anointed was apparently a very serious crime, so Isaiah's use of the phrase here suggests an effort to silence doubts about Cyrus.[9]

Why would Isaiah have been concerned about a reaction against Cyrus? Perhaps because his anointing as king was a violation of the Mosaic law, which said: "you may indeed set over you a king whom the LORD your God will choose. One of your brothers you may set as king over you; *you are not permitted to put a foreigner over you,* who is not your brother" (Deut 17:15).[10] That was the word of the Lord—but now the Lord has changed his mind.

※

Ideas have effects, and you don't have to go to the New Testament to see the logical outcome of these surprising prophetic views. If God has actually been at work in the histories of many nations—if God's plan for the earth includes even the salvation and establishment of one's enemies—then how could it make sense to go to war against them?

The end of war is envisioned in various ways in the prophets, but one expression of this vision was so important that it occurs verbatim in two different books (Isa 2:4, Mic 4:3):

> they shall beat their swords into plowshares,
>   and their spears into pruning hooks;
> nation shall not lift up sword against nation,
>   neither shall they learn war any more.

This is idealistic talk, of course. Some call it "eschatological," meaning that it can never come to pass within human history, but only at an end time when God will renew the heavens and the earth and bring sin and suffering to an end. But the kingdom of God is not only a future reality. Rarely has a group of people read the Bible and concluded that there is nothing they can do to bring about God's will. Every community that seeks to live by God's ideals ought to testify to its faith by seeking to show what the kingdom of God is like. As Jesus proclaimed, "the kingdom of God is *among you*" (Luke 17:21). And the kingdom of God is peaceable, as Isaiah said:

> They will not hurt or destroy
>   on all my holy mountain;
> for the earth will be full of the knowledge of the LORD
>   as the waters cover the sea. (Isa 11:9)

Just as for Abram and for Jesus's disciples, the ultimate call of the prophets is to be a part of something larger than our ethnic and national identities—not to renounce who we are, but to get a glimpse of a world more gracious and merciful than our tribalisms would allow. Although this is in some way present in the beginning of the biblical story, the differences in divine pronouncements require us to consider it another example of God's widening mercy. These texts invite us to expand our boundaries, rather than defending them.

6

"I Knew That You Are a Gracious God, and Merciful"

Most of the authors of the Old Testament were not lucky enough to live in peaceful times. When the upheavals afflicted foreign nations, it was easy to view them as divine wrath, from the decimation of Egypt in Exodus, to the oracles against Israel's neighbors in the prophets, to the overthrow of Greek kingdoms in Daniel, to the final devastation of Rome in Revelation. But the canon as a whole suggests that, as Paul said in Romans 2:11, "God shows no partiality." Israel is not excepted from the judgment that other nations were subject to. Indeed, Israel's story with God revolves around the national cataclysm of the Babylonian exile—the destruction of Jerusalem and the temple of the Lord that stood there, and the death and exile of many of the people.

It is an understatement to say that it would have been easy to lose faith—to conclude that the Lord was not so powerful after all, not so benevolent, not so worthy of worship. To interpret these events as judgment against oneself, and then make this the touchstone of one's national story, is a remarkable choice, akin to taking a man as one's Messiah who was crucified and dead. But Israel's theologians clung fiercely to the idea of God's grace and mercy—in spite of all.

Chapter 2 touched on one of the most ancient and important confessional statements about the Lord, which God spoke to Moses in Exodus 34 and Moses quoted back to God in Numbers 14 in his effort to save the people from God's wrath:

> Yahweh! Yahweh!
> A God merciful and gracious,
> slow to anger,
> and abounding in steadfast love and faithfulness . . .
>   (Exod 34:6)[1]

Some might be tempted to object that this overlooks the end of the passage where God reminds people he will visit the iniquity of the parents on future generations (34:7). But God's steadfast love is said to be to the thousandth generation, while judgment extends only to the third or fourth. Thus, some quick, back-of-the-napkin math reveals that God's love is 250 to 333 times more durable than his wrath.

The history of this one formula in the Bible embraces God's entire history with the nation, from the Exodus onward. It is used repeatedly in the Psalms like a refrain and alluded to in numerous other contexts in addition to the ones discussed in this chapter.[2] Not surprisingly, it is quoted in Jonah as a truism about God that everyone knows.

The Hebrew prophets present an extended meditation on the judgment and mercy of God in relation to the fates not only of Israel and Judah, but also those of nearly all of the neighboring nations. God destroys in wrath, but God also repeatedly repents of his wrath. God changes his mind about his methods and decisions.

Sometimes this takes the form of realizing after the fact

that punishment has gone too far. Much later in Israel's history, in the wake of the destruction of Jerusalem and the exile of the people to Babylon, God speaks the beloved words of Isaiah 40:

> Comfort, O comfort my people,
> > says your God.
> Speak tenderly to Jerusalem,
> > and cry to her
> that she has served her term,
> > that her penalty is paid,
> that she has received from the LORD's hand
> > double[3] for all her sins. (Isa 40:1–2)

Something similar is implied in Isaiah 10:5–19 and 14:16–17: that the Assyrian king went too far in conquering and destroying, even though he was designated as the rod of the Lord's anger.

These texts assert the Lord's imperial rule over the nations of the earth and their histories. Yet one can infer from them that, even in this role, God does not mechanically control all events: He speaks tenderly to his people because their punishment was twice what it should have been. He has to punish Assyria because it went beyond its divine mandate.

The idea that God does not foresee and control everything, and feels pity and regret even concerning his past judgments, is troubling for some theological views, but if we take the Bible seriously, it is hard to deny.

God may also change his mind about judgment before ever executing it—which is easier for many readers to appreciate. In some cases the prophets act as mediators, pleading for mercy on the people much like Moses did in the wilderness. In Amos 7, God shows the prophet a swarm of locusts ready to devour Israel. Amos cries out:

> "O Lord GOD, forgive, I beg you!
> How can Jacob stand?
> He is so small!" (Amos 7:2)

And so, "The LORD changed his mind [*nacham*]," and said, "It shall not be" (7:3).[4] Then God shows Amos a shower of fire devouring the earth and sea. Amos makes the same objection, and again the Lord changes his mind.

One of the clearest statements that God changes his mind about the fate of nations is in Jeremiah 18:7–10, in which God says:

> At one moment I may declare concerning a nation or a kingdom, that I will pluck up and break down and destroy it, but if that nation, concerning which I have spoken, turns from its evil, *I will change my mind* [*nacham*] about the disaster that I intended to bring on it. And at another moment I may declare concerning a nation or a kingdom that I will build and plant it, but if it does evil in my sight, not listening to my voice, then *I will change my mind* [*nacham*] about the good that I had intended to do to it.

That is, the prophet may announce judgment only to have God change his mind about it.

Jeremiah's statement becomes the plot of the book of Jonah: Jonah announces judgment on the Assyrian capital, Nineveh, and the whole city promptly repents. In fact, in a comically exaggerated spasm of repentance, the Ninevites even put sackcloth on their animals and force them to fast (Jonah 3:7–8). And so, "When God saw what they did, how they turned from their evil ways, God changed his mind [*nacham*] about the calamity that he had said he would bring upon them; and he did

not do it" (3:10). Jonah goes on to say that this is simply who
God is known to be: "Isn't this what I said while I was still in my
own country? That is why I fled to Tarshish at the beginning;
for I knew that you are a gracious God and merciful, slow to
anger, and abounding in steadfast love, and *one who changes his
mind [nacham]* about punishment" (4:2).[5]

The book of Jonah is an interesting reflection on the potential piety of foreigners, with an optimistic view not shared
by all the biblical authors. But Jonah's insight about the nature
of God is of course hardly a new one; rather, it's a quotation
from one of the oldest and most widespread theological formu-
lae in the Bible about God. As we have seen, it can be traced all
the way back to Exodus 34:5–7, in which the Lord descends in a
cloud, stands with Moses, and proclaims his merciful character.

In light of the Genesis stories that we looked at earlier,
God's response to Jonah is revealing: Pressed to explain his change
of mind, he says, "should I not be concerned about Nineveh,
that great city?" (Jonah 4:11). The verb here could also be translated "spare" or "look compassionately upon" Nineveh. God
seems to want to emphasize that the concern Abraham raised
about Sodom and Gomorrah in Genesis 18 is not forgotten in
the case of Nineveh: There are people there who are worth spar-
ing. Specifically, God continues, "there are more than a hundred and twenty thousand persons *who do not know their right
hand from their left,* and also many animals" (4:11). Now, clearly
God was impressed by the Assyrian animals in sackcloth, but
the emphasis here is on the ignorance of the Ninevites: They're
as clueless as their animals (or maybe more so, as Isa 1:3 says of
Israel). The lessons of those early experiences with humans seem
to have taken root in God's heart, though: Whereas figuring out
that the hearts of humankind were evil and disobedient came
as a surprise in Genesis 3–6, the evil of the Ninevites elicits a
bemused shrug, as long as they're repentant.

Jonah, of course, is not happy about this, and he spends chapter 4 pouting. The grumpy Jonah is a bit of a comic character—but a lot of theologians in more recent times have been equally unhappy about God changing his mind. I nod again to the paradigmatic story of Samuel and Saul: By tracing the use of the verb *nacham* through 1 Samuel 15, we saw not only that God changes his mind, but that people are prone to try to deny it, because it makes it too difficult and messy to speak for God. A prophet is a sort of spokesperson. So is a preacher. A spokesperson often just wants a clear and consistent message.

For many theologians, the plain testimony of these texts has not been enough to convince them that God changes his mind. One of the most prominent of these theologians is a touchstone for my own Reformed tradition: John Calvin. Calvin is perhaps most (in)famous for his doctrine of "double predestination," the belief that God has predestined some to heaven and others to hell. In his *Institutes of the Christian Religion*, Calvin takes on those who "contend that God has not determined the affairs of men by an eternal decree, but that, according to each man's deserts or according as he deems him fair and just, he decrees this or that each year, each day, and each hour." Calvin wants to correct this misconception: "That is far removed from the intention of the Holy Spirit, who in the very reference to repentance says that God is not a man so that he can repent [1 Sam 15:29]. . . . By these words openly and unfiguratively God's unchangeableness is declared."[6]

So although God and the narrator both say in 1 Samuel 15 that God changed his mind about Saul, Calvin takes the irritated Samuel's word for it that he doesn't. Calvin goes on to explain that "the change of mind is to be taken figuratively," like every instance in which God is described in human terms. These descriptions of God are "accommodated to our capacity so that we may understand it."[7]

Calvin has other prooftexts on his side as well. For example, Samuel's words are almost the same as those of the prophet Balaam in Numbers 23:

God is not a human being, that he should lie,
    or a mortal, that he should change his mind.
Has he promised, and will he not do it?
        Has he spoken, and will he not fulfill it? (Num 23:19)

It is interesting that Samuel quotes these words in 1 Samuel 15. The two religious professionals were in fact in quite similar situations, being asked to reconsider the divine judgments that they have just spoken. In Balaam's case, he was hired by Balak, the king of Moab, to hex the Israelites as they enter the promised land—but instead, he pronounces divine favor on them. Balak sputters: "What have you done to me? I brought you to curse my enemies, but now you have done nothing but bless them" (23:11). Balaam's response is simply a refusal to recant what he has just said. It is certainly phrased categorically, but in light of all of the countervailing biblical testimony, it cannot be taken as the last word on the subject of God changing his mind.

Calvin also mentions Malachi 3:6: "I the LORD do not change"—but this statement is in the perfect tense and should better be translated, "I the LORD *have not changed*."[8] God is emphasizing he has not changed his mind about a specific list of sins—adultery; swearing falsely; and oppressing workers, widows, orphans, and aliens. God is *not* saying that he *never* changes; rather, he is encouraging the "children of Jacob" to marvel that they have not perished in spite of transgressing these specific, enduring principles.

All this tends to undermine the relevance of these statements. But in light of what we know about the Bible as a whole, it may be better to admit that there are indeed contrasting perspectives in dialogue with each other in the Bible. So if the Bible as a whole is the word of God, then perhaps we should say that God changes his mind about whether he changes his mind.

The tension between God's plan and its surprises is in fact hardwired into Old Testament theology. The later portions of the book of Isaiah, where Israel's monotheism is most explicitly crystalized, focus on both poles of the tension. God is both the one

> declaring the end from the beginning
>   and from ancient times things not yet done,
> saying, "My purpose shall stand,
>   and I will fulfill my intention . . . " (Isa 46:10)

. . . and also the one who declares new things (42:9) and does new things (43:19).

It is notable that the Ninevites, in their agnosticism, are more in tune with God than Jonah is. "Who knows?" they say, "God may relent and change his mind" [*nacham*; 4:9]. And they're right. We have seen the danger of "knowingness" in Samuel's case, and we see it in Jonah as well: He is not surprised by God, as Samuel seems to have been, but like Samuel he has very clear ideas about who God *should* be, and he is angry when God does what he does.

Educators sometimes face the problem of students who think they already know everything, or ought to. But surely the problem of knowingness is nowhere as severe as in theology. The philosopher Jonathan Lear has written about the problem of knowingness as a substitute for thought. He describes knowingness as a sickness in which "reason is being used to jump ahead to a conclusion, as though there is too much anxiety involved in simply asking a question and waiting for the world to answer."[9] This anxiety seems to me to characterize much religious conservatism. Paradoxically, such conservatism proceeds as if God were dead, or were at least done with the world. If God were done with us, then we could simply add up the sum of the texts and arrive at a right answer, once and for all. (This, I'm afraid, is not too far from what *Moral Vision* did in regard to homosexuality, although it seems to me that my father was always uneasy about the answers.) But scripture repeatedly testifies that we have a living God who does new things. Faithfulness to a living God means seeking to know him face-to-face, as Moses did—to bring questions and wait for the answers.

Paul said it more simply to the Corinthians who thought they already had knowledge: "Knowledge puffs up, but love builds up" (1 Cor 8:1–3).

Waiting for mercy is probably always difficult, and it is sometimes excruciating. Sometimes mercy is long delayed. In the passage above from Amos 7, the patience and mercy that Amos secures from the Lord eventually run out. A third oracle follows with a judgment against Israel that is not delayed. It foretells the destruction of Israel and its sanctuaries. Samaria was, in fact, destroyed in the late eighth century, and these same oracles were later seen as relevant to the destruction of Jerusalem a century and a half later.

The prophetic books are rarely content to end on such a note, however. They sense that for God, judgment is not meant to be the last word. And so, in the case of Amos, the book ends with this oracle from the Lord:

I will restore the fortunes of my people Israel,
      and they shall rebuild the ruined cities and inhabit
            them;

they shall plant vineyards and drink their wine,
and they shall make gardens and eat their fruit.
I will plant them upon their land,
and they shall never again be plucked up
out of the land that I have given them. (Amos 9:14–15)

This vision of restoration was probably added after Amos's time, but that only reinforces the point: This sort of enduring hope for divine mercy is difficult for anyone to grasp in the limitations of our personal histories, but the "great cloud of witnesses" that make up our canons of scripture have a longer view.

Another late prophetic voice, Zechariah, explicitly reflects back on God's history with the people. The book pronounces peace and bounty to the people (Zech 8:11–13). Anticipating doubts, God says to them: "Just as I purposed to bring disaster upon you when your ancestors provoked me to wrath, and I did not relent [*nacham*], says the LORD of hosts, so again I have purposed in these days to do good to Jerusalem and to the house of Judah; do not be afraid" (8:14–15). This has in view more than a century in which Judah and its people suffered greatly, and in which God did not change his mind. But even where God punishes, there is hope for the longer run.

It is not easy to put a neat bow on a work of biblical theology such as this one, because of the complexity of the texts themselves: The canon of the Hebrew Bible reads differently depending on whether one reads it as the Jewish Tanakh or the Christian Old Testament. The Old Testament ends with the prophets, while the Tanakh ends with the writings, and specifically with Ezra-Nehemiah-Chronicles. Neither canon is complete in itself: In Christian tradition, the Old Testament prophets are believed to prefigure the Messiah (note the ending of Malachi) and are supplemented by the New Testament); in Jewish tradition, Ezra-Nehemiah-Chronicles are meant to point beyond themselves to the restoration of Judah and Jerusalem (and are supplemented by the Oral Torah).

These different arrangements of texts give rise to quite different interpretations and theological conclusions—in some cases. Yet we find both canons emphasizing to the end a God who is "gracious and merciful, slow to anger and abounding in steadfast love." Nehemiah, one of the latest historical figures in the Tanakh, invokes that formula when he retells the story of the people's rebellion against God in Numbers 14, in a sermon summoning the people to repent and rebuild. He concludes: "You did not forsake them" (Neh 9:17).

Among the prophets, Joel is one of the latest and most beloved by Christians, with his apocalyptic visions leading to the divine promise, "I will pour out my spirit on all flesh; your sons and your daughters shall prophesy" (Joel 2:28; cf. Acts 2:17). Along the way Joel exhorts the people:

> Rend your hearts and not your clothing.
> Return to the LORD your God,
>   for he is gracious and merciful,
> slow to anger, and abounding in steadfast love,
>   and relents [*nacham*] from punishing. (2:13)

In neither Nehemiah nor Joel can we say that the implications of God's widening mercy are fully realized. The realization of the kingdom of God is still incomplete today. But no matter what trajectory we take from the Hebrew Bible, its authors embrace that mercy as a crucial article of faith. Whether we aspire to *tikkun ʿolam* (repairing the world) or *imitatio Christi* (imitating Christ), the widening mercy of God for the whole earth stands at the center.

7

"Besides Those Already Gathered"

Sometimes the word of God is not large enough to contain the character and plan of God. Or at least, that was Isaiah's opinion. This is not, in itself, surprising. We have seen that, from Moses onward, it was part of the prophetic calling to turn aside and notice where the spirit of God has caught fire, and to listen for God's will in new situations.

Up to this point in the story, we have encountered different prophetic perspectives and even different legal judgments, but we have not yet really encountered the tension we live with today when we consider the will of God: the weight of scripture.

Early in the Old Testament period, contrasting traditions seem to have coexisted more easily; perhaps the differences came into sharp focus only when they were combined later. As existing texts took on greater importance, and the idea of a canon began to emerge, new words from God that conflicted with past ones would have been more readily scrutinized.

The story of Ezra reading "the scroll of the law [Hebrew *torah*] of Moses" before the assembly of the people, in Nehemiah 8, is often taken to be the earliest reference to the Torah in something like its current form. Prophetic proclamation did not cease after the exile, but the weight of older traditions meant that postexilic prophets often had to be even more forceful in their witness about God—to the point that some of their contemporaries would have seen them as rending the very fabric of scripture. These prophets created conflicts, or at least waded into them.

It can be hard to fully appreciate these ancient conflicts when we read the Bible today. It's one thing to read the words, and something else again to hear them the way their original audience would have. Most of us today don't understand their original cultural contexts, and we don't feel their impact.

Isaiah 56:1–8 is a great example of a prophetic re-envisioning of the divine will that doesn't make much of an impression on most readers now but was scandalous in its time. It undermined some key things that people thought they knew. In fact, it took a couple of the prevailing ideas about God and the temple, looked them in the eye, and contradicted them. To explain why requires a bit of time.

The passage begins in this way:

> Thus says the LORD:
>   Maintain justice, and do what is right,
> for soon my salvation will come,
>   and my deliverance be revealed.
>
> Happy is the mortal who does this,
>   the one who holds it fast,
> who keeps the sabbath, not profaning it,
>   and refrains from doing any evil. (Isa 56:1–2)

The prophet opens with a few simple admonitions. This kind of summary of the law was a familiar trope in early Jewish biblical interpretation. According to the Talmud, the law contained

613 laws, but Isaiah was able to sum them up here in two: "Maintain justice, and do what is right" (b. Mak. 23b–24a).[1] This boils down the law considerably—a bit like Jesus's later statement that love of God and love of neighbor are the whole basis for the law (Matt 22:40). In Isaiah 56, only the Sabbath commandment contributes any specifics. This seems like typical biblical rhetoric: Sabbaths and covenants and doing the right thing.

The prophet promises salvation and happiness—blessedness—to anyone who keeps this brief list of commandments. Again: not surprising. That was a basic idea: that those who did the right things (Ps 1:1) and followed the paths of wisdom (Prov 3:13, 8:34) would be blessed.

A few verses later, the passage ends with a promise to gather people so that "my house shall be called a house of prayer / for all peoples" (Isa 56:7–8). To many contemporary readers, it will sound familiar and normal to invite everyone to the house of God for prayer, but this inclusive vision was not necessarily the norm for an ancient temple. The one in Jerusalem had originally been the private, royal sanctuary for the Davidic kings, not a community synagogue.

Because the passage's ideas are somewhat novel, Isaiah spends much of it answering objections. Immediately after the injunction to do justice and keep the Sabbath, he goes on:

> Do not let the foreigner joined to the LORD say,
>> "The LORD will surely separate me from his people";
> and do not let the eunuch say,
>> "I am just a dry tree." (Isa 56:3)

Why would the foreigner and the eunuch think that they were excluded from the circle of blessing that was supposed to be for God's people? Why would they have lower expectations and hopes?

These would in fact have been quite understandable reactions in light of earlier biblical traditions. Isaiah is explicitly
welcoming two groups who were previously excluded from temple worship, for different reasons. He's throwing open the doors
to a wider group of people, and not everyone was on board with
that plan.

Since we don't live in ancient Israel or Judah, it's useful to
look at how foreigners and eunuchs were talked about and treated
in Isaiah's time, each in turn. Isaiah started with the eunuchs,
so we will too:

> For thus says the LORD:
> To the eunuchs who keep my sabbaths,
>> who choose the things that please me
>> and hold fast my covenant,
> I will give, in my house and within my walls,
>> a monument and a name
>> better than sons and daughters;
> I will give them an everlasting name
>> that shall not be cut off. (Isa 56:4–5)

Eunuchs were castrated men, whose genitals had been excised
or mutilated. In that sense, they were a sexual minority. Castration was sometimes practiced as a punishment for conquered
elites and was also prevalent among palace officials in some
ancient Near Eastern cultures.[2]

The problem that this later passage in Isaiah 56 perceives
is that the eunuchs will have no memory, no heritage—a very
understandable concern for a group of men who could not father children. One way in which people in the ancient world
hoped to live on after death was through the invocation of their
names by future generations.[3] This is also reflected in the decision of Absalom to "set up for himself a pillar that is in the

King's Valley, for he said, 'I have no son to keep my name in remembrance'" (2 Sam 18:18). Conversely, Isaiah 14:21–22 calls for the death of the sons of a Mesopotamian king so that the name of Babylon would be "cut off."

So that this will not happen to the eunuchs, the prophet offers them "an everlasting name" on behalf of the Lord—meaning, presumably, a mortuary monument in the temple itself. Assuming this text dates from around the period of the construction of the second temple, this monument may have served as a record of their service or gifts.

The "monument and name" are thus connected, and the Hebrew term for "monument" is a somewhat cheeky pun by the prophet: The Hebrew word is *yad*, which most commonly means "hand" but is also used widely in Semitic languages for "stela" (1 Sam 15:12, 2 Sam 18:18, Ezek 21:24) . . . and as a euphemism for "penis" (Isa 57:8, 10). Thus Isaiah is saying that although key parts of the eunuchs' genitalia (*yad*) have been cut off, they will still have a *yad*, a monument, to preserve their name.

The other side of Isaiah's message to eunuchs involves access to the temple and participation in its practices. Castration was not generally practiced in Israelite or Judahite culture, and the biblical lawmakers describe eunuchs as damaged goods in the eyes of God. Leviticus 21:17–23 states, "No one of your [Aaron's] offspring throughout their generations who has a blemish may approach to offer the food of his God," and goes on to name specifically those with damaged testicles among those considered blemished. They are thus forbidden from serving as the priests who make offerings at the tabernacle and temple. It would seem that just as blemished offerings were not good enough for God (Lev 22:20–25), neither were blemished people good enough to bring them.

Leviticus at least allows that eunuchs could share in consuming sacrificial food (Lev 21:22). Deuteronomy is even stricter, banning men with crushed testicles (along with foreigners and illegitimate children) from even entering "the assembly of the LORD" (Deut 23:1).

If conservatives today find scriptural warrant for excluding sexual minorities, how much more did religious leaders in Isaiah's time have warrant to exclude eunuchs?

The prophet has no time for those traditions.

In Isaiah's prophecy, the Lord makes it clear that the eunuchs will not only have a legacy, but they will have it "in my house and within my walls." He throws open the doors. They won't just be admitted to the sanctuary; they will be given an everlasting memorial there to comfort and compensate them. Furthermore, the eunuchs' legacy will not be inferior to other members', but rather "better than sons and daughters." They are no longer second-class citizens.

There are hints in scripture that help us imagine whom Isaiah was speaking of. Isaiah warned Hezekiah when faced with an Assyrian threat in 701 BCE: "Some of your own sons who are born to you shall be taken away; they shall be eunuchs in the palace of the king of Babylon" (Isa 39:7). Although there is no record that this happened, the Assyrian king did boast of taking Hezekiah's daughters back to Assyria, and so he may have taken sons as well. The reference to Babylon also suggests a later context, such as when Jehoiachin gave himself and his family up to the Babylonians in 597 BCE (2 Kgs 24:12–15); Jehoiachin, his sons, and other men of Judah did in fact live and receive rations at the palace of the Babylonian king for many years (2 Kgs 25:27–30, Jer 52:32–34). Some of Jehoiachin's descendants might have been among the returnees to Jerusalem who had seen the first temple, and who wept when the foundations of the second one were laid (Ezra 3:10–13).

Among the others who returned from Babylon to Jerusalem was Nehemiah. It has also often been assumed that Nehemiah was a eunuch: He was a high-ranking servant in the Persian court at Susa (Neh 1:1, 11); no family is ever attributed to him; and he is preoccupied with the way that he will be remembered, appealing directly to God rather than relying on descendants (5:19; 13:14, 22, 31). He also suggests that someone like him should not enter the Temple (6:11).[4] If this is so, then readers have a prominent example in the Bible of a eunuch's longing for inclusion in the story of God.

Either way, the uncertainty about the identities of the eunuchs is telling: Other biblical authors were probably reticent to speak of such things in relation to important figures in national history. Isaiah 56 is breaking a taboo in acknowledging the eunuchs' existence and proclaiming their full inclusion in the temple community. As is the case with sexual minorities today, the people he sought to include may have had gifts and leadership potential that the community needed.

Foreigners had even more reason to expect to be excluded. They are regularly condemned and demonized in biblical law. They were forbidden by law from sharing in the Passover (Exod 12:43) and excluded from entering the sanctuary (Ezek 44:9). More generally, they seem to have been viewed by some with suspicion and contempt—for example, Psalm 144:11 portrays foreigners as those "whose mouths speak lies, / and whose right hands are false."

Although Chapter 5 showed that Israel was from its origins a nation that incorporated a "mixed multitude" (Exod 12:38),[5] the definition of Israel's ethnic boundaries was still under constant negotiation. The United States is also a nation of immigrants, and yet anti-immigrant and racist sentiments flourish here as well.

Antiforeigner views thrived in the time when Isaiah 56 was being composed. Even more than most biblical eras, the

Persian period was one of serious ethnic tensions. Ezra and Nehemiah both advocated separation from foreigners and their ways (e.g., Neh 9:2, 13:23–30),[6] even to the point of castigating men to compel them to send away their foreign wives. In the face of a long tradition of suspicion toward foreigners and a culture of ongoing, aggressive xenophobia, the prophet rolls out the red carpet and unhooks the velvet rope to the temple sanctuary.

Before going any further, we should acknowledge that not all types of foreigners and outsiders were the same. There was a distinction in Hebrew between foreigners who were not attached to the people (Hebrew *nēkār/nokri*) and "resident aliens/ sojourners" (Hebrew *gēr*) who were presumed to be living in Israel's land for an extended time. Resident aliens were theoretically protected by certain laws, and this was justified by memories that Israelites had been sojourners in Egypt (Exod 23:9). They are listed as a protected class along with widows, orphans, and the poor (Deut 24:19–21), because all these groups were assumed to be disempowered and vulnerable, since various legal rights and social privileges were grounded in land and family.

The story of the Israelites' sojourn in Egypt illustrates the situation: Their land was granted by the Egyptian pharaoh (Gen 47:4–6), and although they were said to flourish under his blessing for a time, it was never really theirs. They were vulnerable to being oppressed when their favored status was forgotten (Exod 1).

Isaiah 56 could have made the case for inclusion more familiar and moderate by appealing to the tradition of the sojourner. Instead, it uses the most explicit term for a foreigner (*nēkār*). But it goes on to describe them as "foreigners who join themselves [*nilvîm*] to the LORD" (Isa 56:6). This invites reflection: Numbers 18:2, 4 use the same verb to describe the Levites joined to the priests. So at a minimum, Isaiah seems to invite foreigners to Levitical service. Pragmatically speaking, this would have given them state support (e.g., Deut 26:11–13) without awarding them land.[7] Indeed, the word "Levite" essentially means "one who accompanies," and the related Hebrew verb is used in a number of late texts to describe converts to a form of early Judaism after the exile (Jer 50:5, Zech 2:11, Dan 11:34, Esth 9:27).

In the wake of the Babylonian exile, ethnic identities in Judah were more fluid than usual. After so much upheaval, identities were in a process of redefinition, so that one who was originally a foreigner might be "joined" to the people and gain a more secure status. Other biblical stories tell of foreigners joining themselves to the people by pledging their allegiance to the royal house (as Ittai the Gittite does to David in 2 Sam 15:19–21) or another household (Ruth 1:16–17, 2:10).

Isaiah 56 goes further than offering to the foreigners to be joined to the people: It invites them into the house of the Lord as priests:

> And the foreigners who join themselves to the LORD,
>> to minister to him, to love the name of the LORD,
>> and to be his servants,
> all who keep the sabbath, and do not profane it,
>> and hold fast my covenant—
> these I will bring to my holy mountain,
>> and make them joyful in my house of prayer;
> their burnt offerings and their sacrifices
>> will be accepted on my altar;
> for my house shall be called a house of prayer
>> for all peoples. (Isa 56:6–7)

This declaration flew in the face of ancient laws concerning the priesthood. To "minister to" the Lord is a technical term for serving as priests, which had been expressly forbidden to foreigners in the Torah. Earlier texts had sought to make it a "perpetual ordinance" that the priesthood was limited to a specific group of Israelites (Exod 29:9), and Nehemiah drove even men *married to* foreigners out of the priesthood: "they have defiled the priesthood, the covenant of the priests and the Levites. Thus I cleansed them from everything foreign" (Neh 13:29–30).

Isaiah is nevertheless quite clear about God's will: The foreigners will be brought to God's holy mountain, they will celebrate in God's temple, and all their sacrifices will be accepted, "for my house shall be called a house of prayer for all peoples" (Isa 56:7).

This is one of the most striking expansions of divine grace in the Old Testament, offering the full rights and responsibilities of leadership to those included. Sometimes minorities are welcomed from the front of the church and then denied the opportunity to lead. Not here.

We can be sure much of the original audience would have been scandalized.

Indeed, the controversy over the meaning of these radical words didn't stop there. The fight over this oracle and the extent of God's grace went on through the centuries. We can see it unfold in the earliest manuscripts and the most ancient translations of the Bible. Texts like this had to be copied by hand and eventually translated for new communities; the scribes who did all this work also clearly saw the challenges to the tradition that this text posed. Practically all ancient copies of the Bible contain minor errors and variations, but we can tell that this one is a particularly controversial one because the copies and translations show a conflagration of attempts to change what it says.[8] One of the Dead Sea Scrolls, for example, simply leaves out the phrase "to minister to him." The Septuagint normally uses a special Greek verb (*leitourgein*) to translate the Hebrew verb "to minister" (*šārēt*); but here, seemingly scandalized by the implications, it makes an exception, instead using a verb for common work (*douleuein*). And so on.

You can almost hear the scribes thinking, "That can't *possibly* be what the prophet meant to say! I've read and copied other texts that say contrary things!" These careful and faithful scribes were sure that God's grace did not extend *that* far. Surely foreigners were not allowed to be priests!

The author of these verses was not naïve; as the climactic verse of the passage reinforces, he was very aware of the impact of this theological and social reimagining of God's intentions:

> Thus says the Lord GOD,
>> who gathers the outcasts of Israel,
> *I will gather others to them*
>> *besides those already gathered.* (Isa 56:8)

A reader working through the whole book of Isaiah has heard earlier that "[The LORD] will assemble the outcasts of Israel" (11:12). Now, God is going to gather more—not just the outcasts of Israel, but other nations as well. God is going to enlarge the tent. Those who were once forcibly excluded from it are now meant to be ushered in.

"The outcasts of Israel" is not a casual phrase. This was a people that traced its lineage to itinerant herders and slaves and that had only recently been defeated by Babylon, scattered across the known world, and finally reconstituted. They were supposed to remember what it was to be outcasts. Just as the law summoned them to remember that their ancestors had been slaves in Egypt, this allusion may have been meant to inspire sympathy for the new arrivals. (In much the same way, United States citizens of European descent might be summoned to remember that they should welcome immigrants because their

ancestors were immigrants.) Isaiah 56:8 uses the same terminology as older texts such as Isa 11:12 to allude to these older
traditions directly and loudly. It's Isaiah's way of making sure
that no one misses the allusion.

All in all, Isaiah 56 is a rhetorical tour de force, challenging both earlier and contemporary views about what it meant
to be a part of the covenant and to serve the Lord. The image
of the Lord's sanctuary as "a house of prayer for all peoples"
(Isa 56:7) remains inspirational. It was composed in a new and
surprising era of history for the people of God. In his coura-
geous willingness to rethink old rules, this prophet is a model
for all who live in such times.

We also do well to remember that this would have been a
difficult stand to take. Christians today may thrill to the vision
of serving as "a light to the nations," to expand and extend God's
salvation "to the end of the earth" (Isa 49:6), and the promise
that those who follow the prophet will "run and not be weary
. . . walk and not faint" (40:31); but the latter parts of Isaiah also
reflect the exhaustion from the ongoing struggles. Despite a
continuing conviction about his calling, the prophet laments:
"I have labored in vain. / I have spent my strength for nothing
and vanity" (49:4). We still live in the tension between Isaiah's
hope and despair. The story is not yet over. The world still needs
not only prophetic proclamation, but also care and sympathy
in the midst of the struggle.

As the present book turns from the Old Testament to the New,
we are poised to appreciate the continuities of the Bible's vision. In the Gospels, Jesus too always seems to be inviting and
welcoming people whom other people don't think should be
welcomed, such as lepers (Matt 8:1–4), tax collectors (Luke 5:27),
Samaritans (Luke 17:16, John 4:7–30), and children (Matt 19:14).
The reactions to this generous welcome reflect that he was

unusual: "Why does your teacher eat with tax collectors and sinners?" (Matt 9:11); "How is it that you, a Jew, ask a drink of me, a woman of Samaria?" (John 4:9).

You might conclude that Jesus's sensibilities were different from those of most of his Judean neighbors because he was God—that he had some special, supernatural insight that was unavailable to others around him. Actually, though, a lot of what Jesus walked around shocking people with was straight from the Hebrew scriptures. In particular, a lot of it was from Isaiah. It's not an accident that when he spoke about his calling, at his home synagogue in Nazareth (Luke 4:16–21), he quoted from Isaiah:

> The spirit of the Lord GOD is upon me
> because the LORD has anointed me;
> he has sent me to bring good news to the oppressed,[9]
> to bind up the brokenhearted. (Isa 61:1)

Isaiah is also quoted at least eight times in Matthew,[10] and in various parallel passages in other Gospels. Jesus quoted Isaiah so much that it's been said that he must have been "brought up on Isaiah"—that it had played a formative role in his childhood.[11]

Christians confess that Jesus was the Son of God and that he revealed God's identity and intentions in a unique way. But at least in this case, he was also preaching something that *any* rabbi working from the Hebrew scriptures could have taught. One reason Jesus welcomed a surprisingly broad range of people was that Isaiah did, too. And like the postexilic prophet, Jesus had to reckon with the weight of scripture when he spoke. In the New Testament, the interpretation of texts by the community becomes a major theme.

The rabbinic tradition out of which Jesus came could serve as a helpful model for Christians, because it inherently records

and recognizes differing opinions. Although the Christian tradition is no less diverse, there is a tendency in some quarters
to talk as if we could simply tally up the biblical passages with
the right keywords and derive the right answers—without having to really encounter God anew. We don't think to bring new
questions to God like Moses, or argue with God like Job.

The fresh encounter with a surprising God sets the trajectory for the reimaginings and revisions that take place in the
New Testament—and continue into our times. It bears repeating: Scripture reflects that God's grace and mercy towards the
whole world was always broader than one might expect. It also
says that God may change his mind and his approaches to the
world to broaden it further. So, faithfulness to God means sometimes doing the same.

II

The Widening of God's Mercy
in the New Testament

8

Jesus Upsets People

Jesus upset a lot of people. He came proclaiming good news of hope, liberation, and healing. But he also troubled many of his own people. Why? Because his teaching and actions penetrated to the heart of Israel's sacred scriptures and disclosed there a generous, unsettling vision of the wideness of God's mercy.

It may seem strange that the good news of God's mercy—so deeply grounded in Israel's own story and traditions—would upset people. But Jesus's message was troublesome because it called his followers to change. He called people to rethink their identities and their relationships to others—including others whom they may have previously regarded as alien, undesirable, immoral, or threatening. In short, he called them not only to receive mercy, but also to give it.

Jesus burst on the public scene at a time when the people of Israel were under the thumb of foreign authority. In the first century CE, the reigning power in the Mediterranean world was the Roman Empire, but Israel had endured a much longer history of suppression by more powerful kingdoms in the ancient Near East. They had experienced a brief period of independence after the Maccabean revolt during the second century BCE, but a couple of generations before the birth of Jesus, in 63 BCE, the Romans had taken control of the land.

Many people in Israel chafed under Roman authority. Some plotted revolution; their simmering resistance movement ultimately led to the catastrophic rebellion against Rome in the years 66–70 CE, as chronicled by the Jewish historian Josephus.[1] Others, including the religious leaders in Jerusalem, adopted strategies of accommodation to Roman governance.

The Gospel of John gives an irony-laden account of this kind of pragmatic strategy. In John 11, some members of a council of Jewish leaders are fretting that if Jesus is allowed to continue performing signs, he will be perceived as a dangerous leader of Jewish resistance: "If we let him go on like this, everyone will believe in him, and the Romans will come and destroy both our holy place and our nation" (John 11:48). The high priest Caiaphas responds with hard-edged realism: "You know nothing at all! You do not understand that it is better for you to have one man die for the people than to have the whole nation destroyed" (11:49–50). There are two layers of irony here: First, John reads Caiaphas's words as an unwitting prophecy that Jesus was indeed to die for the nation, and not for the nation only. But retrospective readers of John's Gospel will also know that in squelching the Jewish revolt against Roman rule, the Romans did in fact eventually destroy the holy place, the temple.

Still others, like the community at Qumran that produced the Dead Sea Scrolls, withdrew into separatist enclaves. And in the midst of it all, many looked to the words of the prophets and to the psalms for signs of hope that someday God would send them a deliverer to restore the long-lost, now almost legendary, kingdom of David—a kingdom where justice and righteousness would finally prevail.

This was precisely the hope of a prophecy spoken by Zech-

ariah, the father of John the Baptist, in the opening chapter of
the Gospel of Luke:

Blessed be the Lord God of Israel,
>   for he has looked favorably on his people and
>   redeemed them.
He has raised up a mighty savior for us
>   in the house of his servant David,
as he spoke through the mouth of his holy prophets from of
>   old,
>   that we would be saved from our enemies and from the
>   hand of all who hate us. (Luke 1:68–71)

Zechariah speaks poetically of future events as though they
had already occurred. But his proleptic prophecy stands in poignant contrast to the facts on the ground: At the time of Jesus's
birth, Israel has *not* yet been saved from its enemies.

Against that historical backdrop of subjugation, longing,
and hope, Luke's Gospel tells the story of Jesus's first recorded
public activity following his baptism by John:

> When he came to Nazareth, where he had been
> brought up, he went to the synagogue on the Sab-
> bath day, as was his custom. He stood up to read, and
> the scroll of the prophet Isaiah was given to him.
> He unrolled the scroll and found the place where it
> was written:
>
> "The Spirit of the Lord is upon me,
>   because he has anointed me
>   to bring good news to the poor.
> He has sent me to proclaim release to the captives
>   and recovery of sight to the blind,

> to let the oppressed go free,
> to proclaim the year of the Lord's favor."

And he rolled up the scroll, gave it back to the attendant, and sat down. The eyes of all in the synagogue were fixed on him. Then he began to say to them, "Today this scripture has been fulfilled in your hearing." (Luke 4:16–21)[2]

Within Luke's story, this is a bombshell. The people of Nazareth are excited by the message. The "year of the Lord's favor" has arrived! They think: *He's saying that the time has come for us, the oppressed people, to be liberated. He is going to drive out our enemies and make Israel great again!* This is a welcome message, and Luke reports, "All spoke well of him and were amazed at the words of grace that came from his mouth" (Luke 4:22).[3]

On the other hand, they do find it a bit odd that Jesus, the hometown boy, is declaring himself God's long-awaited anointed messenger. Understandably, some of the congregation in the synagogue are incredulous ("Isn't this Joseph's son?" they ask).

Furthermore, Jesus goes on to explain that he has a different vision of the intended recipients of Isaiah's good news, a wider understanding of "the year of the Lord's favor" than the interpretation apparently held by his fellow townspeople. To elaborate, he alludes to two stories from the scriptures in which outsiders—one from the region of Sidon and another from Syria—receive God's mercy:

> But the truth is, there were many widows in Israel in the time of Elijah, when the heaven was shut up three years and six months and there was a severe famine over all the land; yet Elijah was sent to none of them except to a widow in Zarephath in Sidon.

There were also many lepers in Israel in the time of
the prophet Elisha, and none of them was cleansed
except Naaman the Syrian. (Luke 4:25–27, referring
to 1 Kgs 17:8–24 and 2 Kgs 5:1–19a)

According to Luke's account, this was *not* what the people wanted to hear. Their hope was for national restoration; they
didn't want to hear that God's effusive mercy might also be lav-
ished on foreigners. They were particularly incensed to hear
Jesus citing stories from scripture in support of this seemingly
unpatriotic idea. They weren't just surprised and disappointed;
they were "filled with rage," so furious in fact that they "got up,
drove him out of the town, and led him to the brow of the hill
on which their town was built, so that they might hurl him off
the cliff" (Luke 4:28–29). But Jesus eludes their grasp and narrowly escapes.

As Luke tells the story, from the very beginning of his
ministry, Jesus interpreted his own work in light of Isaiah's prophetic message. And he understood Isaiah's message to signify—
as we have seen earlier in this book—not only the restoration
of Israel, but also an expansion of the grace of Israel's God to
encompass foreign nations and to embrace outcasts.[4]

Jesus's prophetic proclamation provoked amazement and
triggered hostility from some of his hearers—particularly those
in positions of authority. That provocation eventually reached
its climax at the end of Jesus's public career, when he drove the
merchants and money changers out of the temple, saying:

"Is it not written,

'My house shall be called a house of prayer for all
    the nations'?
        But you have made it a den of robbers."

> And when the chief priests and the scribes heard
> it, they kept looking for a way to kill him; for they
> were afraid of him, because the whole crowd was
> spellbound by his teaching. (Mark 11:17–18)[5]

As Jeremiah had discovered earlier, criticism of the temple was
a sore subject for many religious leaders in Jerusalem.[6]

It's important to notice that *Jesus was not condemning
temple worship itself.* Instead, he was defending its purity and
integrity against those who were exploiting and corrupting it.
Christian interpreters have too often made the disastrous mistake of thinking that Jesus was opposing Judaism and seeking
to replace it with a more universal, purely spiritual religion
(Christianity). On the contrary, Jesus was firmly rooted in Jewish prophetic tradition. Both his critique of the Jewish authorities of his time and his expansive vision of God's mercy were
grounded in Israel's scriptures. For an analogy in recent history,
consider the way in which the Reverend Martin Luther King
Jr. stood squarely in the biblical tradition and in the highest
ideals of American history in order to summon both church
and nation to repent and change, to live into a truer vision of
social and racial equality.

Similarly, Jesus stood directly in the tradition of Isaiah
and Jeremiah, both of whom he quoted in his condemnation of
the merchants and money changers. "My house shall be called
a house of prayer for all the nations" is an explicit quotation of
Isaiah 56:7, and his announcement resonates strongly with Isaiah's withering critique of the people's hypocrisy and injustice:

> Shout out, do not hold back!
>> Lift up your voice like a trumpet!
> Announce to my people their rebellion,
>> to the house of Jacob their sins.

Yet day after day they seek me
        and delight to know my ways,
as if they were a nation that practiced righteousness
        and did not forsake the ordinance of their God. . . .
Look, you serve your own interest on your fast day,
        and oppress all your workers.
Look, you fast only to quarrel and to fight
        and to strike with a wicked fist.
Such fasting as you do today
        will not make your voice heard on high. (Isa 58:1–4)

Furthermore, Jesus's portrayal of the commercially compromised temple as "a den of robbers" is taken directly from Jeremiah's scathing indictment of hypocritical temple practices (Jer 7:1–11).

So Jesus should be understood first of all as a radical Jewish prophet. There is more than that to be said about who he was, but not less.

Before him, Jesus's mother, Mary, stands in that same prophetic stream. After she conceived Jesus, she sang a song of praise to the Lord (known to later Christian tradition as the Magnificat). Her prophetic song drew from the deep well of Israel's scriptures (cf. Hannah's prayer in 1 Sam 2:1–10; Ps 113) to proclaim the coming reversal of fortune: God will bring down the proud and powerful while lifting up the poor and lowly.

My soul magnifies the Lord,
        and my spirit rejoices in God my Savior,
for he has looked with favor on the lowliness of his servant.
        Surely, from now on all generations will call me
        blessed;
for the Mighty One has done great things for me,
        and holy is his name.

His mercy is for those who fear him
> from generation to generation.
He has shown strength with his arm;
> he has scattered the proud in the thoughts of their
> > hearts.
He has brought down the powerful from their thrones,
> and lifted up the lowly;
he has filled the hungry with good things,
> and sent the rich away empty.
He has helped his servant Israel,
> in remembrance of his mercy,
according to the promise he made to our ancestors,
> to Abraham and to his descendants forever.
> > (Luke 1:46–55)

Mary rejoiced in the confidence that God's mercy was for *all* who fear him, from generation to generation. (To "fear" God does not mean to quake in terror; rather, it means to stand in reverence, respecting God's holiness and power.)

Perhaps, then, it is no surprise that her son Jesus came to embrace a similar confidence that God's mercy and blessing would be poured out freely on the lowly and on those who have suffered rejection and oppression. This is the message he proclaimed:

> Blessed are you who are poor,
> > for yours is the kingdom of God.
> Blessed are you who are hungry now,
> > for you will be filled.
> Blessed are you who weep now,
> > for you will laugh.
> . . . .
> But woe to you who are rich,

> for you have received your consolation.
> Woe to you who are full now,
>> for you will be hungry.
> Woe to you who are laughing now,
>> for you will mourn and weep.

Woe to you when all speak well of you, for that is what their ancestors did to the false prophets. (Luke 6:20–21, 24–26)[7]

Jesus's message turns the world upside down. This theme of *eschatological reversal* is hardwired into the Gospel accounts of Jesus's teaching: not only in the Beatitudes, but also in his parables, such as that of the prodigal son (Luke 15:11–32), and his aphorisms—for example, "But many who are first will be last, and the last will be first" (Matt 19:30).[8]

The term "eschatological" refers to "last things," the ultimate fulfillment of God's gracious purposes for history. Interpreters of Mary's Magnificat and Jesus's Beatitudes sometimes suppose that the great reversal—the pouring out of blessing on the poor and hungry and on those who weep—is a promise only for the far future or for the afterlife. As Paul writes in his Letter to the Romans, "we hope for what we do not see" (Rom 8:25). To be sure, that is true; we don't yet see the final fulfillment of God's promises.

But the entire New Testament also bears witness that God's powerful, healing future has already begun breaking into the present time. Jesus declares again and again, in his words and actions, that the kingdom of God has drawn near. The greatest sign of that inbreaking new age is, of course, Jesus's resurrection. The power of death is already defeated—and because of his resurrection the community of Jesus's followers is already experiencing signs and foretastes of the new creation.

Readers of C. S. Lewis's *The Chronicles of Narnia* will recall the scene in *The Lion, the Witch, and the Wardrobe* where the coming of Aslan to Narnia prefigures the end of the White Witch's cruel reign, and the unrelenting winter of Narnia begins to thaw. That story mirrors the New Testament's portrayal of Jesus's life-giving incursion into our history of pain, loss, and death. Where the good news is proclaimed and the Spirit is present, the reversals proclaimed by Mary and Jesus are already happening. It's been a long, cold, lonely winter. But when the sun appears, the ice begins to melt.

Once we grasp this message of reversal, it is only another short step to imagine that God's good news is meant not just for his band of early followers and not just for the people of Israel but also for a wider circle of those who were previously—as the Letter to the Ephesians later declares—"aliens from the commonwealth of Israel and strangers to the covenants of promise, having no hope and without God in the world" (Eph 2:12). Might they—or better, might *we*—also be counted among the poor, captive, blind, and oppressed for whom the year of the Lord's favor has dawned? If so, we might also ask ourselves how our own lives, our own communities, reflect and embody the great reversal that Jesus proclaimed. How do we become conduits for the unexpected mercy that we have received?

In the following chapters, we explore several stories in which Jesus challenged or transformed previously settled understandings of God's will for those who seek to live rightly. Many of these stories will be familiar to readers of this book, but their very familiarity may have hindered our ability to discern how they might cast fresh light on the church's contemporary struggles with questions of sexuality. Of course, if we go to the four Gospels looking for Jesus's explicit teachings about homosexuality, we will look in vain; there's not a word on this topic in the Gospels. But these foundational texts might offer us some-

thing else, perhaps something better: a collection of stories
that teach us how to reframe ethical questions in light of God's
scandalously merciful character. As we revisit these well-known
stories, I propose that we keep asking ourselves this question:
How might the Gospel stories of Jesus's convention-altering
words and actions affect our thinking about norms for sexual
relationships in our time?

But that is to get ahead of ourselves. The Gospels focus
on the stories of Jesus's own earthly lifetime. For that reason,
they offer only hints and foreshadowings of the momentous
conclusions that the church was later to draw about rereading
Israel's scripture as a witness for the expansiveness of God's
gracious welcome. Before we can ponder those hints and foreshadowings, it's necessary to begin where the Gospels begin—
by tracing some of the specific ways in which Jesus *directly* proclaimed and enacted the wideness of God's mercy.

9
Sabbath as a Time for Healing

A re there times when the human desire for conscientious obedience to biblical law actually produces actions contrary to the spirit and intent of God's commandments? This paradoxical tension is nowhere more clearly illustrated than in the Gospel stories of Jesus's healings on the Sabbath day.

The Gospels tell several stories of Jesus's conflicts with Pharisees or other Jewish leaders for performing healings on the Sabbath. The details vary, but the plot is similar in each case. On the Sabbath, Jesus encounters a person who is suffering from some physical affliction: a man with a withered hand (Matt 12:9–14, Mark 3:1–6, Luke 6:6–11), a crippled woman unable to stand up straight (Luke 13:10–17), a man suffering from edema[1] (Luke 14:1–6), a man unable to walk (John 5:1–18). Each time, Jesus has compassion for the sufferer and performs a miraculous healing, despite the disapproval and resistance of wary religious authorities.

These accounts appear prominently in all four Gospels; the emphasis given to them suggests that the Gospel writers saw something crucial in these healing/controversy stories. Clearly, the evangelists tell and retell these stories not merely to demonstrate Jesus's great healing power but also to teach something about his controversial interpretation of Israel's law.

The requirement to observe the Sabbath by resting and refraining from work is one of the foundational elements of Jewish piety. In both lists of the Ten Commandments given in Israel's scriptures, this particular commandment is spelled out in full detail. But, as the italicized sentences below reflect, these two versions of the Sabbath commandment give different warrants for observance of the day:

Remember the sabbath day and keep it holy. Six days you shall labor and do all your work. But the seventh day is a sabbath to the LORD your God; you shall not do any work—you, your son or your daughter, your male or female slave, your livestock, or the alien resident in your towns. *For in six days the LORD made heaven and earth, the sea, and all that is in them, but rested the seventh day; therefore the LORD blessed the sabbath day and consecrated it.* (Exod 20:8–11)

Observe the sabbath day and keep it holy, as the LORD your God commanded you. Six days you shall labor and do all your work. But the seventh day is a sabbath to the LORD your God; you shall not do any work—you, or your son or your daughter, or your male or female slave, or your ox or your donkey, or any of your livestock, or the resident alien in your towns, so that your male and female slave may rest as well as you. *Remember that you were a slave in the land of Egypt, and the LORD your God brought you out from there with a mighty hand and an out-*

stretched arm; therefore the LORD *your God com-*
manded you to keep the sabbath day. (Deut 5:12–15)

In Exodus, the mandate to rest is patterned on God's resting
on the seventh day of creation. In Deuteronomy, that mandate
is rooted in the memory of the people's liberation from slavery.
The opportunity to rest is a sign of freedom, and even the slaves
of the people of Israel must be given a day of Sabbath rest. There
is no contradiction between these two accounts of the reasons
for keeping the Sabbath. *Creation* and *liberation* are complementary aspects of God's gracious action.

Given how important the Sabbath was, it isn't surprising
that the Pharisees and synagogue leaders were seeking to enforce scrupulous observance of these solemn Sabbath restrictions. They were not just picking nits; they were concerned for
careful and rigorous observation of a divinely given ordinance
that had deep theological justification in the scriptural stories
of creation and redemption. In short, they believed that Israel's survival depended on it. In Deuteronomy 28, for instance,
Moses instructs the people that if they "diligently" observe God's
commandments, they will receive overflowing blessings and
prosperity; however, if they do not "diligently" obey all God's
commandments and decrees, terrible curses will befall them,
including military defeat and horrifying abuse at the hands of
their enemies. So the stakes were high for meticulous observance of the law's teachings.

The scribes and Pharisees have gotten a bad rap in much
Christian preaching, but in fairness they should be understood
as earnestly devout people concerned to maintain a high view
of scriptural holiness and scriptural authority. No doubt their
motives for opposing Jesus were mixed—as most human motives are—but their concern about Jesus's flouting of Sabbath
rules was logically and theologically consistent. Although there

is no specific prohibition in Torah of *healing* on the Sabbath, Jesus's opponents were operating on the basis of a traditional interpretation that sought to safeguard the sanctity of the Sabbath day.[2]

Jesus certainly didn't disapprove of Sabbath observance, either. Instead, as the Gospels make clear, he sought to deepen the meaning and intent of the day in a way that recognized the expansive scope of God's mercy.

For purposes of illustration, let's look more closely at two of the Gospel accounts of Jesus's healing activity on the Sabbath, one in Mark and the other in Luke.

Mark 3:1–6 is the culminating episode in a cycle of brief stories near the beginning of Mark's Gospel that dramatize Jesus's emergent conflict with scribes and Pharisees (Mark 2:1–3:6). As in several of these controversy stories, the action occurs in a synagogue:

> Again he entered the synagogue, and a man was there who had a withered hand. They watched him to see whether he would cure him on the sabbath, so that they might accuse him. And he said to the man who had the withered hand, "Come forward." Then he said to them, "Is it lawful to do good or to do harm on the sabbath, to save life or to kill?" But they were silent. He looked around at them with anger; he was grieved at their hardness of heart and said to the man, "Stretch out your hand." He stretched it out, and his hand was restored. The Pharisees went out and immediately conspired with the Herodians against him, how to destroy him. (3:1–6)

Jesus takes the initiative in provoking debate. He frames his healing of the man with a pointed question: "Is it lawful to do good or to do harm on the Sabbath, to save life or to kill?" The silence of the legal authorities reveals their recognition of the compelling force of the question: It challenges them to reflect on the *purpose* of the Sabbath law—and to interpret it as an ordinance given for the sake of human wholeness and flourishing.

We tend to imagine this scene from the perspective of Jesus or of the man who is healed. But it's also poignant to read the story from the standpoint of these faithful Pharisaic scribes. Here they are, faced with human suffering; their silence in the face of Jesus's question may indicate that they are internally conflicted about how to answer. They feel unable to help or react in any way because of their strong beliefs and their determination to uphold the authority of scripture. And so their sacred space becomes a place of withholding and suffering.

In the silence of these scribes in the synagogue, I see a reflection of my own longstanding reticence to speak about the question of same-sex relationships in the church: uncomfortably aware of aching human need but constrained by my interpretation of scripture from responding with grace or generosity. And so I kept silent.

What Jesus says about the Sabbath is consistent with Isaiah's interpretation of "a day acceptable to the LORD":

Is not this the fast that I choose:
> to loose the bonds of injustice,
> to undo the thongs of the yoke,
to let the oppressed go free,
> and to break every yoke?
Is it not to share your bread with the hungry,
> and bring the homeless poor into your house;
when you see the naked, to cover them,
> and not to hide yourself from your own kin?

Then your light shall break forth like the dawn,
    and your healing shall spring up quickly;
your vindicator shall go before you,
    the glory of the LORD shall be your rear guard.
Then you shall call, and the LORD will answer;
    you shall cry for help, and he will say, Here I am.
        (Isa 58:6–9a)

Isaiah's powerful words are part of his indictment of a people who . . .

. . . seek me
    and delight to know my ways,
as if they were a nation that practiced righteousness
    and did not forsake the ordinance of their God. (58:2)

But in Isaiah's view, their hypocrisy is shown by their behavior: Even while fasting, they oppress their workers, quarrel with each other, and "strike with a wicked fist" (58:4).

Like Isaiah's audience centuries earlier, the Pharisees believe they are seeking to practice righteousness—but their silence is self-condemning: They refuse to change their minds about the rightness of Jesus's healing. Their strict adherence to their traditional interpretation of the law overrides any concern for the afflicted man who stands before them. That is why Jesus is both angry and "grieved at their hardness of heart." I now suspect that the Lord may have been also grieved with me.

In Luke 13:10–17 we encounter a similar story, again unfolding in a synagogue on the Sabbath:

Now he was teaching in one of the synagogues on
the sabbath. And just then there appeared a woman

with a spirit that had crippled her for eighteen years. She was bent over and was quite unable to stand up straight. When Jesus saw her, he called her over and said, "Woman, you are set free from your ailment." When he laid his hands on her, immediately she stood up straight and began praising God. But the leader of the synagogue, indignant because Jesus had cured on the sabbath, kept saying to the crowd, "There are six days on which work ought to be done; come on those days and be cured, and not on the sabbath day." But the Lord answered him and said, "You hypocrites! Does not each of you on the sabbath untie his ox or his donkey from the manger, and lead it away to give it water? And ought not this woman, a daughter of Abraham whom Satan bound for eighteen long years, be set free from this bondage on the sabbath day?" When he said this, all his opponents were put to shame; and the entire crowd was rejoicing at all the wonderful things that he was doing.

In this case, Jesus *sees* the suffering woman and heals her; he simply lays hands on her and pronounces that she is set free. Luke's account, unlike Mark's briefer story, emphasizes the response of the person healed: She "stood up straight and began praising God." Her action of standing up straight signifies that this event is not just a healing but also an act of liberation.

As Jesus says, she has been *"set free,"* and she has found a voice of gratitude to God. As readers of Luke's Gospel, we should recall what Jesus said at the beginning of his public mission: He has been anointed by the Spirit of the Lord to proclaim *release* to the captives and "to let the oppressed go free" (Luke

4:18). This woman, now set free on the Sabbath, embodies the meaning of that good news.

Up to this point, there is no controversy; it appears that this is a straightforwardly joyful healing story. But the leader of the synagogue protests retrospectively. Interestingly, rather than scolding *Jesus* directly for his offensive healing action, he begins exhorting *the crowd* to come back some other day, not the Sabbath day, to be healed. There is something oddly pathetic in this appeal; even though he is unable to undo the merciful healing that Jesus has performed, he wants to head off any more such embarrassing violations in the space where he holds authority.

And once again, Jesus responds angrily: "You hypocrites!" (The plural noun suggests that the leader of the synagogue is not alone in his disapproval of what Jesus has done; others must be supporting his resistance.)

When Jesus refers to untying and leading an ox or donkey to water on the Sabbath, he is alluding to an already established practice of interpreting Torah. The rabbis carried on extended debates about what actually counts as "work"; they sought to articulate precisely the conditions under which exceptions could be made to the strictest prohibition of Sabbath-day activity.[3] In light of these debates, Jesus's reply to the synagogue leader employs the logic of reasoning from the lesser to the greater: We are not arguing here about an ox or a donkey. If you approve of the task of giving water to thirsty animals, how could you not approve of healing this afflicted woman? This is a woman, a daughter of Abraham! If Satan has bound her for eighteen years, what could be more appropriate on the Sabbath day than to set her free from this bondage?

In the Greek text of Luke's Gospel, the same verb (*luei*, "to loose") is used for both the untying of a thirsty animal and the freeing of the bent-over woman from her condition. Again, the echoes of Isaiah are loud:

> Is not this the fast that I choose:
> > to *loose* the bonds of injustice,
> > to *undo the thongs* of the yoke,
> to let the oppressed go free,
> > and to break every yoke? (Isa 58:6)

Luke concludes the story by telling us something important. Jesus's opponents are put to shame, but "the entire crowd was rejoicing at all the wonderful things that he was doing." This shows that the worshipers in the synagogue are not scandalized by Jesus's gracious actions and words; nor are they intimidated by their scrupulous, disapproving leader. They recognize God's grace when they see it in action, and they rejoice.

In these Sabbath healing stories, then, Jesus acts with compassion and justifies what he has done by appealing to *the wideness of God's mercy.* Healing on the Sabbath, he says, is not defiance of God's law but rather an embracing of its deeper intent. Healing on the Sabbath is a decision to do good and to save life rather than to do harm. The command to rest on the Sabbath is not an arbitrary restriction; it is given for the sake of human well-being. That means that actions done for healing and human wholeness should be welcomed rather than forbidden, *even if they appear to violate a particular scriptural prohibition.* As Jesus proclaims elsewhere, "The Sabbath was made for humankind and not humankind for the Sabbath" (Mark 2:27). If the well-meaning attempt to honor God's law leads to hardness of heart and blindness to the need of afflicted people, something has gone badly awry.

10

Mercy, Not Sacrifice

The last chapter traced the way Jesus advocated—both in word and in action—a generous reading of Israel's law that highlighted the wideness of God's mercy. As a Jewish prophet, a passionate voice in Israel's prophetic tradition, he encountered resistance from other devout Jews who held to a narrower interpretation of scriptural law. In other cases, however, Jesus encountered resistance from his contemporaries not because he was seen to be violating a divinely given law but rather because he was willing to associate freely with *others* who were seen as lawbreakers—or simply as disreputable. In fact, one of the hallmarks of Jesus's public mission was his scandalous practice of eating with "tax collectors and sinners."

The Gospel of Matthew tells the story of Jesus's calling of a tax collector named Matthew to follow him.[1] As the story unfolds, we see a clear picture of Jesus's practice of table fellowship with socially unacceptable people—and of the offense it caused:

> As Jesus was walking along, he saw a man called Matthew sitting at the tax booth; and he said to him, "Follow me." And he got up and followed him.

> And as he sat at dinner in the house, many tax collectors and sinners came and were sitting with him and his disciples. When the Pharisees saw this, they said to his disciples, "Why does your teacher eat with tax collectors and sinners?" But when he heard this, he said, "Those who are well have no need of a physician, but those who are sick. Go and learn what this means, 'I desire *mercy*, not sacrifice.' For I have come to call not the righteous but sinners." (Matt 9:9–13)

Why was it objectionable for Jesus to eat with tax collectors? Tax collectors were despised by many because they were in collaboration with the Roman authorities; their job was to collect tribute payments from the people.[2] Furthermore, there was good reason to believe that some of them were lining their own pockets by extortionate gathering of money, taking a cut of what they collected (cf. Luke 19:8). Thus, they were seen as traitors to their own people. Today, some people in the United States feel a similar contempt for politicians who receive large contributions from wealthy corporate donors in exchange for supporting legislation that creates tax breaks for the rich while disregarding the interests of the majority of less affluent citizens.

What about the "sinners"? Who were they? Other stories in the Gospels might imply that this slur refers particularly to people habitually engaged in sexual misconduct (prostitutes and adulterers), but actually the term has a far broader meaning; in principle, it could include everyone who failed to obey the law scrupulously. For advocates of strict legal purity, the category of "sinners" could include a wide range of "undesirables." In the context of the Gospel accounts, the term "sinners" is a catchall designation used by people who regard themselves as righteous (in this case, the Pharisees) to express disdain for people they perceive as being less respectable. And so, the pervasive human impulse toward what we today call "cancel culture" kicks in when the Pharisees see Jesus dining with tax collectors and sinners.[3]

In Matthew's account, the Pharisees don't challenge Jesus directly for associating with unseemly dinner companions. Instead, they confront his disciples: "Why does your teacher eat with tax collectors and sinners?" Jesus overhears and intervenes to answer their question directly. His answer has two components.

First, Jesus explains his action by using the metaphor of a physician whose calling is to help the sick. He declares that he has come for the precise purpose of calling those who are actually in need of help, not the self-proclaimed "righteous" who have no need of healing. (One suspects that Jesus's concessive description of the Pharisees as "those who are well" is heavy with irony.) This first part of Jesus's answer would suggest that his purpose in breaking bread with tax collectors and sinners is to summon them to repent and change their ways.

But there is a second crucial component in Jesus's answer. In Matthew's distinctive telling of the story,[4] Jesus also points the objectors to a key text (Hos 6:6) from Israel's scriptures: "Go and learn what this means: 'I desire *mercy* [*eleos*], not sacrifice.'"[5] This text from Hosea might seem like an odd justification for hanging out with tax collectors, but in fact it opens up a wider field of vision on interpreting scripture. Jesus is suggesting that his decision to sit down with the disreputables is neither a careless violation of propriety nor a calculated evangelistic stratagem; instead, it is a symbolic acting-out of the *mercy* that lies at the heart of God's own desire.

Matthew's quotation of Hosea 6:6 follows the Greek Septuagint, which uses the word *eleos* to translate the Hebrew *ḥesed*. This word carries the connotation not of "pity," but rather of

"passionate, steadfast love." So the passage doesn't call readers
to *feel sorry* for "sinners"; rather, it calls them to participate in
God's desire to embrace sinners in love. When Jesus says "Go
and learn what this means," he's telling the Pharisees to go back
and study Hosea; he is pointing them back to Hosea's prophetic
revelation of the all-encompassing, restorative love of God. In
Hosea 6, to "know the LORD" is to know him as one who will
heal and bind up wounds rather than condemn:

> His appearing is as sure as the dawn;
> he will come to us like the showers,
> > like the spring rains that water the earth. (Hos 6:3b)

Mercy stands near the heart of Jesus's teaching. The theme
is sounded already in the Beatitudes, Jesus's opening discourse
on the meaning of discipleship: "Blessed are the *merciful,* for
they will receive *mercy*" (Matt 5:7). Matthew underscores the
importance of this theme by repeating it again and again.

In a later controversy discourse about plucking grain on
the Sabbath, Jesus once again challenges the Pharisees to rethink their restrictive scruples in light of the broader meaning
of Hosea 6:6: "But if you had known what this means, 'I desire
mercy and not sacrifice,' you would not have condemned the
guiltless" (Matt 12:7). Jesus is suggesting that mercy is the overriding message of scripture; Hosea 6:6 becomes the key that
unlocks what Israel's scripture is actually all about.

Mercy belongs to the very short list of what Jesus calls
"the weightier matters of the law: justice and *mercy* and faith"
(Matt 23:23). In the grain-plucking controversy in Matthew 12:1–8,
Jesus accuses the Pharisees of being blind to these weightier
matters, because their morally tidy hermeneutic is straining out
gnats (by protesting against plucking grain on the Sabbath to
feed hungry people) but swallowing a camel (cf. 23:23–24).

The Gospel accounts, taken as a whole, suggest that Jesus's act of sitting down at table with tax collectors and sinners was not a one-time event; it was a controversial and regular practice that drew criticism from many of his contemporaries. Jesus laments that "this generation" of hearers were unreceptive to the messengers that God was sending to them: "For John [the Baptist] came neither eating nor drinking, and they say, 'He has a demon'; the Son of Man came eating and drinking, and they say, 'Look, a glutton and a drunkard, a friend of tax collectors and sinners!'" (Matt 11:18–19, Luke 7:33–34).

That label stuck for one reason: It was true. Jesus really was a friend of tax collectors and sinners, for his mission was to embody the wideness of God's mercy.

In the Gospel of Luke, Jesus drives home this point by telling the parable of the Pharisee and the tax collector (Luke 18:9–14). The Pharisee says, "God, I thank you that I am not like other people: thieves, rogues, adulterers, or even this tax collector." But the tax collector beats his breast and prays, "God, be *merciful* to me, a sinner." The tax collector throws himself on God's *mercy,* and he is the one who is said to be "justified."[6] To make sure that we don't miss the point, Luke frames this parable with an explanatory word. Why did Jesus tell this parable? He was speaking "to those who trusted in themselves that they were righteous and regarded others with contempt."

This story holds up a mirror to all of us in the church who are tempted to consider ourselves righteous and to look with contempt at others. We the community of Jesus's followers—whatever our sexual orientation—will disregard this parable at our own peril. Indeed, those of us who are heterosexual Christians might need to look critically at the disordered state of sexual relations in our own lives and communities and breathe the tax collector's prayer: "God have mercy."

Luke gives us one final story about a tax collector, in this case, a "chief tax collector" (*architelōnes*), Zacchaeus (Luke 19:1–10). This rare word, which does not appear elsewhere in the New Testament, apparently means that he oversaw a team of other tax collectors and profited handsomely from his job. Luke pointedly remarks that he "was rich." No doubt this made him all the more offensive to the ordinary Jewish people whose taxes went to support his affluent lifestyle. But Jesus surprisingly invites himself to Zacchaeus's home. This time it is not only the Pharisees who are scandalized: "*All who saw it* began to grumble and said, 'He has gone to be the guest of one who is a sinner.'" As so often in the Gospels, Jesus incurs guilt by association; his acceptance of hospitality from Zacchaeus is interpreted by the onlookers as tacit condoning of Zacchaeus's oppressive tax-farming operation.

But something startling happens: Confronted by the presence of Jesus, Zacchaeus declares, "Look, half my possessions, Lord, I will give to the poor, and if I have defrauded anyone of anything, I will pay back four times as much." Zacchaeus's promise to repay "four times as much" is in the spirit of the law of Exodus 22:1, which prescribes restitution of four or five times the value of stolen livestock. This is what authentic repentance looks like: the generous setting right of economic wrongs.[7] And rather than scolding Zacchaeus for his past misdeeds, Jesus simply proclaims the good news of God's grace: "Today salvation has come to this house."

What we have seen in these stories about tax collectors holds equally true for Jesus's generous fellowship with other "sinners." Let us consider the story of Jesus's encounter (Luke 7:36–50) with "a woman in the city who was a sinner." We are not told what she had done wrong to be classified as such a notorious sinner. She has often been depicted in the tradition as a prostitute, but the text offers no explicit indication of that.[8] Jesus says near the end of the episode that her sins were many, but neither he nor she discloses what they may have been. The important thing is that she interrupts the dignified dinner party by extravagantly anointing his feet with expensive ointment, bathing them with her tears, and drying them with her hair—surely an erotically charged act.

This time the story is taking place not in the house of a disreputable tax collector, but in the home of a Pharisee named Simon. The fact that Jesus is now dining with a Pharisee shows that he is an equal opportunity dinner guest, willing to sit down at table not only with "sinners," but also with upright citizens who pride themselves on careful observance of the law and its purity standards.

Simon, however, is scandalized by Jesus's embarrassing indulgence of this weeping woman: "Now when the Pharisee who had invited him saw it, he said to himself,[9] 'If this man were a prophet, he would have known who and what kind of woman this is who is touching him—that she is a sinner'" (Luke 7:39). Horrors! Of course, as the story unfolds, we see that Jesus does in fact know perfectly well that she is a sinner—and precisely for that reason he welcomes her touching expression of "great love" (7:47), which he contrasts to Simon's stingy hospitality.

The climax of the story is Jesus's pronouncement to the woman, "Your sins are forgiven"—a pronouncement that triggers wonderment and dismay from the other dinner guests: "Who is this who even forgives sins?" They are saying, "Who does he think he is, anyway, to claim that authority?" As readers of Luke's Gospel, we know the answer to the question: He is the One anointed by the Spirit to let the oppressed go free and to proclaim the year of the Lord's favor.

The deep plot structure of this story closely parallels the structure of Jesus's mission-defining parable of the prodigal son (Luke 15:11–32). The younger son wanders off and squanders his inheritance in "dissolute living" in a far country; he winds up mucking around feeding pigs, who were regarded as unclean animals. Eventually, he drags himself home repentantly, hoping to be received no longer as a son but, at best, as a hired hand. But here is the surprise turning point of the story: "while he was still far off, his father saw him *and was filled with compassion;*[10] he ran and put his arms around him and kissed him." The father in Jesus's parable corresponds to the passionate God of Israel who says, "I desire mercy and not sacrifice"—and who goes on later in Hosea to say this to Israel:

> How can I give you up, Ephraim? . . .
> My heart recoils within me;
> > my compassion grows warm and tender. . . .
> for I am God and no mortal,
> > the Holy One in your midst,
> > and I will not come in wrath. (Hos 11:8–9)

(Note carefully: This is a classic expression of God changing his mind, rescinding his earlier declaration of judgment and destruction.)

But the older son in Jesus's parable wants to hear none of this. He has been a diligent and dutiful son, following all the rules. Like Simon the Pharisee, he sees his younger brother as a sinner unworthy of his father's compassion, and he begrudges the party that the father is throwing to welcome him back. Sadly, he exemplifies the truth of Jesus's maxim spoken to Simon: "the one to whom little is forgiven, loves little" (Luke 7:47). Nonetheless, the father continues to invite the petulant older brother to come and join the celebration.

Those who, like the older brother, begrudge Jesus's welcoming of those deemed sinful and despised are unwittingly placing themselves in the shoes of the chief priests and elders of the people, to whom Jesus gave a dire warning: "Truly I tell you, the tax collectors and the prostitutes are going into the kingdom of God ahead of you" (Matt 21:31).

It should not escape our attention that the parable of the prodigal son is the climax of three parables that Jesus tells in reply to the grumbling of Pharisees and scribes who complain, "This fellow welcomes sinners and eats with them" (Luke 15:2). It's true: Indeed, he does.

11

Mercy to Foreigners and Outsiders

So far we have seen that Jesus consistently interpreted the particular commandments of Israel's scriptures within the wider horizon of God's mercy. And we have also seen that Jesus upended some established conventions of his time and culture by welcoming fellowship with "tax collectors and sinners." In the latter case, he was not breaking any laws, even though he may have appeared to some of his contemporaries to be flirting dangerously with "the path that sinners tread" (Ps 1:1).

In light of these surprising indicators of *the wideness of God's mercy*, let us return now to the issues Jesus raised at the beginning of his public mission when he suggested that in "the year of the Lord's favor" (Luke 4:19), God's liberating mercy might overflow the national/ethnic boundaries of Israel and fall upon foreigners (4:25–27).

In Jewish parlance, all non-Jews were simply called "the nations"—*goyim* in Hebrew, *ethnē* in Greek. "Gentiles," the standard translation in English, is derived from the Latin *gentes* ("nations"). In reading modern translations of the New Testament, it is important to remember that references to "the gentiles" always presuppose a Jewish perspective: "Gentiles" are seen as foreigners, outsiders to the people of God, "aliens from the commonwealth of Israel and strangers to the covenants of promise" (Eph 2:12). Some observant Jews were wary of associating too closely with gentiles: They were uncircumcised, ate unclean foods, were regarded as sexually immoral, and generally were implicated in idolatry—the worship of other gods.[1]

Jesus, during his short public career, did not pursue a mission of outreach to the gentiles. Quite the contrary: In Matthew's Gospel, he explicitly instructs his disciples to stay away from them. He sent the twelve out with these instructions: "Go nowhere among the Gentiles, and enter no town of the Samaritans, but go rather to the lost sheep of the house of Israel" (Matt 10:5–6).[2]

Nonetheless, the actual conditions on the ground in first-century Israel were such that contact with gentiles was not unusual, given the Roman presence in the land and the reality of commerce in the empire. The Galilean town of Sepphoris, rebuilt by Herod Antipas as "the ornament of all Galilee," was only four miles from Nazareth.[3] Modern excavations have found signs of Greco-Roman cultural influence in this urban setting, within walking distance of Jesus's small hometown.[4] Though the Gospels do not mention Sepphoris, they do narrate a few incidents in which Jesus encounters gentiles/foreigners. These episodes offer hints and anticipations of the church's later mission, after Jesus's resurrection, to the gentile world. As we shall see in following chapters of this book, that mission proved controversial. But some of the seeds from which that mission grew can be found in Jesus's surprising interactions with these foreigners.

In Matthew 8:5–13, a Roman centurion approaches Jesus with an entreaty for help:

> When he entered Capernaum, a centurion came to
> him, appealing to him and saying, "Lord, my ser-

vant is lying at home paralyzed, in terrible distress."
And he said to him, "I will come and cure him." The
centurion answered, "Lord, I am not worthy to have
you come under my roof; but only speak the word,
and my servant will be healed. For I also am a man
under authority, with soldiers under me; and I say
to one, 'Go,' and he goes, and to another, 'Come,' and
he comes, and to my slave, 'Do this,' and the slave
does it." When Jesus heard him, he was amazed and
said to those who followed him, "Truly I tell you, in
no one in Israel have I found such faith. I tell you,
many will come from east and west and will eat with
Abraham and Isaac and Jacob in the kingdom of
heaven, while the heirs of the kingdom will be thrown
into the outer darkness, where there will be weeping and gnashing of teeth." And to the centurion Jesus
said, "Go; let it be done for you according to your
faith." And the servant was healed in that hour.

This story includes several surprises. A Roman military
official approaches Jesus (a member of the subjugated Jewish
populace) in an unexpected posture of humility, addressing him
as "Lord" (*kyrie*). The English translation "Lord" may reflect a
later Christian interpretation of the Greek text; the vocative
kyrie in common Greek usage could simply mean "sir." Even
so, it is an address indicating respect for Jesus, not what one
would expect from a Roman officer. In the parallel account in
Luke 7:1–10, the centurion sends Jewish elders as intermedi-
aries who vouch for him, saying he is "worthy of having you
do this for him, for he loves our people, and it is he who built
our synagogue for us." He is thus depicted as a "godfearer," a
gentile who reveres Israel's God and the Jewish people, without
having undergone full proselyte conversion. Matthew's version

of the story, however, provides none of this shock-softening justification; he tells the bare tale as an inexplicable instance of a gentile official who trusts in Jesus's power to heal.

Perhaps equally surprising is that Jesus, without further ado, immediately volunteers that he will come and heal the servant. And most remarkable of all is the centurion's abject avowal, "I am not worthy to have you come under my roof," along with his confidence that Jesus has the authority to perform a long-distance healing simply by speaking a word.

This bold speech of the centurion elicits from Jesus a startled pronouncement: "Truly I tell you, in no one in Israel have I found such faith." This gentile foreigner has expressed an unanticipated faith that is lacking in many of Jesus's own people. Jesus declares that he sees here a foreshadowing of the great eschatological banquet when "many will come from east and west" to sit at table with Israel's long-dead patriarchs.[5] This prophecy portends an extension of table fellowship to outsiders (not only to sinners but also to foreigners) in the future life of the resurrection. And the inclusion of foreigners is coupled with an equally shocking exclusion of "the heirs of the kingdom," Jesus's own ethnic community.

At this point in the story, Jesus does not yet take the centurion's faith as a cue for initiating a new program of mission to the gentile world. It simply stands as a marvelous anomaly. But Jesus discerns in the centurion's faith a prefiguration of the life of the world to come, a world in which many gentiles will join the celebration along with the people of Israel—or at least some of them.

If this encounter with the gentile centurion seems to be an anomaly, its repercussions continue to echo in Matthew's second story about Jesus's brush with gentiles (Matt 15:21–28). Jesus leaves his home territory in Galilee and goes away to the district of Tyre and Sidon—that is, onto gentile turf.[6] A desperate woman seeks him out, begging for help for her daughter who is tormented by a demon. In contrast to Mark, who describes her as "a Gentile, of Syrophoenician origin" (Mark 7:26), Matthew pointedly calls her "a Canaanite woman." This description evokes the old biblical stories of the pagan Canaanites who inhabited the promised land before Israel drove them out; consequently, the epithet heightens the narrative tension by suggesting that she is not merely a foreigner but also part of a historic enemy people. Thus, Matthew's description of her evokes "traditional prejudices."[7]

Jesus first ignores her, and the disciples try to shoo her away, but she persists. Finally, Jesus explains why he is giving her the cold shoulder: "I was sent only to the lost sheep of the house of Israel" (cf. Matt 10:5–6). But she refuses to take no for an answer; she kneels before him and continues pleading. Jesus gives her one more dismissive answer: "It is not fair to take the children's bread and throw it to the dogs." Her reply is a brilliant, witty riposte that seizes the metaphor and turns it into an argument in support of her plea: "Yes, Lord, yet even the dogs eat the crumbs that fall from their masters' table." Finally Jesus recognizes in her—perhaps once again with amazement—the same luminous quality of faith that he had first seen in the gentile centurion: "Woman, great is your faith! Let it be done for you as you wish."[8]

Perhaps two points make a line: A gentile centurion and a Canaanite woman, both distanced from Jesus and Israel by ethnicity and culture, turn to Jesus with faith and hope. Both receive the healing they seek. Both of them foreshadow the hope that "for those who sat in the region and shadow of death / light has dawned" (Matt 4:16b). Still, at this point in the story, Jesus shows no inclination to embark on a mission to foreign outsiders.

But Matthew has already planted another clue, a bit earlier in the plot. After a general account of Jesus's healing activity, he admonishes the crowds "not to make him known" (Matt 12:16). Matthew then introduces one of his characteristic fulfillment quotations, an adaptation of Isaiah 42:1–4:

> This was to fulfill what had been spoken through the prophet Isaiah:
>
> "Here is my servant, whom I have chosen,
>> my beloved, with whom my soul is well
>>> pleased.
> I will put my Spirit upon him,
>> and he will proclaim *justice to the Gentiles.*
> He will not wrangle or cry aloud,
>> nor will anyone hear his voice in the streets.
> He will not break a bruised reed
>> or quench a smoldering wick
> until he brings justice to victory.
>> And in his name *the Gentiles* will hope."
>>> (Matt 12:17–21)

The quotation from Isaiah—the longest biblical quotation in Matthew's Gospel—makes two references to gentiles: The servant will proclaim justice to the *gentiles* (*ethnē*), and *gentiles* will place their hope in him. These prophecies seem oddly unconnected to the story, since there is no specific mention of gentiles in the immediate narrative context of Matthew 12. Nonetheless, Matthew's citation of Isaiah 42 foreshadows the goal toward which his Gospel is driving, as we shall see.

Matthew is not the only Gospel writer who describes Jesus's encounters with foreigners. The Gospel of John features an account of Jesus's extended conversation with a Samaritan woman. (Recall, by contrast, Jesus's stricture for his disciples' mission in Matthew 10:5: "enter no town of the Samaritans.") There was an abiding and mutual disdain between Jews and Samaritans, despite their geographical and cultural/religious proximity. The Samaritans traced their ancestry and their religious practices back to the ancient Northern Kingdom of Israel. In common with the Jews, they received the five books of Moses (the Pentateuch) as their scripture. But they did not accept the temple in Jerusalem as their cultic center. In light of the tension and mutual distrust between Samaritans and Jews, the encounter described in John 4:4–42 contains several boundary-breaking elements.

Jesus is returning to Galilee from Judea, passing through Samaria on the way. John tells us that he was tired from the journey and stopped to rest near the Samaritan city of Sychar, by a well. In this story, in contrast to the cross-cultural contacts we have seen in Matthew where gentiles take the initiative to seek out Jesus for help, Jesus initiates the conversation; he asks a Samaritan woman who comes to the well to give him a drink. Her incredulous response is explained by the narrator in an aside: Jews don't share things in common with Samaritans.[9] She therefore asks, "How is it that you, a Jew, ask a drink of me, a woman of Samaria?" She doesn't dance around the awkward question: She lays the cultural conflict out in the open. This leads to an extended conversation in which Jesus enigmatically offers to give her "living water."

When she eventually comes to recognize that Jesus is a prophet, she raises the ante by asking him a fundamental theological question about the difference between Jewish and Samaritan religious practices: "Our ancestors worshiped on this mountain [i.e., Mount Gerizim in Samaria], but you [Jews] say that the place where people must worship is in Jerusalem." Jesus's reply effectively annihilates the significance of this difference. While affirming that "salvation is from the Jews," he declares that the hour is coming, and is now here, when this debate about different places of worship will be inconsequential, because "God is spirit, and those who worship him must worship in spirit and truth." This declaration effectively removes the barrier, the rationale for conflict between Jews and Samaritans about the right location of the cultic center: The worship of God can no longer be tied to a specific place. It is a revolutionary claim. But even this is not yet the climax of the conversation.

The woman, perceptively recognizing the authoritative voice of someone greater than she could have imagined, extends a deft probe to test what she is sensing: "I know that Messiah is coming. . . . When he comes, he will proclaim all things to us." And Jesus at last pulls away the veil of indirection: "I am he [*egō eimi*], the one who is speaking to you."

At just this climactic moment, Jesus's disciples blunder onto the scene. (John is nothing if not a brilliant dramatist.) And they are "astonished that he was speaking with a woman"— perhaps particularly, a *Samaritan* woman. We are meant to understand that their conversation has broken down a barrier wall. The barrier between Jews and Samaritans—and perhaps also the barrier erected to restrict conversation between men and women—has been breached.

Jesus has pronounced that the hour has arrived when a new community of worshipers in the spirit will transcend the Jewish/Samaritan divide, and he has breathtakingly revealed himself to this Samaritan outsider. She, in turn, has grasped his true identity, and she returns to the city to spread the word, with the result that "many Samaritans from that city believed in him because of the woman's testimony" (John 4:39). Jesus then agrees to spend two more days staying with the Samaritans (another surprising boundary transgression),[10] and they in turn come to say, "we have heard for ourselves, and we know that this is truly the Savior of the world" (4:42). Thus, the connection between the Jew Jesus and this anonymous Samaritan woman has opened up a new community for the reception of God's good news.

Of course, when we think of Jesus's connection to Samaritans, we can't help recalling the parable he told about another Samaritan who reached across conventional boundaries (Luke 10:25–37). This Samaritan is conjured out of Jesus's imagination in response to a self-justifying question from an earnest Torah scholar who is seeking to clarify the terms necessary for inheriting eternal life.[11] The legal scholar asks, "Who is my neighbor?" Rather than answering directly, Jesus tells a story. In the story, a Jewish priest and a Levite delicately pass by and decline to help a man who has been mugged on the road from Jerusalem to Jericho. It is the despised foreigner, the Samaritan, who stops to rescue the victim. This leads up to Jesus's decisive question: "Which of these three, do you think, was a neighbor to the man who fell into the hands of the robbers?" The question explodes any narrow definition of "neighbor." Why is this crucial? Because Jesus and the scholar have already agreed that the central imperatives of the Torah are the commandments to "love the Lord your God with all your heart, and with all your soul, and with all your strength, and with all your mind; *and your neighbor as yourself*" (Luke 10:27, quoting Lev 19:18). In Leviticus the intended "neighbor" is one of "your people," that is, a fellow Israelite. Jesus, however, has spun a mind-expanding story that forces the Torah expert to acknowledge a more expansive definition of "neighbor."

Here, as we saw in the controversies about Sabbath observance, Jesus is not overturning the law; instead, he is arguing for a wider interpretation of it, driven by a vision of God's mercy. In this case, the widening tears open the veil of ethnic separation.

That tearing open should remind us of another rending of a veil. In the passion narratives of Mark and Matthew, at the moment of Jesus's death the curtain of the temple in Jerusalem is torn in two, from top to bottom. Precisely at that moment it is a *gentile* observer, the Roman centurion standing at the foot of the cross, who blurts out an astonished confession: "Truly this man was God's Son!" (Mark 15:39, Matt 27:54). This cry is particularly poignant in Mark's Gospel, where this foreigner becomes the first human figure in the story to utter the confession that Jesus is the Son of God (cf. Mark 1:1).[12]

Mark is a subtle, mysterious narrator. He offers no comment on the fact that after a long story in which Jesus has been consistently misunderstood, even by his own followers, it is a gentile who at last perceives Jesus's identity. Mark doesn't go on to set forth a program for a church that will include gentiles alongside Jews in the community of Jesus's followers. He leaves us only with hints and anticipations.

Matthew's Gospel is a different story. Matthew frames his whole narrative in a way that leads up to the mandate— counterintuitive for many Jewish readers—of a mission that will embrace gentiles and Jews together in one people of God. We don't know for sure, but it seems likely that Matthew wrote his Gospel for an emerging church community that found itself in controversy with other early communities of Jesus-followers who resisted the inclusion of gentiles. If so, Matthew's Gospel should be seen as an *apologia* for a gentile-inclusive church.

Matthew foreshadows this gentile mission in the opening chapters of his Gospel. Jesus is identified as "the Messiah, the son of David, the son of Abraham" (Matt 1:1), who will "save his people [Israel] from their sins" (1:21). But among the first to acclaim him are the Magi—gentile sages from the east—who come to worship him (2:1–12). Already they foreshadow the eventual widening of God's kingdom. Jesus will be not just "king of the Jews," but of all who may come from afar to worship him.

As Matthew's story unfolds, this theme is highlighted again and again. Jesus acknowledges and celebrates the faith of the gentile centurion and the Canaanite woman. And Matthew drops into the middle of his narrative a prophecy of Isaiah, declaring that Jesus is the servant on whom God's spirit rests, so that he will proclaim justice to the gentiles and bring them to hope in his name. And then, finally, at Jesus's death, the centurion and the Roman soldiers with him testify that truly Jesus was the Son of God. It is as if the crumbs under the table that the Canaanite woman sought have become, in Matthew's hands, a trail of breadcrumb clues. Those clues lead to the grand final scene of Matthew's Gospel, in which the risen Jesus appears to his disciples on a mountain in Galilee and solemnly gives this commission to them: "All authority in heaven and on earth has been given to me. Go therefore and *make disciples of all the gentiles,* baptizing them in the name of the Father and of the Son and of the Holy Spirit, and teaching them to obey everything that I have commanded you. And remember, I am with you always, to the end of the age" (Matt 28:18–20).[13]

Matthew leaves us expecting to hear more about whether and how the disciples carried out this commission. But it seems that Matthew never wrote a sequel to his Gospel. That task fell to the evangelist Luke, who carried forward the story into a second volume about the earliest expansion of the good news of Jesus into the gentile world. We follow that part of the story in the next chapter of this book.

For now, we are left to ponder the stories we have traced in the four canonical Gospels. We have heard many stories about the ways in which Jesus proclaimed the wideness of God's mercy. These stories narrate how Jesus's teaching and actions encouraged his followers to think more broadly about the expansive grace of Israel's God.

A consistent theme of these stories is that Jesus does not

reject Israel's scriptures; instead, like the prophets before him, he insists on reinterpreting them in light of the conviction that love and mercy lie at the root of God's purposes. That insistence on God's wide-ranging mercy brought him into conflict with some others, including scholars and religious leaders, who were passionately committed to the authority of Israel's God-given law but interpreted it in a more restrictive way, a way that sought to protect Israel's obedience, purity, and distinctiveness. Here we should pause to reflect: Should this contrast of perspectives inform the church's present conflicts over sexuality?

As we have walked through these stories, we have found again and again the element of *surprise*. Jesus challenges conventional norms and startles his contemporaries. The consistent theme of his surprising words and actions is that God's mercy is wider and stronger than we might expect. The ultimate demonstration of that surprising truth occurred in the resurrection of Jesus: God's power and God's mercy are stronger than death.

12

The Holy Spirit Begins to Change the Church's Mind

The first half of the Acts of the Apostles tells the story of how Jesus's followers surprisingly changed their minds. Or rather—more precisely—it tells the story of how the Holy Spirit surprised these early disciples and changed their minds.

Most people today think of "Christianity" and "Judaism" as separate religions. But that distinction did not exist so clearly twenty centuries ago, in the first decades of the church's existence. In fact, after the death and resurrection of Jesus, the burning controversial issue for his early followers was whether gentiles could join the church at all without first becoming converts to Judaism. Could gentiles be accepted in the community of Jesus-followers? If so, should they be required to undergo circumcision and begin observing the food laws, sexual norms, and other customs that set the Jewish people apart from their pagan environment?

The earliest churches quickly developed factions that took different sides on this hot-button issue. The divisions were no less passionate and painful than the differences that divide Christians today in debates about sexuality, race, and nationalist ideology. To see how the argument about inclusion of gentiles developed in the church's early years, we can turn to the account given by Luke in the Acts of the Apostles.[1]

Throughout the first fifteen chapters of Acts, we see the Spirit at work, bearing witness to the resurrection of Jesus and transforming the minds of the church's leaders, especially Peter and Paul. The Holy Spirit was leading them to "read backwards," deepening and reshaping their understanding of scripture and tradition.[2] As Acts tells the story, the Spirit was shaping a new community: expanding the church's understanding of the wideness of God's grace and opening the early leaders up to embrace gentiles, whom they previously would have shunned.

Although Jesus's words and actions had given significant pointers toward the expansion of God's mercy to gentiles, his followers were slow to take the hint. Their hesitancy is not really surprising, for they were faithful Jews who understood that God had made a special covenant with the people of Israel. This was the message that God had spoken to Moses at Mount Sinai:

> Then Moses went up to God; the LORD called to him from the mountain, saying, "Thus you shall say to the house of Jacob, and tell the Israelites: You have seen what I did to the Egyptians, and how I bore you on eagles' wings and brought you to myself. Now therefore, if you obey my voice and keep my covenant, you shall be my treasured possession out of all the peoples. Indeed, the whole earth is mine, but you shall be for me a priestly kingdom and a holy nation. These are the words that you shall speak to the Israelites." (Exod 19:3–6)

Over time, the awareness of Israel's special calling to be "a holy nation" had caused many devout Jewish people to be wary of close contact with idolatrous gentiles. This deeply religious impulse found ample grounding in some portions of Israel's scripture, such as the Deuteronomistic commands to drive other nations out of the land and the fervent xenophobia of Ezra-Nehemiah.[3] At the same time, within the cosmopolitan Mediterranean culture of the first century, other Jews were much more open to free association with their gentile neighbors. Judaism was no more monolithic than is Christianity in the twenty-first century; there was a wide spectrum of belief and practice.

Within that wide spectrum, many of the earliest followers of Jesus, as faithful Jews, saw themselves as carrying forward a vocation to be a special people set apart for God's service. This conviction is powerfully articulated in the First Letter of Peter, which clearly echoes Exodus 19: "you are a chosen people, *a royal priesthood, a holy nation, God's own people,* in order that you may proclaim the excellence of him who called you out of darkness into his marvelous light" (1 Pet 2:9).[4]

Accordingly, the default assumption of many of the earliest Jewish Jesus-followers was that they—as bearers of the good news of the coming kingdom of God—should maintain a judicious separation from corrupting foreign influences. That is why the earliest church endured a painful struggle to reach a common understanding concerning inclusion of gentiles in the community.

When the curtain opens on the book of Acts, the risen Jesus is giving instructions to his disciples. His final words before his ascension into heaven give them both a promise and a commission: "you will receive power when the Holy Spirit has come upon you; and you will be my witnesses in Jerusalem, in all Judea and Samaria, and to the ends of the earth" (Acts 1:8). That mandate sketches the broad outline of all that follows in Acts: It is the story of the Spirit-empowered expansion of the early church in the Mediterranean world.

Acts 2 gives a vivid account of the coming of the Holy Spirit on the day of Pentecost. The Spirit falls like the rush of a violent wind upon the small band of believers gathered in Jerusalem. Luke's story highlights the presence of a crowd of people from all over the known world; they are spectators to the event and hearers of the proclamation of "God's deeds of power." Miraculously, all of them hear the message spoken in their own languages (Acts 2:1–13).

Despite the geographical and cultural diversity of the crowd, Luke takes pains to say that they are all "*devout Jews* from every people under heaven" (Acts 2:5).[5] Some of them are visitors, perhaps in Jerusalem for the festival, while others may be living there. Whatever the reason for their presence, it is a *Jewish* crowd. The outreach to gentiles has not yet begun. Nonetheless, this launching event of the church's mission prefigures the worldwide reach of the gospel. The Pentecost event is not simply the proclamation of good news for Aramaic-speaking Jews in the land of Israel; the scope of the mission is wider.

The message that Peter preaches on this occasion foreshadows that wider scope. He quotes from the prophet Joel to proclaim that the dramatic descent of the Spirit is the fulfillment of God's promise: "I will pour out my Spirit upon *all flesh,* / and your sons and your daughters shall prophesy" (Acts 2:17, citing Joel 2:28).[6] At the conclusion of his message to the assembled crowd, he declares that "the promise is for you, for your children, *and for all who are far away, everyone whom the Lord our God calls to him*" (2:39).

As subsequent events in the story will show, it had not yet occurred to Peter that "everyone whom the Lord our God calls" might include gentiles as well as Jews. Speaking to a crowd of Jews from far-flung places around the Mediterranean world, he may simply assume that God's promise applies to Jews from the diaspora as well as to Jews in the Holy Land. If that is what he thinks, the unfolding story will reveal to him that his words meant even more than he had understood when he first spoke them.

In Acts 8, we begin to see the fulfillment of Jesus's charge to his followers to be his witnesses in widening geographic circles, "in Jerusalem, in all Judea and Samaria, and to the ends of the earth" (Acts 1:8). According to Luke's account, the members of the church in Jerusalem were driven from the city as a result of persecution, and they were "scattered throughout the country-side of Judea and Samaria" (8:1). The story next focuses on Philip, one of the leaders who had previously been chosen to supervise the distribution of food to Hellenist widows in Jerusalem (6:5).[7] He now ventures out to Samaria and begins preaching there about Jesus as Messiah. His message receives an enthusiastic reception: Many Samaritans are converted and baptized, and Philip performs signs of exorcism and healing among the people (8:4–13).

We should recall that Jews in this era tended to regard Samaritans with hostility and disdain. Samaritans were not exactly "gentiles," but they were seen as illegitimate cousins and apostates who, although they accepted a variant version of the law of Moses, rejected the temple in Jerusalem as the central place for sacrifice and worship. As we have seen, the Gospels tell several stories that highlight the tension between Jews and Samaritans. In light of this context, Philip's preaching mission in Samaria was a boundary-crossing initiative.

The apostles in Jerusalem heard reports of Philip's successful mission and dispatched Peter and John to investigate and to pray that the Samaritan converts would receive the Holy Spirit in the same way that the believers in Jerusalem had (Acts 8:14–17). The unexpected gift of the Spirit to the Samaritans (8:17) is the decisive seal of divine approval for this expansion of the Jesus movement, bringing Jewish and Samaritan believers into fellowship on equal footing.[8] The actions of Philip, Peter, and John in Samaria fulfill part of Jesus's postresurrection charge to the original circle of disciples.

This episode ends with a brief, almost throwaway, note that confirms the significance of what has taken place: "Now after Peter and John had testified and spoken the word of the Lord, they returned to Jerusalem, *proclaiming the good news to many villages of the Samaritans*" (Acts 8:25). The fact that Peter and John are now also preaching to Samaritan villagers demonstrates that these authoritative apostles have been led by the Spirit to a transformed attitude about Samaritans. Peter and John not only approve and bless Philip's bold boundary-crossing mission but now are participating in it themselves.

Jesus had said, "You will be my witnesses in Jerusalem, in all Judea and Samaria." It does not take a great leap of imagination to guess where Luke's narrative might be headed next.

As Luke's story of Spirit-inspired surprises continues, it provides still more foreshadowing of what is to come. The account of Philip's work in Samaria now segues into the curious story of the Ethiopian eunuch (Acts 8:26–40).

Philip is abruptly commanded by an angel of the Lord to leave Samaria and head south on the wilderness road between Jerusalem and Gaza. There he encounters an unlikely figure: an Ethiopian eunuch who is the official in charge of the treasury of the queen of the Ethiopians.[9] Luke tells us that "he had come to Jerusalem to worship" and is now on his way back home.

This sketch portrays the eunuch as an ambiguous figure: He is a foreigner—indeed, an inhabitant of "the ends of the

earth" from the viewpoint of Mediterranean culture. The fact
that he has come to Jerusalem to worship is surprising, for there
is no extant evidence for the existence of a Jewish community
in Ethiopia in this historical period. Some interpreters have
conjectured that the man might have been a proselyte to Judaism. But, as many commentators have suggested, this is unlikely, because Deuteronomy explicitly excludes eunuchs: "No
one whose testicles are crushed or whose penis is cut off shall
come into the assembly of the LORD" (Deut 23:1).[10] Thus, the
Ethiopian eunuch is both a wealthy and powerful figure (holding high office and possessing a chariot) and, at the same time,
a marginal figure who likely would have been barred from full
participation in some aspects of Jewish religious life.[11]

It appears that he is also a seeker. He has made a long and
arduous journey to worship in Jerusalem. (Even if he was not
accepted as a proselyte, he would have been allowed to make
sacrificial offerings along with other gentiles in the outer court
of the Jerusalem temple.)[12] As he returns home in his chariot,
he is reading a scroll of the prophetic book of Isaiah and wondering how to interpret it.

Philip, at the explicit command of the Spirit, runs up to
the chariot and overhears the man reading aloud. He strikes
up a conversation with the eunuch, who invites him to come
up into the chariot to help interpret the mysterious text he is
reading:

> Like a sheep he was led to the slaughter,
> and like a lamb silent before its shearer,
> so he does not open his mouth.
> In his humiliation justice was denied him.
> Who will tell his family history?
> For his life is taken away from the earth. (Acts 8:32–33,
>   quoting Isa 53:7–8 [Septuagint])[13]

Critical commentators on Acts sometimes digress into wondering why Luke doesn't quote more of the passage from Isaiah 53 that would point to the vicarious redemptive nature of the servant's suffering. (For example, the passage that Luke cites does not include Isa 53:4–6 or 53:12.) This line of questioning, however, overlooks the subtle, poignant suggestion of the narrative: that the eunuch is wondering whether to see *himself* reflected in the prophetic text. "About whom," he asks Philip, "does the prophet say this, about himself or someone else?" (Acts 8:34). Precisely because he is a eunuch, perhaps the man sees himself—despite his wealth and status—included in the category of "someone else": as one who has been led to slaughter (by castration) and humiliated, as one whose life will be "taken away from the earth" because he is incapable of generating descendants who will carry forward his story.[14] If so, the eunuch's question parallels the aching question posed in the musical *Hamilton:* "Who lives, who dies, who tells your story?"[15]

Whomever he had in mind, the eunuch's question provides a starting point for Philip to tell the story of Jesus. He explicates Isaiah 53 as a prophecy concerning "the good news about Jesus." This interpretation accords with a consistent theme of Luke-Acts that Moses and the prophets prefigure Jesus's life, death, and resurrection.

The Ethiopian eunuch receives this message gladly. Seeing a body of water, he asks a hopeful, but no less poignant question: "Look, here is water! What is to prevent me from being baptized?" (Acts 8:36). "What is to prevent me," indeed? No doubt he has already faced barriers on his visit to Jerusalem. No doubt he has encountered the stern biblical prohibition in Deuteronomy that prevents him from being admitted to "the assembly of the Lord." Now, however, Philip erects no barrier. They immediately get out of the chariot, go down into the water, and Philip baptizes him. In baptism the eunuch becomes united with Christ and—as Paul wrote in his letters—a member of the body of Christ.

The story has a startling and abrupt ending: Philip has done what he was sent to do, and so "the Spirit of the Lord snatched Philip away," and the eunuch "went on his way rejoicing" (Acts 8:39).

Acts provides no explanation for Philip's thinking. Why did he decide to embrace this gentile eunuch and to initiate him without hesitation into the new community of God's people in Christ, despite the proscription of Deuteronomy 23:1? Perhaps it was because Philip had been explicitly directed by the Spirit to encounter this man and to tell him about the good news of Jesus. Perhaps Philip, on the basis of his experience in Samaria, was able to recognize that God was doing a new thing to widen Philip's previous understanding of the boundaries of the people of God.

Or did Philip know that if the eunuch kept reading Isaiah, he would soon come to the word of assurance in Isaiah 56:3–5?

Do not let the foreigner joined to the LORD say,
　　"The LORD will surely separate me from his people";
and do not let the eunuch say,
　　"I am just a dry tree."
For thus says the LORD:
To the eunuchs who keep my sabbaths,
　　who choose the things that please me
　　and hold fast my covenant,
I will give, in my house and within my walls,
　　a monument and a name
　　better than sons and daughters;
I will give them an everlasting name
　　that shall not be cut off.

Perhaps Philip was mindful of this text; if so, Luke doesn't tell us. Philip simply acts in response to the Spirit and without hesitation decides—despite the Deuteronomic prohibition (Deut 23:1)—that there is nothing to prevent the eunuch from being baptized. And so, the baptism of this foreign eunuch offers a vivid foreshadowing of how the good news of Jesus will spread to the ends of the earth.

13

The Conscripted Apostle

The stories of Philip's boundary-crossing outreach in Acts 8 (as seen in the foregoing chapter) are framed by Luke's account about Saul (later to be known as Paul), the resolute persecutor of the earliest Jesus-followers who was stopped in his tracks by the Lord and astonishingly recruited as a chosen apostle to the gentiles (Acts 7:58–8:3, 9:1–31). The roughly chiastic "sandwich" structure of this section of the story creates an illuminating contrast:

> **Acts 7:54–8:3**—We first meet Saul as an approving witness to the stoning of Stephen (7:54–8:1). At this point he is simply described as "a young man," not an instigator of persecution but an accomplice to the violence, serving as a coat-check boy for the stone-throwers. Soon after that, however, he becomes a leading enforcer: "Saul was ravaging the church by entering house after house; dragging off both men and women, he committed them to prison" (8:3).
>
> **Acts 8:4–25**—The narrative focus shifts away from Saul to the figure of Philip. Philip journeys to Samaria, where he preaches to Samaritans and

baptizes them. The apostles Peter and John lend support, lay hands on the Samaritan believers, and join the preaching mission.

Acts 8:26–40—The next segment of the story continues to follow Philip, as he encounters another outsider; Philip greets and baptizes the Ethiopian eunuch.

Acts 9:1–30—Then the narrative swings back to the figure of Saul, who is "still breathing threats and murder against the disciples of the Lord" (9:1). But suddenly he is struck blind on the road to Damascus by a vision of Jesus. Ananias lays hands on him; he is filled with the Spirit and baptized. He begins preaching the gospel.

The contrast is striking: Philip generously reaches across cultural and ethnic boundaries to extend grace to outsiders, while Saul zealously polices the boundaries of God's people and punishes those who deviate from his strict norms.

We don't know exactly why Saul, before his visionary call experience, found the followers of Jesus so offensive, but we do get a few clues from his rueful retrospective remarks in some of the letters he wrote to the churches after he became an advocate of the new faith. A key passage appears in his Letter to the Galatians: "You have heard, no doubt, of my earlier life in Judaism. I was violently persecuting the church of God and was trying to destroy it. I advanced in Judaism beyond many among my people of the same age, for I was far more zealous for the traditions of my ancestors" (Gal 1:13–14). And again, in his later Letter to the Philippians, he offers this autobiographical account of his background and former life: "If anyone else has reason to be confident in the flesh, I have more: circumcised on the eighth day, a member of the people of Israel, of the tribe of Benjamin, a Hebrew born of Hebrews; as to the law, a Pharisee; as to zeal, a persecutor of the church; as to righteousness under the law, blameless" (Phil 3:4b–6).

A few common threads connect these passages. First, Saul/Paul readily acknowledges not only that he had violently persecuted the church but that he had seen this action as an *achievement* that showed him to be "more advanced" than his contemporaries. Second, he describes his attitude as one of "zeal." Third, he saw himself as an ardent defender of "the traditions of my ancestors."

These passages still don't explain precisely what it was about the message of the early church that the young Saul found so objectionable or threatening. Perhaps he found the notion of a crucified messiah scandalous, because according to Israel's law, "Cursed is everyone who hangs on a tree" (Gal 3:13, quoting Deut 21:23). Or perhaps he saw the Jesus-followers as guilty of carelessness about keeping the law, because of the freedom with which Jesus had treated Israel's laws about the Sabbath and food. Or perhaps he was worried that the new movement was already becoming susceptible to contamination by its emerging contacts with gentiles.

Significantly, Saul/Paul directly connects his persecution of the church to his "*zeal*" for tradition. In Israel's scripture, "zeal" is distinctively connected with the figure of Phinehas, who zealously opposed the threat of foreign influence and idolatry by gruesomely killing an Israelite man and his foreign Midianite wife and thereby (according to Num 25:6–9) stopped a plague that was afflicting the Israelite people. The story seems to suggest that he impaled the couple together in the very act of sexual intercourse: "Taking a spear in his hand, he went after the Israelite man into the tent, and pierced the two of them, the Israelite man and the woman, through the belly" (25:7–8).

In Numbers 25:10–13, we read this approving verdict on Phine-has's *zealous* intervention:

> The LORD spoke to Moses, saying: "Phinehas son of
> Eleazar, son of Aaron the priest, has turned back my
> wrath from the Israelites by manifesting such *zeal*
> among them on my behalf that in my jealousy I did
> not consume the Israelites. Therefore say, 'I hereby
> grant him my covenant of peace. It shall be for him
> and for his descendants after him a covenant of per-
> petual priesthood, because *he was zealous for his*
> *God,* and made atonement for the Israelites.'"

A similar laudatory assessment of Phinehas's zealous violence
is repeated in Psalm 106:28–31, where we are told that Phine-has's lethal action "has been *reckoned to him as righteousness /*
from generation to generation forever [!]."

All of these considerations may have played a role in shap-ing the young Saul's self-image as a heroic, zealous, righteous
defender of the true worship of Israel's God, following the ex-ample of Phinehas.[1]

This is a spiritual and psychological profile that is still all
too familiar to us today. Saul was a bit like the self-appointed
vigilantes who patrol the US border with Mexico to try to main-tain the boundary. At the extremes, this kind of zeal for purity
and boundaries can inspire terrorists who fly airliners into sky-scrapers or plant bombs in abortion clinics or carry out mass
shootings of immigrants. The perpetrators of such violence often
see themselves as noble defenders of a righteous cause.

But in the case of Saul, God intervened to stop him. The
story is a familiar one. Here is a quick recap of the events (Acts
9:1–22).

Saul was on his way to Damascus to apprehend and arrest "any who belonged to the Way, men or women," that is,
followers of Jesus. But he was suddenly blinded by a light from
heaven and fell to the ground. He heard a voice saying, "Saul,
Saul, why do you persecute me?" His companions led him on
to Damascus, where he continued to be blind and unable to
eat or drink. The Lord appeared to a man named Ananias in a
vision and instructed him to go to Saul and lay hands on him
so that he might regain his sight. Ananias protested, because
he knew all too well "how much evil he has done to your saints
in Jerusalem." But the Lord answered: "Go, for he is an instrument whom I have chosen to bring my name before Gentiles
and kings and before the people of Israel. I myself will show him
how much he must suffer for the sake of my name." Ananias
then did as he had been instructed, Saul regained his sight, and
within days he began proclaiming in the synagogues that Jesus
is the Son of God. Soon—just a few pages farther into the narrative of Acts—we find Paul and various companions traveling
around the Mediterranean, preaching the gospel to Jews and
gentiles alike and establishing churches that sought to bridge
these divisions.[2]

Thus Saul, the rigid and self-righteous defender of a narrowly rigorous vision of Israel's traditional faith, found himself
overthrown and conscripted by God to become the apostle
Paul, a "chosen instrument" to carry the message of Jesus to the
gentiles. Paul himself was not unaware of the irony of his vocation as apostle to the gentiles. Writing to the church at Corinth,
here is how he assessed his own career: "I am the least of the
apostles, unfit to be called an apostle, because I persecuted the
church of God. But by the grace of God I am what I am, and
his grace toward me has not been in vain" (1 Cor 15:9–10a).

Eventually Paul's letters to the churches in Galatia and
Rome were to become the definitive theological defense of the

conviction that in Christ there is no longer Jew or Greek, and that gentiles in Christ need not be circumcised or follow Jewish dietary laws. As a young man in Jerusalem, Saul would have found this position appalling.

It was a remarkable reversal: a paradigmatic demonstration of the way in which the gospel of grace can knock people off their high horses and lead to surprising transformations. Knowing what it was to have his mind dramatically changed by the Lord, Paul later wrote this to the believers in Rome, who were embroiled in disputes with one another: "I appeal to you therefore, brothers and sisters, on the basis of God's mercy, to present your bodies as a living sacrifice, holy and acceptable to God, which is your reasonable act of worship. Do not be conformed to this age, but *be transformed by the renewing of the mind*, so that you may discern what is the will of God—what is good and acceptable and perfect" (Rom 12:1–2).[3] That transformation of mind led Paul ultimately to embrace those he had once feared and hated, and to articulate this summary of the entire meaning of Israel's law: "Love does no wrong to a neighbor; therefore, love is the fulfilling of the law" (13:10).

14

"Who Was I That
I Could Block God?"

Is it possible for human beings to block God's gracious action by insisting on the strict application of God's own
biblical commandments? Or, to turn the question around,
are there times when God's Spirit breaks down conscientious
human resistance by doing something new that revises previously given laws and judgments?

The Acts of the Apostles tells a story that forces these
questions into the foreground.

In the first nine chapters of Acts, we encounter several
stories hinting that God's mercy would extend beyond Israel
to the non-Jewish world. In none of these anticipatory episodes,
however, is there a clear case of *gentiles* coming to embrace faith
in Jesus. (The Samaritans and the Ethiopian in Acts 8 are lim-
inal cases whose relations to Jewish identity are ambiguous.)
Nor have we seen an explicit decision by leaders of the church
in Jerusalem to endorse a mission to non-Torah-observant gentiles. When we arrive at Acts 10, however, all that is about to
change.

Acts 10 narrates the conversion of a gentile centurion, Cornelius, along with his household, in response to Peter's preaching. Subsequently, both Acts 11 and 15 go on to explain how the church in Jerusalem came to terms with this unexpected development. Luke retells the key events again and again, highlighting them through repetition. This special emphasis suggests that we need to look carefully at how these watershed events unfolded, how the church discerned what the Holy Spirit was doing, and what practical decisions followed from that discernment.

At the beginning of Acts 10, we meet Cornelius. He is introduced as a Roman centurion, a military officer overseeing troops whose responsibility was to maintain the empire's oversight in Judea. He is described as "a devout man who feared God . . . , gave alms generously . . . , and prayed constantly to God" (Acts 10:2). In other words, he was a "godfearer," a gentile drawn to the monotheistic faith of the synagogue, without having become a full proselyte to Judaism and undergoing circumcision.

Yet the story is set in motion neither by Cornelius's piety nor by any intentional evangelistic strategy of Peter or the other disciples, but by the initiative of God.

Cornelius and Peter receive simultaneous complementary visions. In his, Cornelius is terrified by the appearance of an angel of God, who instructs him to send for Peter to come to his house. Despite his terror—or perhaps because of it—he obeys and sends emissaries to Joppa to look for Peter.

Peter, for his part, dozes off while waiting for his lunch and experiences a vision in which the Lord instructs him to eat a decidedly unappetizing meal: a bag full of unclean animals, including reptiles (!). He protests, saying, No way Lord, "for I have never eaten anything that is profane or unclean." But then he hears a voice saying, "What God has made clean, you must not call profane" (Acts 10:14–15). This is a disturbing dream for a devout Jew who seeks to observe the Jewish dietary laws. After all, it was the explicit command of God that had declared certain classes of animals unclean (Lev 11:1–47, Deut 14:3–20). What sense could it make for God now to command Peter to eat these disgusting animals?

This troubling vision happens three times, leaving the drowsy Peter puzzled about how to interpret it. But just then the Spirit speaks to him again, announcing the arrival of three men who are looking for him.

When Peter finds out that these men have been sent by a Roman centurion, he might well be apprehensive. After all, it was Roman officials who tortured and crucified Jesus as a potential troublemaker. Perhaps now the authorities are trying to round up Jesus's prominent followers? But the Spirit has told Peter to go with them without hesitation, so he agrees.

When Peter arrives in Caesarea, the Roman administrative headquarters for Judea, a remarkable thing happens: Cornelius falls at Peter's feet and begins to worship him! This seems bizarre: Why is this Roman military officer showing veneration for a Galilean fisherman turned itinerant preacher? Peter tells the groveling centurion to cut it out and get up, for "I am only a mortal" (Acts 10:26).[1] Presumably the centurion's strangely awkward welcome allays any lingering apprehension that Peter might have about being summoned by a Roman authority.

After seeing the assembled crowd in the centurion's house, however, Peter makes things still more awkward. Looking around, he says, "You yourselves know that it is improper for a Jew to associate with or visit an outsider" (Acts 10:28a).[2] Not exactly a warm and friendly conversation opener.

Though the 2021 updated edition of the NRSV uses the word "improper," the 1989 NRSV said it was "unlawful" for a Jew to associate with a gentile. That translation overstated what the text actually says. There is no legal prohibition in the Torah of Jewish association with gentiles.[3] The Greek word here in Acts

10:28a is *athemitos,* which describes a breach of tradition or conventional social norms, not a legal transgression. "Improper" is a better translation, or one might use "unseemly"—or perhaps even "politically incorrect."

The major barrier to Jewish association with Gentiles would have derived from Jewish laws about food and drink; an observant Jew would be wary of receiving forbidden food from a gentile host or participating in mealtime customs associated with idolatry.[4] For that reason, in point of fact, it must not have been unusual for Jews to be hesitant about accepting gentile hospitality. To be sure, on this matter as on many others, actual Jewish practices varied; some Jews, especially in the diaspora, sought ways to accommodate their meal practices to the dominant gentile cultures of the Greco-Roman world. Nonetheless, the extant evidence shows that the observance of the Torah's dietary restrictions did generally mark the Jewish community as culturally distinctive, binding them together in solidarity.[5]

In any case, after his off-putting opening remark, Peter qualifies it by recounting what he was told three times in his visionary trance: "God has shown me that I should not call anyone profane or unclean" (Acts 10:28b). At this point, we learn for the first time that Peter has now decoded the symbolism of his vision. The vision was not really about food. Peter doesn't say, "God has shown me that I should not call any *food* unclean." He says, "God has shown me that I should not call *anyone* profane or unclean." So Peter has now opened the door a crack—wide enough to step inside Cornelius's house and say, "Now may I ask why you sent for me?" (10:29).

Cornelius, from his side, opens the door further by telling about his own vision and concluding with an open invitation: "So now all of us are here in the presence of God to listen to all that the Lord has commanded you to say" (Acts 10:33).

Peter begins to speak—and we can almost hear the new conviction dawning upon him as he hears himself saying, "I truly understand that God shows no partiality, but in every people anyone who fears him and practices righteousness is acceptable to him" (Acts 10:34–35).[6]

Anyone who knew Israel's scripture would already take it as axiomatic that "God shows no partiality." But that maxim would have been understood chiefly in relation to God's care for the poor, as in Deuteronomy 10:17–18: "For the LORD your God is God of gods and Lord of lords, the great God, mighty and awesome, *who is not partial* and takes no bribe, who executes justice for the orphan and the widow, and who loves the strangers, providing them food and clothing."[7] Peter newly interprets and expands the principle of divine impartiality: It must mean also that God accepts *anyone* in *every nation* ("every people") who fears him.[8]

Peter then launches into an elegantly concise summary of the good news about Jesus (Acts 10:36–43), concluding with an open invitation that flings the door open wide for gentiles to walk through: "*everyone* who trusts in him receives forgiveness of sins in his name."[9] Just at this point, the Spirit falls on everyone in the room. It is a replay of Pentecost, but no longer with an exclusively Jewish crowd; this time it is a roomful of *uncircumcised gentiles* speaking in tongues and praising God.

Peter and his circumcised companions are "astounded" because "the gift of the Holy Spirit had been poured out *even on the gentiles*" (Acts 10:45). That way of putting it indicates that Peter and his friends understood the paradigmatic significance of what they were witnessing. This is not just the outpouring of the Spirit on one particularly pious godfearer and his family; rather, it is the beginning of an outpouring of the Spirit on "the gentiles" more broadly. The dam has broken and the Spirit is rushing over it. So Peter asks a momentous question that can have only one right answer: "Can anyone with-hold the water for baptizing these people who have received the Holy Spirit just as we have?" (10:47). Case closed.

Luke concludes the scene with one more telling bit of narrative detail: "Then they [Cornelius and the other gentiles] invited him [Peter] to stay for several days" (Acts 10:48). Peter had ventured cautiously into the house, expressing wariness about associating with a gentile. Now he becomes a house guest for several days. His continued presence in a gentile home signals that the traditional barriers are coming down.

When Peter returns to Jerusalem, however, he learns that not everyone is delighted by these events (Acts 11:1–18). He finds himself being cross-examined by his circumcised associates. Fascinatingly, their complaint does not focus on Peter's preaching or baptizing. Instead, they say, "Why did you go to uncircumcised men *and eat with them?*" Their objection underscores the point that the tradition of Jewish social distancing from gentiles focused primarily on issues of food impurity and table fellowship.

Peter responds by explaining "step by step" how it all went down.[10] His orderly account repeats the story we have already read in Acts 10, but with one salient addition. When Peter gets to the climax of the story, when the Spirit fell upon the gentiles, he explains *what he thought at the time* upon witnessing this unexpected outpouring: "And I remembered the word of the Lord, how he had said, 'John baptized with water, but you will be baptized with the Holy Spirit.' If then God gave them the same gift that he gave us when we believed [or better, 'trusted'; Greek *pisteusasin*] in the Lord Jesus Christ, who was I that I could hinder God?" (Acts 11:16–17, recalling Luke 3:16 and Acts 1:4–5).

So when Peter saw another outpouring of the Spirit, he

recognized a pattern and intuitively linked this outpouring of Spirit also with baptism. The work of the Spirit was playing out palpably before his eyes.

All this led Peter to an inescapable conclusion: This was God at work, doing a new thing. *"If then God gave them the same gift that he gave us when we believed [trusted] in the Lord Jesus Christ, who was I that I could hinder God?"* Peter's question neatly summarizes the import of the story up to this point.

Unfortunately, many translations, including the NRSV, obscure the way that Peter's question links the foregoing episodes together. The verb translated here as "hinder" is *kōluō*. It can refer to any sort of oppositional blocking action.[11] The English language offers a wide range of possible translations: It could be rendered as "hinder," "prevent," "obstruct," "block," "deny," "withhold," "oppose," "forbid," "stand in the way," and so on. The NRSV chooses three different options for translation of this verb in three passages in this pivotal section of Acts. Here are the three texts, presented with a consistent translation of *kōluō* as "block":

> Acts 8:36—[A]nd the eunuch said, "Look, here is water! What can *block* [*kōluei*; NRSV: 'prevent'] me from being baptized?"

> Acts 10:47—"Can anyone *block* [*kōlusai*; NRSV: 'withhold'] the water for baptizing these people who have received the Spirit just as we have?"

> Acts 11:17—"If then God gave them the same gift that he gave us when we believed in the Lord Jesus Christ, who was I that I could *block* [*kōlusai*; NRSV: 'hinder'] God?"

My point is not that "block" is a better translation than "prevent," "withhold," or "hinder"—the NRSV's translations offer perfectly reasonable and idiomatic choices in these three passages. My point is, rather, that Luke's threefold repetition of *kōluō* encourages a hearer of the Greek text to sense the interconnection of these three accounts, as well as the climactic effect of the third. The first two passages speak of (and reject) the hypothetical blocking of a human action of baptism. The third passage then performs a crucial variation of the motif: Attempting to block the baptism of Cornelius's household would be not merely to hinder the action of an apostle. It would be not merely to oppose a humanly proposed innovation. Rather, Peter says, it would be attempting to block *God*.

It is the Holy Spirit who has orchestrated this whole episode, through visions and angelic visitations, through direct instructions to Cornelius and Peter, through opening the door for Peter to enter a gentile home, and most of all, through pouring out spiritual gifts on the gentile hearers of Peter's short sermon. All this is the work of the Spirit.

And so, Peter insists, he had no alternative. He had to recognize the correspondence—the metaphorical fit—between his own experience of receiving the Spirit and the experience of Cornelius's household. He had to recognize God's Spirit at work and stand out of the way.

Peter's critics in Jerusalem, hearing his account, were silenced. After pondering the story for a moment, they too began praising God and drew the inevitable conclusion: "Then God has given even to the gentiles the repentance [*metanoia:* transformation of the mind] that leads to life" (Acts 11:18). So they too stood aside and acknowledged the Spirit's work.

15

The Jerusalem Council
Community Discernment

Alas, the apparent happy ending of Peter's testimony to his circle of skeptical associates in Jerusalem was not yet the end of the story. Disputes about group identity and boundaries are never easily settled—particularly if they involve fundamental changes in a community's self-understanding. Peter's account had satisfied one group of objectors, but it had not yet brought about a wider consensus in the emergent Jesus movement, nor had it adequately addressed the vexing question of what gentile believers in Jesus would be required to do *after* baptism. And so, in Acts 15, the controversy continued.

We might put it this way: It was not only the new gentile converts who required a transformation of mind.

The movement to welcome gentiles into the community of Jesus-followers was gaining momentum, especially in the major urban center of Antioch. This was the place where adherents of this new movement were first called "Christians" (Acts 11:26). Paul and Barnabas were sent out from Antioch on a missionary trip that included the island of Cyprus and parts of Anatolia (modern-day Turkey), where they preached the gospel to both Jews and gentiles. They of course encountered opposition along the way, but they also enjoyed some notable successes. To take just one example, in the town of Iconium, "a great number of both Jews and Greeks became believers" (14:1). At the end of their journey, they returned to Antioch and reported on the fruitfulness of their work.

But there they also encountered a group of Jewish Christians who had come from Judea teaching, "Unless you are circumcised according to the custom of Moses, you cannot be saved" (Acts 15:1). Paul and Barnabas vigorously debated against this position, and there was significant dissension in the church. Eventually, the church at Antioch decided to send a delegation to Jerusalem "to discuss this question with the apostles and the elders" (15:2). The ensuing meeting (often later described as the Jerusalem Council) was to make fateful decisions about the future shape of the emerging Christian movement.

Within the community of the Jerusalem church, there was a group of believers associated with the Pharisees who argued that gentile converts should not only be circumcised as a token of membership (a fairly severe initiation ritual) but also be required to keep the law of Moses in its entirety (Acts 15:5). This view was an entirely coherent position: These Pharisaic believers saw the fellowship of Jesus-followers as an integral development within Judaism as traditionally practiced. On this view, the gentiles who were coming to follow Jesus should be viewed as proselytes to Judaism—more precisely, proselytes to a specific new movement *within* Judaism that understood Jesus as Messiah.

Peter, Barnabas, and Paul, on the other hand, argued that God was doing something radically different, creating a new sort of community. They envisioned a community in continuity with Israel but in which there was "no distinction between them and us" (Acts 15:9). Jewish and gentile believers may have different practices, but as Peter contended, "we believe that we will be saved through the grace of the Lord Jesus, just as they will" (15:11).[1] Peter's way of putting the point is interesting: He doesn't say, "*They* will be saved through the grace of the Lord Jesus, just as we will." Instead, he reverses the emphasis in order to remind his Jewish-Christian hearers that *they themselves* will be saved by the grace of Jesus, not by adhering to the requirements of Torah. Paul was later to make exactly the same point in his Letter to the Romans: "*There is no distinction* [between Jew and gentile], since *all* have sinned and fall short of the glory of God; *they are now justified by his grace as a gift*, through the redemption that is in Christ Jesus" (Rom 3:22b–24).

At this point in the story, after "much debate" (Acts 15:7), both sides of the case have been presented. Peter's dramatic account of the giving of the Holy Spirit to gentile converts had silenced the contentious assembly (15:12). Barnabas and Paul then buttressed Peter's argument by telling of "the signs and wonders that God had done through them among the Gentiles" (15:12). The force of their testimony was to argue that the Holy Spirit was already doing miraculous things in communities of non-law-observant gentiles: Those were the facts on the ground. Those facts, they contended, signified God's endorsement of the gentile mission. Indeed, they insisted, God was not just endorsing that mission but driving it.

In light of all that has been said on both sides, James— the brother of Jesus, who was recognized as a leader in the Jerusalem church (cf. Gal 1:19)—speaks up to offer a resolution of the matter. His proposal has two key components: (1) He cites *a prophetic text* to demonstrate that the innovative gentile mission was actually in accordance with scripture and with God's previously revealed will; and (2) he offers *a compromise proposal*, articulating terms that would allow gentiles to participate fully in this new community of Jesus-followers without undergoing circumcision and taking on the "yoke" of comprehensive Torah observance.

The citation of scripture is crucial to the fledgling church's effort to understand what is happening. Once the community had listened carefully to the stories about the *experience* of gentiles who have responded to the preaching of the gospel and received the Spirit, it was necessary for the church corporately to consider whether and how this unexpected set of experiences could be understood in light of Israel's long tradition of hearing and responding to God's word. To put it another way, how was the community's new experience of the Spirit's action to be interpreted *within* the story of Israel? This process of "reading backwards" to discover previously unrecognized meanings in Israel's scripture occurs pervasively throughout the New Testament, including in many of the apostolic speeches in Acts.[2]

James summarizes Peter's testimony concerning the descent of the Holy Spirit upon the gentiles in Caesarea as a claim that God has now "looked favorably on the gentiles, to take from among them a people for his name" (Acts 15:14). This is a remarkable assertion: Traditionally, Israel had understood itself as a people for God's name, distinct from other nations, a special chosen people. James recognizes that Peter's story breaks open that narrative of Israel's special election. His account is nothing less than a bold claim that God has expanded his elective purpose to embrace (at least some) gentiles as a part of the chosen people. Although this assertion was both novel and radical, James now declares, "This agrees with the words of the prophets" (15:15). In support of that judgment, he cites a single prophetic text from Amos:

After this I will return,
and I will rebuild the dwelling of David, which has fallen;

from its ruins I will rebuild it,
        and I will set it up,
so that all other peoples may seek the Lord—
        even all the gentiles over whom my name has been
        called.
Thus says the Lord, who has been making these things
   known from long ago. (Acts 15:16–18)

The passage as cited in Acts 15 corresponds loosely to Amos 9:11–12 in the Greek Septuagint version, rather than to the Hebrew text of Amos. These verses in the Hebrew text speak simply of the restoration of the Davidic kingdom and its territory, with no reference to the novel inclusion of gentiles as God's people. Therefore, James's interpretation (in Luke's narrative) depends upon a different (i.e., Greek) textual tradition.[3] The last line of James's quotation, however, doesn't come from Amos 9 at all; instead, it echoes Isaiah 45:21. And the following verse in Isaiah depicts the Lord as saying:

"Turn to me and be saved,
        all the ends of the earth!
        For I am God, and there is no other." (Isa 45:22)

Thus, the echo of Isaiah 45 in Acts 15:18 may be meant to invoke this sweeping invitation to the gentile world, although the point is not made explicit in Luke's account of James's speech.[4]

Despite the exegetical complexities surrounding this citation, the significant point *within the story-world of Acts* is simply this: James is seeking (and finding) scriptural confirmation that the incorporation of gentiles into the people of God was part of God's long-intended purpose, as foreshadowed in scriptural texts.

Other texts within the New Testament point to different

scriptural passages to affirm that God's ultimate intention was the inclusion of all nations. For example, Matthew cites prophetic oracles from Isaiah (Matt 12:17–21), while Paul points to the example of God's call of the "ungodly" pagan Abraham (Rom 4) and to the complexities of the biblical accounts of unmerited election (Rom 9–11, 15:7–13). These examples are somewhat more straightforward than James's surprising reading of Amos 9:11–12. But even if James's speech asserts a creative reinterpretation of Amos, the theological intention of the story is clear: Luke is seeking to assure his readers that this unexpected event of gentile inclusion is not an aberration based solely on reports of recent spiritual experiences. Instead, it is part of what Luke elsewhere calls simply "the plan of God" (e.g., Acts 2:23, 20:27).

So, according to James's argument, the gentiles are to be embraced within God's mercy and included in the community of God's people. But even after James finds scriptural support for the acceptance of gentiles, the original problems still remain unresolved. What requirements or ethical standards should apply to gentile followers of Jesus living alongside the original Jewish followers? Do gentile converts need to be circumcised and keep the law, or not? Are they free simply to carry on with their own customs and practices? What guidance will the Jerusalem Council offer the new gentile Christians in Antioch?

The second part of James's response is a proposed set of practical guidelines for the conduct of the newly incorporated gentile believers. The guidelines are minimal and simple: "Therefore it is my judgment[5] that we should not trouble those gentiles who are turning to God, but we should write to them to abstain only from things polluted by idols and from sexual immorality and from whatever has been strangled and from blood" (Acts 15:19–20).[6]

According to Luke's account, James's compromise proposal

was accepted by the assembly. Subsequently, "the apostles and the elders, with the consent of the whole church" (Acts 15:22), deputized representatives to accompany Paul and Barnabas back to Antioch with a letter summarizing the agreement reached in Jerusalem (15:23–29). That letter states clearly that the hardliners who wanted to require circumcision and law observance for gentiles do not speak for the gathered community of believers in Jerusalem. It then restates James's proposal in the following way, with the same four requirements listed in a different order: "For it has seemed good to the Holy Spirit and to us to impose on you no further burden than these essentials: that you abstain from what has been sacrificed to idols and from blood and from what is strangled and from sexual immorality. If you keep yourselves from these, you will do well" (15:28–29).[7]

This concise resolution of the problem represented an ingenious mediating position, with far-reaching consequences for the church. On the one hand, the rigorous demands from the law-observant faction (cf. Acts 15:1, 5) are rejected: The gentile believers are not required to be circumcised, nor are they subjected to most of the law's requirements (e.g., Sabbath-keeping, sacrifices, the calendar of Jewish festivals, prohibition of eating pork, etc.).

On the other hand, neither are they given carte blanche to keep doing whatever they may please. They are required to "abstain" from certain practices that were common in their cultural environment. First of all, they are to distance themselves from idolatry; the abstention from things "sacrificed to idols" would set them dramatically apart from the ordinary social and religious customs of the Mediterranean world. The second and third restrictions stated in the letter have to do with eating meat: These rules assume the binding character of Leviticus 17:10–16, the stern prohibition of consuming blood. The effect of obeying these first three strictures would be to signify publicly that the gentile converts have left behind their former identities and assumed a new posture of solidarity with the Jewish community.

But what about the last requirement? The one other restriction proposed by James, and endorsed by the council, is that the gentile converts should abstain from "sexual immorality" (Greek *porneia*). Some English versions translate this term as "fornication," but it is instead a nonspecific umbrella term for any kind of sexual immorality—presumably including any and all of the forms of illicit sexual relations elaborated in Leviticus 18 (adultery, incest, lying "with a male as with a woman," and so forth).

If so, the implicit connection to the other three required abstentions in the council's letter comes more clearly into focus. Here is the common thread: *The four "essential" requirements have the effect of classifying the new gentile converts as analogous to aliens who reside among the people of Israel.*

In the Levitical Holiness Code (Lev 17–26), resident aliens are explicitly required to observe the rules about abstention from idolatrous sacrifices, eating blood, and forbidden forms of sexual activity (see, e.g., 17:8, 12; 18:24–30). A major purpose of those rules was to set Israel apart from the other nations around them: "Do not defile yourselves in any of these ways, for by all these practices the nations I am casting out before you have defiled themselves" (18:24; see also 18:3–5, where the statutes and ordinances of Israel's law are contrasted to the practices of the Egyptians and the Canaanites).

This interpretation brings into focus the careful compromise that James crafted. Gentile converts who observe the four "essentials" are thereby renouncing idolatry; they are symbolically leaving behind their identity as citizens of the pagan social world and entering a relation of solidarity with the Jewish community of Jesus-followers. At the same time, however, they are implicitly placed in a category that could allow the hardline law-observant faction in the church to see them as analogous to resident aliens, rather than fully integrated into the people of Israel.

None of this is explicitly stated, either by James or in the letter from Jerusalem to Antioch. No texts from Leviticus are cited, and no explicit inferences are drawn about the "resident alien" status of the gentile converts in Antioch. On the central controversial points, the council's decision validates the position of Peter, Barnabas, Paul, and other advocates of the law-free gentile mission: Gentile converts do not have to be circumcised in order to be saved, nor are they required to observe the whole law of Moses. But at the same time, the letter from the apostles and elders posits practical requirements that guard against idolatry and sexual misconduct, while maintaining symbolic continuity with Jewish tradition. This mediating position does not resolve all possible issues, but it allows the community to go forward, at least for a time, in unity.

Was the decision of the Jerusalem Council simply a smart political compromise? It was at least that, to be sure, for politics is the art of the possible. But the Jerusalem letter claims more. The letter introduces its proposals with a remarkable formula: "*It has seemed good to the Holy Spirit and to us.*" This is more than throat-clearing rhetoric. Three observations may be especially noteworthy here:

1. *The community's discernment depends on an imaginative reinterpretation of scripture.* The apostles and elders do not say, "We are imposing these rules because scripture teaches them." Instead, it seems that the stipulations of their letter are derived by *analogical inference* from the Levitical laws pertaining to resident aliens. A moment's

reflection will show that the application of these restrictions to gentile Christians is indeed a creative leap. The gentile converts in Antioch are, after all, not ancient Canaanites dwelling in the land of Israel. It appears that the representatives at the Jerusalem Council considered the Levitical laws about sojourners in the land and *imaginatively transferred them* to address the controversy about what gentile converts must do. This is a good illustration of what I described in *The Moral Vision of the New Testament* as the formation of ethical judgment through "metaphor-making."[8]

2. *The community's discernment depends on paying attention to stories about where God was currently at work.* In the context of the story of Acts, the claim that the decision "seemed good to the Holy Spirit" alludes to the Spirit's falling upon the gentiles (as in Peter's narrative) and working signs and wonders. These signs and wonders, as reported by Barnabas and Paul, are said to be things that "*God had done* through them among the gentiles." And Peter, for his part, explains the story of the conversion of Cornelius's household in this way: "*God, who knows the human heart, testified to them by giving them the Holy Spirit,* just as he did to us; and in cleansing their hearts by faith he has made no distinction between them and us" (Acts 15:8–9). So when the apostles and elders say "it seemed good to the Holy Spirit," they aren't referring to some ineffable sense of unanimity that descended mysteriously like a fog upon the assembly in Jerusalem; instead, they are referring to specific events in which God's

Spirit *testified* to the inclusion of gentiles in the church by transforming their lives. The Jerusalem church listened carefully and believed these stories.

3. *The discernment is made in and by the community.* James, as a leader in the Jerusalem church, articulates his understanding of the implications of the testimony that the community has heard, but he is not an autocratic decider. The letter that goes out from the meeting is sent "with the consent of the whole church" (Acts 15:22). And the letter says, "it has seemed good to the Holy Spirit . . . *and to us*" (15:28). It was not a private discernment, but *a discernment made in community* after hearing different sides of a debate. They have listened to the accounts of the Spirit's work, they have noted the testimony of scripture, and they have made a creative discernment about the best course of action. At the end of the day, it was their own discernment. It is a wise and honest thing that they say so.

Does Luke's account of the Jerusalem Council offer a model for how the church today might address controversial issues concerning inclusion of sexual minorities?[9] Indeed, it is a promising model, fully consistent with the flow of the Bible's ongoing story of God's expansive grace.[10] The model suggests that just as the early Christians deliberated together and decided to remove barriers to gentile participation in the community of Jesus-followers, so also the church today should open its doors fully to those of differing sexual orientations.

If we want to follow that model faithfully, we will recognize that the council's letter did also call the newly welcomed gentiles to observe certain practical requirements that set them apart from their pagan environment. The letter admonishes the gentile believers that if they follow these few restrictions, "you will do well" (Acts 15:29). One of the requirements was to abstain from *porneia*—sexual misconduct. If the church today looks to the council as a pattern—and if it decides that same-sex unions are no longer to be automatically classified as *porneia*—we would need to ask what analogous transformative guidance the church would offer to its members of differing sexual orientations. This is a conversation that will require careful listening on all sides. One reasonable suggestion is that same-sex relationships should aspire to the same standard of monogamous covenant fidelity that the church has long commended and prescribed for heterosexual marriage. And, at the same time, the church should be no less careful to uphold that same standard consistently for its members of heterosexual orientation.

In any case, if we do decide to look to the Jerusalem Council as a model and precedent for the church's present-day controversies about sexuality, we will need to give careful attention to each of the three factors listed here: imaginative attention to scripture, attentive listening to stories of how God is already at work, and careful conversation in community.[11] If we follow these examples of the Jerusalem Council, we—like the early church that recognized the freedom of God at work in their midst—"will do well."

16

Mercy All the Way Down

Groups grounded in a common history or a set of foundational documents find themselves, necessarily, in a constant state of review and revision, asking, *What do these things from the past mean for us?* A case in point: the endless debates in the US Supreme Court about which laws and practices are "constitutional" and which are not.

Things were no different in the earliest communities of Jesus-followers. They were grounded in Jewish scripture and tradition, but they found themselves arguing about whether to welcome gentiles and, if so, on what terms. They had to ask whether Jesus's teachings, along with the community's recent experiences, required them to rethink previously settled norms and practices.

Though the council in Jerusalem provisionally resolved some issues about the surprising grafting of gentiles into the people of God, it hardly marked the end of controversies. Indeed, the entire New Testament bears witness that from the church's beginnings there have always been fierce arguments about ethical standards and identity-defining boundaries. Never was there an idyllic time of unanimity in the community. Luke's preliminary sketches of the earliest church in Jerusalem do suggest that the believers were "of one heart and soul" (Acts 4:32), but the succeeding chapters of the story show how quickly any such unity disintegrated, so that there was "no small dissension and debate" in the community (see, e.g., 6:1, 15:1–5, 36–41).

Likewise, the letters of Paul vividly demonstrate the ongoing struggle in the earliest churches to clarify their relationship to the diverse cultural worlds (both Jewish and Greco-Roman) in which their mission was taking shape.[1] Paul, writing as a missionary to emergent communities of Jesus-followers, confronted the pastoral task of *resocialization:* teaching communities to reconsider their "commonsense" cultural patterns of thinking and living in light of the new things God was doing. That process of resocialization inevitably produced numerous conflicts.

The conflicts were fought out on several fronts. In some of his letters, such as Galatians and Philippians, we find Paul battling the same teachings that provoked debate in the Jerusalem Council: pressures for gentile believers to undergo circumcision and/or to embrace Torah-observant practices.[2] In other letters, such as 1 Corinthians and Colossians, the lines are drawn differently, as the apostle urges his fledgling communities (mostly gentile in composition) to rethink their inherited cultural assumptions about social status, eating and sharing food, sexual practices, and social customs associated with idolatrous worship.[3] In short, on all fronts, these young churches faced internal fights over doctrine and practice, as well as conflicts over leadership. And on all fronts, Paul was calling the nascent communities that confessed Jesus as Lord to undergo *a conversion of the imagination.*[4]

Here is how he explained the basis for this call to conversion:

> So if anyone is in Christ, there is a new creation: everything old has passed away; see, everything has become new! All this is from God, who reconciled

us to himself through Christ, and has given us the
ministry of reconciliation; that is, in Christ God was
reconciling the world to himself, not counting their
trespasses against them, and entrusting the message
of reconciliation to us. (2 Cor 5:17–19)

In the new vision that Paul was sharing, the death and resurrection of Jesus marked the turn of the ages, the beginning of
a whole new world—a world so different that it could only be
called a new creation. In that new creation, all who were once
far off and estranged have been reconciled to God. For that
reason, Paul declares, the whole community in Christ is called
to participate in "the ministry of reconciliation."

The ministry of reconciliation—that is the mission of the
church. To be reconciled to God is to be drawn into the task of
making reconciliation real in embodied human communities.
And yet within these new communities of Jesus-followers conflicts persisted. That explains why Paul's letters repeatedly and
urgently call for *unity* in the church. Consider these examples,
excerpted from several of his letters to these struggling young
communities of believers:

Now *I appeal to you, brothers and sisters, by the
name of our Lord Jesus Christ, that all of you be in
agreement and that there be no divisions among you
but that you be united in the same mind and the same
purpose.* For it has been reported to me by Chloe's
people that there are quarrels among you, my brothers and sisters. What I mean is that each of you says,
"I belong to Paul," or "I belong to Apollos," or "I belong to Cephas," or "I belong to Christ." Has Christ
been divided? Was Paul crucified for you? Or were
you baptized in the name of Paul? (1 Cor 1:10–13)

And so, brothers and sisters, I could not speak to you as spiritual people, but rather as people of the flesh, as infants in Christ. I fed you with milk, not solid food, for you were not ready for solid food. *Even now you are still not ready, for you are still of the flesh. For as long as there is jealousy and quarreling among you, are you not of the flesh, and behaving according to human inclinations?* (1 Cor 3:1–3)

For you were called to freedom, brothers and sisters; only do not use your freedom as an opportunity for self-indulgence, but through love become slaves to one another. For the whole law is summed up in a single commandment, "You shall love your neighbor as yourself." *If, however, you bite and devour one another, take care that you are not consumed by one another.* (Gal 5:13–15)

If then there is any encouragement in Christ, any consolation from love, any sharing in the Spirit, any compassion and sympathy, make my joy complete: *be of the same mind, having the same love, being in full accord and of one mind. Do nothing from selfish ambition or conceit, but in humility regard others as better than yourselves.* Let each of you look not to your own interests, but to the interests of others. (Phil 2:1–4)

I, therefore, the prisoner in the Lord, beg you to lead a life worthy of the calling to which you have been called, with all humility and gentleness, with patience, *bearing with one another in love, making every effort to maintain the unity of the Spirit in the*

bond of peace. There is one body and one Spirit, just
as you were called to the one hope of your calling,
one Lord, one faith, one baptism, one God and Father of all, who is above all and through all and in
all. (Eph 4:1–6)[5]

The specific circumstances of these communities, scattered
throughout Asia Minor and Greece, differ. But in case after
case, as Paul addresses their confusions, concerns, and conflicts, he returns to an appeal for *unity.* That is not because he
is conflict-averse: One could hardly accuse Paul of that! Rather,
it is because his vision of the church as the body of Christ lies at
the beating heart of his gospel: It is a body united in one Lord,
one faith, one baptism.

For readers today, picking our way across the scorched
earth of bitter divisions and media-driven resentments (both
in the church and in broader political culture), this vision of
unity and peace falls upon us like gentle rain from heaven upon
the place beneath. Yet it may also seem wildly idealistic. In order
to understand why Paul thought it was possible for his communities to live in unity, we need to explore more deeply the
theological basis of his hope.

A careful reading of Paul's Letter to the Romans offers
important insights about how and why the church might over-
come difficult divisions. Romans—for all its complex theological twists and turns—should be understood at its root as *Paul's
passionate appeal to the Christians at Rome to accept one another in love despite strong differences of opinion and cultural
norms.* Because of the letter's length and theological density,
it hasn't always been interpreted that way. In order to see what
Paul is driving at, let's chart a fresh overview of his argument.

✺

Paul announces the theme of the letter in a programmatic statement near the beginning of the text: The gospel is "the power
of God for salvation to everyone who has faith, to the Jew first
and also to the Greek. For in it the righteousness [or 'justice']
of God is revealed through faith for faith" (Rom 1:16–17a). The
key words in this programmatic statement are not easy to translate simply into English. The noun *dikaiosynē* is often translated as "righteousness," but it can also mean "justice," and it
ordinarily has that meaning in Greek texts outside the New
Testament. Likewise, the Greek word *pistis* is generally rendered in English translations of Paul as "faith," but its semantic
range includes the ideas of "trust" and "faithfulness." For example, see Romans 3:3: "Will their faithlessness [*apistia*] nullify
the *faithfulness* [*pistin*] of God?"[6]

Encapsulated in Romans 1:16–17 are three ideas that drive
the argument of the entire letter. First, the gospel is not just an
idea or a proposition; instead, it is God's *power* that transforms
the human condition and brings new realities into being. Second, the gospel is not the product of human ingenuity; it is
revealed (*apokalyptetai*) as a mysterious, surprising message
that declares God's justice and faithfulness. Third, the gospel is
"the power of God for salvation to everyone who has faith" (or
better: "for everyone who *trusts*"); it embraces Jews and Greeks
alike on exactly the same terms.

Following this strong opening declaration, Paul argues
throughout Romans 1–4 that all humans, Jews and non-Jews
alike, are "under the power of sin" (Rom 3:9) and have fallen
short of the glory of God so that there is "no distinction" (3:22–
23). But now God has acted to set all things right, justifying
everyone through the atoning faithfulness of Jesus. Though this
is a fresh revelation of God's justice, it is consistent with what
was previously revealed in Israel's scripture, as shown by the
example of Abraham (4:1–25).[7]

In the next four chapters, Romans 5–8, Paul offers a profound exploration of the condition of all who have been embraced by God's grace: It is a life of mysterious union with Christ, a life of participation in his dying and rising. Even though God's people still struggle with the power of sin, even though we still groan and suffer, Paul insists, we are already experiencing the life-giving power of the Holy Spirit that enables us to look forward in confident hope to "the redemption of our bodies" (Rom 8:23), knowing that *nothing in all creation can finally separate us from the love of God* (8:31–39).

But in view of this comprehensive vision of God's saving mercy, what about the people of Israel? In Paul's own experience, many of his kin have rejected his preaching of the gospel message. As Paul describes the situation, "they have not submitted to God's righteousness [or 'justice']" (Rom 10:3). Their unfaithfulness creates a situation in which Paul says he experiences "great sorrow and unceasing anguish in my heart" (9:2). And so, in Romans 9–11, Paul works through a convoluted argument insisting that "God has not rejected the people whom he foreknew" (11:2). Despite their present resistance, in the end "all Israel will be saved" (11:26). If so, how should Paul's readers understand the present state of affairs, in which it seems that most of the adherents to the new faith in Jesus as Lord are gentiles, rather than Jews? Here is Paul's remarkable answer:

> . . . the gifts and the calling of God are irrevocable.
> Just as you [gentiles] were once disobedient to God
> but have now received *mercy* because of their [Jews']
> disobedience, so they [Jews] have now been dis-
> obedient in order that, by the *mercy* shown to you,
> they too may now receive *mercy*. For God has im-
> prisoned all in disobedience *so that he may be mer-
> ciful to all*. (11:29–32)

The necessity for this strange reversal remains shrouded in mystery, but at least one thing is clear: God's ultimate intention is to embrace all within his mercy. *The gospel is a word about mercy, all the way down.* No one deserves mercy, but we all need it.[8] And in the end—in some unfathomable way—God will show mercy to all.

That is the fundamental conclusion that Paul has reached after eleven chapters of searching theological reflection. From that bedrock conviction, Paul turns to offer practical counsel about the implications and outworkings of the gospel message for life in community: "I appeal to you therefore, brothers and sisters, on the basis of God's *mercy,* to present your bodies as a living sacrifice, holy and acceptable to God, which is your reasonable act of worship. Do not be conformed to this age, but be transformed by the renewing of the mind, so that you may discern what is the will of God—what is good and acceptable and perfect" (Rom 12:1–2).[9] The reference in 12:1 to "God's mercy" is not accidental. It explicitly links the preceding argument to all the exhortations that follow: The good news of God's mercy calls us all to devote our lives radically to the service of God. That is the logical and appropriate response to God's *mercy.* And, Paul promises, as we offer ourselves to God, our minds will be transformed to discern the good things that God desires for the community of his people.

What does such a community look like in practice? In Romans 12 and 13 Paul spells out some of the particular marks of a community living with minds renewed by God's mercy:

- It is a community characterized by humility, recognizing diverse and complementary gifts within the one body.
- It is a community characterized by rejoicing in hope, patient suffering, and hospitality to strangers.

- It is a community that blesses its persecutors, rejoices with those who rejoice, weeps with those who weep, and lives in harmony with one another.
- Above all, it is a community that fulfills the law by obeying the commandment, "Love your neighbor as yourself."

We might think that is the end of the sermon: We can sing a final hymn and walk away cheerfully, saying, "Yes, that was a lovely portrayal of what life in the Christian community should look like." But no, Paul has not finished preaching yet. In Romans 14 and 15 he focuses the spotlight on what is *actually* happening in the Roman house churches. What he sees there is not pretty.[10]

It seems that the followers of Jesus in Rome had broken into quarreling factions that Paul labels "the weak" and "the strong." What were they fighting about? "Some believe in eating anything, while the weak eat only vegetables" (Rom 14:2). Really? That is a church-dividing issue? Paul appeals for a truce: "Those who eat must not despise those who abstain, and those who abstain must not pass judgment on those who eat; for God has welcomed them" (14:3).

The verbs "despise" (*exoutheneō*) and "pass judgment" (*krinō*) provide the key to understanding what is amiss. It is "the strong" who *despise* "the weak" for their excessive scrupulousness about food. They look down on the weak ones as legalistic, timid, and unenlightened. According to the strong, the weak are uptight fundamentalists who want to enforce narrow boundaries, barring harmless ordinary behavior. According to the strong, the weak fail to recognize the freedom that Jesus Christ offers.

On the other hand, "the weak" certainly would not have

characterized themselves that way. Instead, they see themselves as strongly committed to following God's commandments. They seek to avoid all entanglement with idolatry and with the defiling foods that were also prohibited by the Jerusalem Council: blood and things strangled. Accordingly, the "weak" *pass judgment* on those who consider themselves "strong." The so-called weak judge the self-proclaimed strong ones as carelessly permissive and arrogantly disobedient to divine precepts given in scripture. (It will not escape careful readers of the present book that the first-century conflict between "the strong" and "the weak" has its haunting parallels in the conflicts that divide the church in our time, not least in conflicts over sexual practices.)

The "weak" in first-century Rome might have been inspired by the example of Daniel and his three Israelite friends in the court of King Nebuchadnezzar of Babylon: young men who refused to "defile themselves" with the king's food and wine and *ate only vegetables* (Dan 1:8–17). Daniel was held up as a great hero for Jews living under gentile rule and pagan culture. Similarly, the Jewish historian Josephus lauds a group of Jewish priests who had been taken as prisoners to Rome, for "even in affliction, they had not forgotten the pious practices of religion, and supported themselves on figs and nuts."[11] Similar ascetic practices might have been a point of pride for those whom Paul provocatively describes as "weak in faith."

There was also a dispute between the factions at Rome about whether some days are especially holy or whether all days are alike (Rom 14:5). This could refer to an argument about Sabbath observance and other Jewish holy days, though Paul's description is sufficiently general to include other possible ways of arguing about calendars and festivals.

In Hellenistic philosophical traditions, some moral philosophers saw it as their role to provide therapy for people of

weak character who held irrational ideas and were burdened
by what we might call psychological issues. The Roman writer
Cicero defines "weakness" as "an unwholesome aversion and
loathing for certain things . . . an intense belief, persistent and
deeply rooted, which regards a thing that need not be shunned
as though it ought to be shunned."[12] So the dichotomy of "strong"
and "weak" may well find its origins in popular philosophical
terminology.

It seems likely that the disputes Paul mentions map neatly
onto gentile and Jewish factions in the Roman house churches.
Perhaps these terms were employed by gentile converts in Rome
(who thought of themselves as "strong") to express condescending disparagement about the more scrupulous Christians of
Jewish origin who wanted to uphold stricter dietary standards
and sharper separation from pagan culture. If so, Paul may
be simply echoing the reproachful term "weak" from the self-
described "strong" party. On the other hand, Paul himself may
have chosen these terms to characterize the disputes flying about
in Rome. Either way—especially in view of Paul's pervasive
concern throughout Romans with questions of Jewish/gentile
parity and his explicit warning to gentiles not to boast and "become proud" over against the Jewish people—it seems reasonable
to assume that the strong/weak dispute is generated by ethnic
and cultural differences between gentile and Jewish believers.

These ethnic distinctions are not, however, strictly deter-
minative. Paul, whose Jewish heritage is unimpeachable, clearly
identifies himself with the liberated "strong" group (Rom 15:1).
And it is quite possible, conversely, that some gentile converts
may have been drawn to more rigorous practices of Torah-
keeping. In that case, they would have been labeled "weak" by
the "strong" faction. Given these blurry boundaries, Paul may
have deliberately selected his terms to allow some latitude of
application. He basically tells the readers of the letter, *if the*

shoe fits, wear it. As it turns out, Paul is going to step on the toes of both sides.

After his initial admonition to the quarreling factions not to despise and judge one another (Rom 14:3), Paul blurts out a stern challenge: "Who are you to pass judgment on servants of another? It is before their own lord that they stand or fall. And they will be upheld, for the Lord is able to make them stand" (14:4).

Having first thrown down this word of reproach, Paul then takes another tack. He diplomatically explains that the believers on both sides of these disputes are seeking to act "for [or 'in honor of'] the Lord"—presumably because they give thanks to God at the table (Rom 14:6). In one of the most moving passages in his letters, Paul calls his Roman readers to recognize that their lives are entirely under the lordship of Jesus and that "whether we live or whether we die, we are the Lord's" (14:8). That is why all their actions should be ordered not toward their own interests and opinions, but toward the one who is "Lord of both the dead and the living" (14:9). That's the big picture.

But finally losing patience, Paul lets his incredulity burst through again: "Why do you *pass judgment* on your brother or sister? Or you, why do you *despise* your brother or sister? For we will all stand before the judgment seat of God" (Rom 14:10). God alone is ultimately our judge, Paul declares, and we are accountable to him alone. In light of that unassailable truth, "Let us therefore no longer *pass judgment* on one another [an admonition to the judgmental 'weak' ones], but resolve instead never to put a stumbling block or hindrance in the way of a brother or sister [an admonition to the condescending 'strong' ones]" (14:13).

At this point, it may be well to acknowledge that this

long-ago dispute among early Christians in Rome holds up a
mirror to our churches today. Many non-Jewish readers today
may reflexively side with "the strong," thinking, "Why are these
dietary scruples such a big deal?" That casual judgment, however, badly underestimates the centrality of meal practices to
Jewish identity. We should recall that three of the four "essentials" stipulated for gentile converts in the letter of the Jerusalem Council (Acts 15:23–29) pertain to foods that may or may
not be eaten. The Torah's dietary laws were no less salient for
devout Jews in antiquity than are rules about sexual morality
for conservative Christians today. Keeping that analogy in mind
may help us comprehend both the intensity of the disputes in
Rome and the extraordinary character of Paul's pastoral response to these controversies.

The "strong" ones today are the liberated advocates of un-
conditional affirmation of same-sex unions; they are tempted
to "despise" the "weak," narrow-minded, rule-following conservatives who would impose limits on their freedom. And the
"weak" ones today are the devout, strict followers of what they
understand to be God's law given in scripture; they are tempted
to "pass judgment" on the sinful laxity of the "strong" who
condone same-sex unions.

Paul makes it clear that he himself is on the side of the
"strong," who believe no food is unclean (Rom 14:14, 15:1)—a
remarkable change of mind for an apostle who describes himself formerly "as to the law, a Pharisee" (Phil 3:5). At the same
time, however, he recognizes that others conscientiously hold
a different opinion. He worries that the strong faction's im-
patient contempt for the scruples of others might create social
pressure for the weak to act against their own conscientious
conviction. Paul sees this as a potential disaster: "If your brother
or sister is distressed by what you eat, you are no longer walk-

ing in love. Do not let what you eat cause the ruin of one for whom Christ died" (Rom 14:15).[13] He is saying, in effect, "Christ died for them—and you can't even change your diet?"

Above all, Paul emphasizes that these disputes are not worth dividing the community: "For the kingdom of God is not food and drink but righteousness [justice] and peace and joy in the Holy Spirit. . . . Let us then pursue what makes for peace and mutual upbuilding. Do not, for the sake of food, destroy the work of God" (Rom 14:17, 19–20a). And what does Paul mean by "the work of God" (*to ergon tou theou*)? It is nothing other than the community of faith, this strange new body of believers who may have been Jew and Greek, slave and free, male and female. God's work has been to bring this surprisingly diverse community into being. Now they are, or should be, one in Christ. Their disputes about food and special days are, within this big new horizon, relatively inconsequential. That is why Paul doesn't issue any ruling on who is right and who is wrong. He doesn't render a judicial ruling; instead, he just appeals for unity in the midst of persisting differences.

Therefore, as he moves to the conclusion of his exhortation, Paul offers a fervent prayer for the quarreling Romans: "May the God of steadfastness and encouragement grant you to live in harmony with one another, in accordance with Christ Jesus, so that together you may with one voice glorify the God and Father of our Lord Jesus Christ" (Rom 15:5–6). Having breathed that prayer, he comes to the point of the whole exhortation—indeed, to the climactic point of the entire lengthy letter: "Welcome one another, therefore, just as Christ has welcomed you, for the glory of God" (15:7).

It's easy for people in churches today to be quite content to be separated from those they disagree with. Whether "the people different from us" are "liberals" or "conservatives," there's surely another church down the road where they'd fit in better. But that's not exactly the ideal symbolized by the metaphor of the church as "the body of Christ."

The vision that Paul offers is quite a different one: *"Welcome one another, just as Christ has welcomed you, for the glory of God."* That's not just a shrugging compromise; it is the climax and consequence of the intricate, passionate argument of the whole letter. Paul proclaims that the gospel is all about the unsearchable, inscrutable *mercy of God* (Rom 11:33–36). All of us are recipients of that mercy. That is why we are called, even in the midst of conflict and difference, to welcome one another.[14]

These words flow from the pen of Paul the former Pharisee who once wanted to arrest and imprison followers of this alleged Messiah Jesus because he saw them as a threat to God's law. By the time he wrote the Letter to the Romans, he had undergone a far-reaching transformation of the mind: The gospel proclaims mercy for all, all the way down.

III

The Widening of God's Mercy
in the Present Day

17

Moral Re-Vision
What We Must Say About Human Sexuality

The freely acting God Himself and alone is the truth of revelation. . . . Exegetical theology investigates the biblical teaching as the basis of our talk about God. . . . Hence dogmatics as such does not ask what the apostles and prophets said but what we must say on the basis of the apostles and prophets.

—Karl Barth, *Church Dogmatics* (I/1, p. 16)

B ecause God sometimes changes his mind and his approaches to the world, faithfulness to God means sometimes doing the same.

This book presents a biblical vision of God that differs from what many people assume about God and the Bible. As we have seen in case after case, the Bible doesn't portray God as static; instead, it tells stories that portray God as a mysterious, dynamic, personal power who can and does change his mind and reveal new and surprising facets of his will. In the stories we have traced, God repeatedly reveals an expansive mercy that embraces ever wider circles of people, including those previously deemed in some way alien or unworthy. Furthermore, again and again, God's widening mercy comes as an unsettling surprise to those who had thought of themselves as God's most resolutely faithful followers.

And so here is the proposal we offer in this book: The many biblical stories of God's widening mercy invite us to re-envision how God means us to think and act today with regard to human sexuality. The biblical narratives throughout the Old Testament and the New trace a trajectory of mercy that leads us to welcome sexual minorities no longer as "strangers and aliens" but as "fellow citizens with the saints and also members of the household of God" (Eph 2:19).[1]

For both of us, this new vision of the implications of scripture's stories represents a change of mind, a *re-vision* of what we thought before.

When the people of God change their minds about things, it is often because someone offers a new vision of God's will. Any time we re*vise* our plans, we literally re-en*vision* things. That is what we have sought to do in this book: to re-envision and reframe the debate about sexuality in the church.

We believe that this debate should no longer focus on the endlessly repeated exegetical arguments about half a dozen isolated texts that forbid or disapprove of same-sex relations. (The regularly cited texts are Gen 19:1–9, Lev 18:22, 20:13, 1 Cor 6:9–11, 1 Tim 1:10, and Rom 1:18–32.) In this book, we have not revisited them. It is relatively clear that these texts view homosexual sex negatively, even if they do not envisage covenanted same-sex partnerships as we know them today.[2] But drawing conclusions based only on these passages would be like basing a biblical theology of slavery on Exod 21:2 (which assumes one can buy a slave) and 1 Pet 2:18 (which tells slaves to be subject to their masters), or a theology of immigration on Ezek 44:9's exclusion of foreigners from the sanctuary.

Instead, we hope to refocus the conversation on larger narrative patterns and precedents in the Bible. The stories we've summarized in the foregoing chapters disclose a deeper logic, a narrative pattern in which God's grace and mercy regularly overflow the prohibitions and restrictions that exclude and condemn fixed classes of human beings—even when those prohibitions were explicitly attributed to God in earlier biblical texts. We believe that our contemporary debates about sexuality should be shaped by that deeper logic. It may be difficult to get our minds around this idea, but if we take the biblical narratives seriously, we can't avoid the conclusion that God regularly changes his mind, even when it means overriding previous judgments.

To say it one more time, our vision is this: *The biblical narratives throughout the Old Testament and the New trace a trajectory of mercy that leads us to welcome sexual minorities no longer as "strangers and aliens" but as "fellow citizens with the saints and also members of the household of God."* Full stop.

But why should anyone credit our vision when other people have other visions?

After all, sometimes new visions are simply misguided. Those who have worked in dysfunctional businesses and institutions know that sometimes there's nothing more terrifying and unwelcome than a new "vision statement." The writers of sitcoms and comic strips have harvested years of material from this basic fact. In religions, harmful visions have a particularly awful and well-documented history. Crusades, pogroms, and witch trials all came out of someone's religious vision.

Sometimes, though, re-vision is necessary.

The Christian church is no stranger to new visions, or to

the controversies that they can generate. Generations before us had to reckon with the validity of new visions as well.

New prophecies, new visions, and new dreams are potentially exciting stuff. They also have the deepest possible roots in the Old Testament. Near the very beginning of Israel's story, Abram has a vision of an unlikely future (Gen 15:1). Samuel is called in a vision (1 Sam 3), Nathan advises David on the basis of visions (2 Sam 7:17), and Ps 89:19–20 speaks of vision as the basis for the Davidic king's coronation. The book of Isaiah is cast as a vision (Isa 1:1) and contains vision reports (most famously Isa 6). Visions are particularly important in Amos, Ezekiel, Daniel, and Zechariah; even foreign diviners like Balaam can see visions of the Almighty (Num 24:4). The lack of visions is seen as a curse (Lam 2:9, Prov 29:18).

In Numbers 12:6, God says, "I the LORD make myself known to them [the prophets] in visions; / I speak to them in dreams." Dreamers and dreams are very similar to visionaries and visions. The dreams of Jacob, Joseph, and Daniel are some of the most beloved Old Testament stories. Joseph's understanding of dreams ultimately saves his people, and Daniel's vindicates Israel's God before a foreign imperial court. Conversely, God's refusal to provide Saul with guidance in dreams plays an important role in his downfall (1 Sam 28:6, 15).

The New Testament also bears witness to dreams as a source of guidance for God's people. Joseph is directed in dreams to take the unexpectedly pregnant Mary as his wife and, later, to flee with her and the child Jesus as refugees to Egypt and eventually to return to the land of Israel (Matt 1:18–25; 2:13–15, 19–21).

The earliest Christian movement was explicitly a visionary one, in a way that revised definitions and polarized communities. The divine sonship of Jesus is revealed in a vision (Matt 17:5–9), and the inspiration of the movement at Pentecost (Acts 2) is explained by Peter, with a quotation from Joel 2:28, in Acts 2:17:

> . . . I will pour out my Spirit upon all flesh,
>   and your sons and your daughters shall prophesy,
> and your young men shall see visions,
>   and your old men shall dream dreams.[3]

One of those visions subsequently directed Peter to proclaim the good news about Jesus to a gentile centurion's household and to approve their baptism, recognizing that God shows no partiality (Acts 10–11). Likewise, the zealous enforcer Saul (later to be known as Paul) was stopped in his tracks by a "heavenly vision" and commissioned to preach to the gentile world the gospel that he had previously sought to eradicate (Acts 9:1–19, 26:19–20).

And yet . . . for such a major component of the Bible's story and theology, visions and dreams were also a source of great *anxiety*. There was a more or less constant fear of false claims about visions, as was the case with prophecy (Deut 18:20–22). Deuteronomy warns about false testimony given by a "dreamer of a dream" (13:1–5). Such false dreamers must be removed from the people lest they turn the people "from the way in which the LORD your God commanded you to walk" (13:5).

Jeremiah's conflicts with false prophets are a theme throughout that book, and such conflicts were often cast in visionary terms, for example in 14:14: "The LORD said to me: The prophets are prophesying lies in my name; I did not send them, nor did I command them or speak to them. They are prophesying to you a lying vision, worthless divination, and the deceit of their own minds" (also Jer 23:16–32, 27:9, 29:8). Ezekiel also warns against those "seeing false visions and divining lies for them, saying, 'Thus says the Lord God,' when the LORD has not spoken" (Ezek 22:28; also 21:9). Interestingly, it is sometimes the most visionary prophets who have the most skeptical things to say about visions; Ezekiel had numerous visions himself, and the visionary Zechariah warns:

> . . . the diviners see lies;
> the dreamers tell false dreams
>   and give empty consolation.
> Therefore the people wander like sheep;
>   they suffer for lack of a shepherd. (Zech 10:2; also 13:4)

Some of the same concerns continued in the period of the New Testament. Despite the importance of visions for the New Testament authors, Jude 8 cautions its audience not to follow "dreamers" who "defile the flesh" and "reject authority." And Colossians 2:18 warns about those who spend their time "dwelling on visions." Writing to the church at Corinth, a community riven by enthusiasm for Spirit-inspired utterances, Paul urges restraint and careful communal judgment: "Let two or three prophets speak, and let the others weigh what is said" (1 Cor 14:29).[4]

There's no simple, exegetical route out of this cul-de-sac. It's not as if there's one Hebrew or Greek word that connotes a true vision and another word that implies a false one. The translations quoted above accurately reflect that the same set of terminology is used for both.

One thing to consider is that true visions were often preserved because they were judged to be true in spite of being inconvenient. Many of them contradicted preconceived notions and undermined the visionaries' own nation or the ruling powers of their times.

That's one reason that accusations of false visionary witness were also wielded against honest prophets: Consider Amos's confrontation with King Jeroboam of Israel and Amaziah, his high priest at Bethel. Like Jeremiah, Amos was suspected of conspiracy to weaken the nation. It would have been inconvenient for the Israelite king and court to take seriously Amos's call to care for the disadvantaged (Amos 5–6). Amaziah simply says to Amos, "O *visionary*, go, flee away to the land of Judah, earn your bread there, and prophesy there; but never again prophesy at Bethel, for it is the king's sanctuary, and it is a temple of the kingdom" (7:12–13).[5] You can hear the threat and condescension dripping from the opening words.

Some may object that the "moral vision" of the Bible is a different matter from the visions of prophets and other visionaries, but the former is inevitably and profoundly based on the latter. The work of the Spirit is ongoing, and the exegesis of texts does not excuse us from the need to recognize it. In fact, on the contrary, faithful exegesis may open our eyes to discern ways in which the Spirit is unexpectedly at work in our midst.

Christian visionaries continue to speak truth to power. Is it a surprise that Martin Luther King Jr.'s most famous speech was about a dream?

Still, why *this vision now*? Why should God's mercy trump and override the Levitical laws about same-sex intercourse? There is of course no simple, irrefutable answer to that question. But we can offer some reasons that seem to us compelling.

First, it isn't hard to find other examples of biblical laws or teachings that the church has subsequently abandoned or overturned. For many readers, the most obvious case is the issue of slavery. Israel's law explicitly permits slaveholding and establishes various regulations concerning the treatment of slaves (e.g., Exod 21:1–11, Lev 25:44–46). Likewise, several New Testa-

ment texts simply presuppose the institution of slavery and ad-
monish slaves to obey their masters (e.g., Eph 6:5–9, Col 3:22–
4:1). To be sure, some of the relevant passages posit rules to
make treatment of slaves more humane, but the bare fact remains that the social practice of slavery is reinforced and treated
as normal in many biblical texts.

These prooftexts were still cited approvingly by slave-
holders in the United States until the middle of the nineteenth
century.[6] Over time, however, the Christian church has come to
a universal conviction—despite the prooftexts to the contrary—
that slavery is incompatible with God's overriding norms of
justice and mercy. Slavery continues to exist (for example in
the deplorable practice of sex trafficking), but no Christian theologian would any longer defend it as permissible "because the
Bible says so."

Likewise, the same Leviticus Holiness Code that prohibits same-sex intercourse also prohibits the eating of blood: "If
anyone of the house of Israel or of the aliens who reside among
them eats any blood, I will set my face against that person who
eats blood and will cut that person off from the people" (Lev
17:10). This prohibition is emphatically reinforced in the New
Testament, in the decree of the Jerusalem Council (Acts 15:19–
20, 28–29). It remains in force for Orthodox Jews who strictly
observe kosher practices, but—despite Acts 15—it is routinely
ignored by Christians who eat nonkosher meat without scruples or pangs of conscience.

We could go on citing other instances, such as the subordination of women (1 Cor 14:33b–36, 1 Tim 2:11–15), Paul's teachings that mandate head coverings for women and prohibit long
hair for men (1 Cor 11:2–16), or Jesus's prohibition of divorce
(Mark 10:2–12). We could fill a whole book with discussion of
such examples, but the general point is clear: Christians across
time have found the Spirit-led freedom to set aside biblical laws

and teachings that they deem unjust, irrelevant, or inconsistent with the broader divine will. It is not hard to see how the prohibition of same-sex relations could fall into the same category.

Second, in many cases where the church has changed its understanding of God's will, the impetus for change has come from careful and compassionate attention to human experience. Why have we rejected slavery? Because we see the suffering it causes, its cruelty and contradiction of human wholeness. Why have many churches rejected the subordination of women to men and supported their full inclusion in church leadership? Because we see in our experience the arbitrary way in which it denies and stifles the evident gifts and graces of half of the human race.[7] For many, the evidence of experience outweighs the inertia of tradition and the force of a few biblical prooftexts on these questions. In the same way, we see LGBTQ Christians all around us who are already contributing their gifts and graces to the work of God in the world and in the church.

When we form moral judgments, we inevitably and rightly pay attention to the evidence of experience. With regard to human sexuality, we have seen over the past generation a cumulatively increasing body of evidence that sexual orientation is (in a way that remains mysterious) deeply ingrained in individuals and not susceptible to change. And for human beings in general, the wisdom of Genesis 2:18 applies, regardless of sexual orientation: It is not good that we should be alone. Some individuals may have a special vocation to celibacy, but that cannot be imposed as a blanket requirement on an entire class of humans. The more we have listened to friends, to our fellow Christians, and to respected voices in the culture more broadly, the more we have been compelled to recognize a tidal wave of evidence that same-sex attraction and partnering is, for some people, hardwired into their identity. And, at the same time, we recognize that the gifts and graces of the Holy Spirit are abundantly present among our LGBTQ friends. That being so, we find ourselves compelled to say, along with Peter, "Who are we that we can block God?"

Third, and most decisively, the vision that informs this book rhymes with the Bible's pervasive portrayals of God's ever-expanding mercy. To put that in more technical theological language: The acceptance of sexual minorities in the church re-enacts a narrative pattern that is pervasive in the Bible. There is a powerful analogy, a *metaphorical correspondence*, between the embrace of LGBTQ people and God's previously unexpected embrace of foreigners, eunuchs, "tax collectors and sinners," gentiles, and people with conflicting convictions about food laws and calendrical observances. When we begin to feel the force of that metaphorical correspondence, we can hardly do otherwise than to declare along with Peter, "God has shown me that I should not call anyone profane or unclean" (Acts 10:28). We advocate full inclusion of believers with differing sexual orientations *not* because we reject the authority of the Bible. Far from it: We have come to advocate their inclusion precisely because we affirm the force and authority of the Bible's ongoing story of God's mercy.

The vision we have presented in this book, then, constitutes a parade example of moral judgment as metaphor-making: the task of "placing our community's life imaginatively within the world articulated in the text."[8] When we make this kind of imaginative connection, we perceive that faithfulness to scripture requires not just following rules or repeating prohibitions; instead, it requires watching and listening to discern where the Spirit is at work.

And so we invite readers of this book to see along with us, looking to where the biblical stories of God's mercy point. In the case at hand, we ask ourselves how God wants people to treat those with different sexual orientations. We find in the

Bible a history in which a lowly people is called to form a great nation, in which foreigners are incorporated, in which youngest brothers are called to be kings, in which we are repeatedly told to pay attention to the most underprivileged. Biblical law warns us to shelter the widow, the orphan, the sojourner; and the prophets could not speak any more loudly about the importance of justice for the poor. We find in the Bible the history of a contentious itinerant from the boondocks, born in questionable moral circumstances, proclaimed by dirty shepherds, who goes around with random fishermen, heals untouchables, and forgives unforgiveable people. It's not surprising that in the midst of that story, there are also moments when someone stands up and says, "Hey, look, if this is who we are and what we stand for, then maybe the grace that we know extends also beyond us, to *those* people." It's not the *only* thing in the Bible, but it's one of the *best* things about the Bible.

Those are the reasons we think that readers should accept our vision for a church that welcomes people of different sexual orientations. We cannot claim direct divine revelation in a dream or visionary experience, but we believe that scripture's portrayal of God's wide and ever-opening mercy provides sufficient warrant for anyone who remains doubtful to come down on the side of generosity and grace. That's what it would mean to live within the biblical story.

This concluding chapter began with Karl Barth's distinction between asking "what the apostles and prophets said" and asking "what we must say on the basis of the apostles and prophets." In light of the freely acting God whom we have encountered in the Bible, we cannot point to the Bible as if it timelessly settled all the issues about human sexuality. It remains *our* responsibility to decide what we must say.

We have thought long and hard about what we must say about human sexuality and have concluded that it is part of the biblical story of God's widening mercy. After spending many years with the Bible, we present this holistic interpretation with full confidence. We believe that sexual minorities who seek to follow Jesus should be welcomed gladly in the church and offered full access to the means of grace available to all God's people: baptism, the Lord's Supper, ordination, and the blessing of covenanted unions, with the same expectations as for heterosexuals.

We hope that this book will start conversations that grow from an awareness of God's free and merciful character revealed in the biblical accounts we have traced. For the sake of the church and those within it, we hope to persuade.

Nevertheless, we know that not everyone who reads this book will begin or end in the same place. On the ground and in our churches, outcomes are going to look different in different places. We hope that at a minimum readers will have a different perspective on God and seek to avoid harm to those around them.

As a practical matter, it is difficult to see how strong differences over same-sex marriages could be maintained within an individual congregation, or even in some cases within an individual denomination. But it is not impossible to imagine that different Christian congregations might hold different norms and practices on this question while still acknowledging one another as members of the one body of Christ—just as Catholic and Protestant churches already do with respect to their different standards on clerical celibacy and women's ordination.

Even among those who agree that those with differing sexual orientations are to be welcomed fully among God's people, there remain some matters where conscientious differences of theological opinion may (and do) continue. These differences are particularly acute with regard to the questions of how to interpret same-sex unions in relation to traditional Christian understandings of marriage.

More than twenty years ago, the theologian Eugene F. Rogers Jr., one of the leading advocates for the church's acceptance of same-sex marriage, articulated the theological complexity of this question and proposed the need for new liturgical forms and ethical guidance:

> Gay and lesbian relationships not only must exhibit the spiritual fruits of faith, hope, and charity but must also exhibit them in sacramental form. Just as marriage gives form or rule to the sanctifying possibilities of heterosexual sex, so gay and lesbian people need sacramental forms, or inspired rules. . . . Conservatives are right to complain about what you might call unformed love: we must mine Scripture and tradition under the Spirit, who will rule new rules for us.[9]

We have sought in the present book to "mine scripture and tradition under the Spirit" to uncover fresh resources for the church's reflection on these matters. We do not, however, presume to offer new rules or liturgies. Only the various ecclesial communities in which debates persist can decide for themselves.

At this point, Paul's pastoral counsel to the contentious believers in Rome may provide a helpful model. (See the discussion of Rom 14–15 in Chapter 16.) He urges them to stop arguing and to welcome one another despite their differences. Love means grace and forbearance toward those with whom we disagree. Therefore, Paul urges, we should welcome one another just as Christ has welcomed us, for the glory of God. It should remain possible for churches with different beliefs and practices to coexist peaceably and work together in an ecumenical spirit as history takes its course. This is not because the issues of sexuality are insignificant. Instead, it is because a church that cannot find more urgent issues than the sexuality debates, given the present state of our faith in the world, is probably not very interested in being the church of Jesus Christ at all.

All that we have said, we have said with sympathy for how difficult it can be to rethink deeply held beliefs. Those who are comfortable with the received wisdom about human sexuality inherited from our elders, comfortable living by it, are likely to feel like the elders in T. S. Eliot's "East Coker," wondering what is "the value of the long looked forward to . . . wisdom of age," if in fact

> . . . the pattern is new in every moment
> And every moment is a new and shocking
> Valuation of all we have been.

But it seems to us that God is moving on again, whether we like it or not. Taking the advice of Phil 2:12–23, we have worked out our own conclusions with fear and trembling, and we invite others to do the same.

We forthrightly offer here a *re-visionary* theology—one that not only re-envisions some ancient realities, but also revises some of our own past thinking. It's the best thing we can think to do at the moment, and we think it would be best for the health of churches to consider it seriously. The old battles and grumblings are nothing if not tired. It's time to see new visions and dream new dreams.

We are not really introducing anything new here. The new was already contained in what is very old. Ecclesiastes asks,

> Is there a thing of which it is said,
> > "See, this is new"?
> It has already been
> > in the ages before us. (Eccl 1:10)

Nor is the tension between the old and the new a new thing. Isaiah first says, "Do not remember the former things, / or consider the things of old" (Isa 43:18); then he says, "remember the former things of old" (46:9). The only resolution to this paradox is to look forward in joy to the new creation:

> For I am about to create new heavens
> > and a new earth;
> the former things shall not be remembered
> > or come to mind.
> But be glad and rejoice forever
> > in what I am creating. (65:17–18)

What we have tried to say in this book is essentially what is already said—in the many passages we have discussed, and also in 1 John 2:7–10:

> Beloved, I am writing you no new commandment, but an old commandment that you have had from the beginning; the old commandment is the word that you have heard. Yet I am writing you a new commandment that is true in him and in you, because the darkness is passing away and the true light is already shining. Whoever says, "I am in the light," while hating a brother or sister, is still in the darkness. Whoever loves a brother or sister lives in the light, and in such a person there is no cause for stumbling.

As it did for the Johannine author, love looms large in our thinking. Is there a simpler or more direct statement about God in the Bible than "God is love"? That definition appears in 1 John 4:8 and 4:16, and between those two is this: "since God loved us so much, we also ought to love one another" (1 John 4:11). Even if we were mistaken in our vision, it is better to be wrong in love. As Paul wrote, "if I have prophetic powers, and understand all mysteries and all knowledge, and if I have all faith, so as to move mountains, but do not have love, I am nothing" (1 Cor 13:2). Paul offers a way to decide whom to follow when visions conflict and people disagree: *Follow the way of love.*

It's not accidental that love also became a key principle for St. Augustine. He wrote, "anyone who thinks that he has understood the divine scriptures or any part of them, but cannot by his understanding build up this double love of God and neighbour, has not yet succeeded in understanding them."[10]

The most significant objection to our interpretation of the God of the Bible is the one that simply says, "This God of widening mercy whom you describe is not one that I have ever experienced." That objection is a condemnation of the church. Although we have known many Christian churches, in many places, where one can see the light of the God whom we've portrayed, we cannot deny the experiences of others who have found in the church a message of rejection and condemnation. For that reason, our argument is also a summons to the church to repent of its narrow, fearful vision and to embrace a wider understanding of God's mercy.

Ultimately, the meaning of scripture is shaped by its reception in communities of faith. Only where the word is embodied in community do we begin to understand what it means. The Bible is capable of inspiring all sorts of things, and our actions activate some meanings and not others. We believe that

welcoming people of different sexualities is an act of faithfulness to God's merciful purposes. Let's not make God's offer of
grace a lie.

This is the exciting thing about living in history: We get
to be a part of it. In fact, we have little choice. Every day, we
wake up and make decisions that make the church and the
world better or worse.

This book is therefore not just an argument about the
meaning of the Bible in the past, but an invitation to readers
to make new meaning in the present by listening to the Spirit
and joining God now in saying, "I will gather others to them /
besides those already gathered" (Isa 56:8). It is only the latest in
the long line of scandals caused by the gospel (1 Cor 1:23–24).

This goes out as an invitation to readers who may have felt
sympathy with LGBTQ friends and neighbors—perhaps along
with some uneasiness about the church's traditional exclusionary practices—but felt constrained by their understanding of
"the authority of the Bible" from offering a full welcome. For
such readers, we hope that this book offers encouragement to
see that the inclusion of sexual minorities is not a rejection of
the Bible's message but a fuller embrace of its story of God's
expansive mercy.

As for those who picked up this book already confident
in this conclusion, but who needed assurance about God and
the church, we hope they are better able to see how God's widening mercy is in evidence throughout much of the Bible, and
how it has already included them, their partners, their friends,
and their families.

Finally, may all of us live into the wisdom of Paul's admonition to the quarreling Christians in Rome: "Welcome one
another, . . . just as Christ has welcomed you, for the glory of
God" (Rom 15:7).

Epilogue

Richard B. Hays

I owe it to readers of this book to explain why my mind has changed.

In our concluding chapter, we described the argument we've made as an attempt to think imaginatively along with the biblical texts and to see how the stories of God's surprising mercies might reshape our moral judgments today. That description of our discernment process referred directly to what I had written a quarter century ago in *The Moral Vision of the New Testament*. In that book's key chapter on methodology, I proposed that if we want to practice New Testament ethics, we shouldn't just look for ethical rules or general principles; instead, we should "seek, under the inspiration and guidance of the Holy Spirit, to reread our own lives within the narrative framework of the New Testament, discerning analogies—perhaps startling ones—between the canonical stories and our community's situation."[1]

I'm now mindful that by quoting myself on the importance of analogical imagination, I am indicting myself for my past blindness. I failed then, and for years afterward, to see how

my own model of analogical moral judgment might have re-
shaped my thinking about homosexuality in the church.[2]

I can't excuse my blindness by claiming I hadn't ever heard
the suggestion that the early church's inclusion of uncircumcised gentiles might serve as a fitting analogy for welcoming
gay and lesbian people in the church. Other interpreters, particularly my friend Luke Timothy Johnson, had clearly made
the argument, pointing to the significance of Acts 10–11 and 15
as an illuminating paradigm.[3] In *Moral Vision*, I opined, "The
analogy is richly suggestive, and it deserves careful consideration."[4] But, having considered it, I rejected it in light of the New
Testament's few but emphatic statements—especially Romans
1:24–27—that portray same-sex intercourse as a tragic distor-
tion of the created order.

I have come to think I was wrong. As we have sought to
show in the foregoing chapters, the argument for God's gracious
inclusion of people of different sexual orientations does not
hang by the thread of a single analogy to Acts 10–15. Instead,
it rests on the broad base of scripture's comprehensive story of
God's counterintuitive but persistent mercy. When writing *Moral
Vision*, I fear, I placed myself in the company of those who
devote intensive scholarly labors to straining out gnats, while
neglecting what Jesus called "the weightier matters of the law:
justice and mercy and faith" (Matt 23:23).

This book is an attempt, belatedly, to attend to those weightier matters. For me, the change of opinion can be described as
metanoia: a turning, a transformation of mind. In most of our
English Bibles, that word is translated as "repentance." The word
connotes more than just "feeling sorry"; it also points forward
toward the transformation of thought and action.

I regret the impact of what I wrote previously. As noted in
the introductory chapter of the present book, I am now mind-

ful that my chapter titled "Homosexuality" in *Moral Vision* has, contrary to my intention, caused harm to many over the past quarter century. Writing at a time when same-sex marriage was illegal in the United States and forbidden in nearly all Christian churches, I intended my chapter as an appeal for compassionate traditionalism, arguing for *acceptance* of gay and lesbian people in the church—but also opining that they should without exception embrace the difficult vocation to remain single and celibate.

That judgment, sadly, was not informed by patient listening to my fellow Christians who found their identity indelibly stamped by same-sex attraction and by the longing for companionship. Instead, it was—to put it bluntly—the presumptuous judgment of an eager young scholar seeking to develop a theoretical model for "doing New Testament ethics," that is, working out a model for processing biblical texts into a clear system of teaching.

I offered that chapter on homosexuality as a thought experiment, a proposal for how to think about a certain type of *methodological* problem in theological ethics: the problem of how to adjudicate a contested moral issue in a case where explicit scriptural teaching was scanty but univocal. The proposal was intended to stimulate conversation, not to end it. Unfortunately, many readers and many churches took my proposal as a definitive pronouncement—a buttress for walls of separation, for rigidly restrictive policies and condemnations. I bear some responsibility for that, and I am grieved by it.

To be sure, my chapter was not solely a head trip, an abstract intellectual exercise. What I wrote was informed by my close friendship with my late friend Gary. I was trying to honor what he had thought and written about his own struggles with his sexual identity. My perception of homosexuality was very much shaped by his experience and his testimony. Nonetheless, in retrospect, I fear that I was using him as a prop for my own theoretical construction. I hope that if he were alive today, he would approve of the argument of this book. (And I know that if he didn't, he would engage me in passionate but generous conversation.)

When I wrote that chapter, I was more concerned about my own intellectual project than about the pain of gay and lesbian people inside and outside the church, including those driven out of the church by unloving condemnation. The present book is, for me, an effort to offer contrition and to set the record straight on where I now stand. Beyond that, it is an effort to sketch a wider reading of the whole witness of scripture to the character of God as a God of mercy.

It has taken me a lot longer to come to this change of mind than it took Moses and Peter and Paul, in the stories we have considered, to change their minds. I can only say to anyone and everyone who has been hurt by my words: I am deeply sorry. The present book can't undo past damage, but I pray that it may be of some help.

The posture from which I write now, as we draw this book to a close, is best expressed in the time-honored prayer of confession that precedes the Eucharist in the Anglican tradition:

> Most *merciful* God,
> We confess that we have sinned against you
> in thought, word, and deed,
> by what we have done,
> and by what we have left undone.
> We have not loved you with our whole heart;
> we have not loved our neighbors as ourselves.
> We are truly sorry and we humbly repent.
> For the sake of your Son Jesus Christ,
> have *mercy* on us and forgive us;

that we may delight in your will,
and walk in your ways,
to the glory of your Name.[5]

    I join with generations of the faithful in praying that heart-felt prayer, recognizing that I, along with all God's people, need God's mercy. May we all walk in God's merciful ways.

Notes

Introduction

1. Authors' translation. Where we vary from the New Revised Standard Version of the Bible (NRSV), we include notes to indicate either our translation; the New Revised Standard Version, Updated Edition (NRSVue); or the New Jewish Publication Society of America Tanakh (NJPS).

2. Authors' translation.

3. Readers of Hebrew will recognize *nacham* as the lexical form of the verb נחם. It comes up again later in the book, and in various inflected forms, but we use this single, informal transliteration for the sake of consistency and pronounceability.

4. Karl Barth, *Church Dogmatics* I/1, trans. G. W. Bromiley (London: T & T Clark, 1975), 16.

5. *The Moral Vision of the New Testament: Community, Cross, New Creation* (San Francisco: HarperSanFrancisco, 1996), 379–406. Subsequent page references to this book are given in parentheses in the text. I would now use the terms "homosexual" and "homosexuality" more sparingly, acknowledging that these terms are a nineteenth-century coinage and that there were no equivalent nouns in the ancient world. Of course, "gay" is equally a neologism, so hardly an improvement. The Bible refers to same-sex *acts,* not to classes of persons who perform them or to persons who have an innate "orientation." The modern debate, therefore, constantly encounters the danger of anachronism.

6. John Wilkinson, "Peace, Unity, and Purity and the Presbyterian Church's Fifty-Year Journey on Human Sexuality," *Interpretation* 74 (2020): 275–88.

7. Thomas Römer, "Homosexualität und die Bibel: Anmerkungen zu einem anachronistischen Diskurs," *JBTh* 33 (2018): 47–63.

8. I think of Jonathan Z. Smith's *Map Is Not Territory: Studies in the History of Religions*, Studies in Judaism in Late Antiquity 23 (Leiden: Brill, 1978), in which he emphasizes the task of the historian to "complicate, not clarify" and to "play between the incongruities." While much of my work does that, here I want to step back from that task for the sake of clarity.

9. Lewis B. Smedes, "Like the Wideness of the Sea?," *Perspectives* (May 1999): 8–12. It is not coincidental that he wrote this after retiring from the faculty. A retrospective on the essay by the journal after Smedes's death recalled that "Smedes met with great hostility and criticism for the essay," even though his views were a "sort of a halfway house: welcoming, but not fully accepting." "Revisiting a Landmark Statement on Homosexuality," *Perspectives* (October 2014), https://reformedjournal.com/revisiting-a-landmark -statement-on-homosexuality/. Some readers of this book have also thought of Clark H. Pinnock's *A Wideness in God's Mercy: The Finality of Jesus Christ in a World of Religions* (Grand Rapids: Zondervan, 1992), but we do not intend any allusion to it.

10. Celeste Kennel-Shank, "J. R. Daniel Kirk to Leave Fuller Seminary Amid Conflict," *The Christian Century*, October 28, 2015. https://www.chris tiancentury.org/article/2015-09/nt-professor-leave-amid-conflict-fuller -seminary.

11. Alejandra Reyes-Velarde, "After Christian College Found Out She Was Married to a Woman, She Was Expelled, Lawsuit Says," *Los Angeles Times*, Nov. 25, 2019.

12. "Maxon *v.* Fuller Theological Seminary," decision date December 13, 2021, Becket: Religious Liberty for All, https://www.becketlaw.org/case /maxon-v-fuller-theological-seminary/.

13. See "Plaintiffs' Memorandum of Points and Authorities in Opposition to Defendants' Motion to Dismiss First Amended Complaint," April 14, 2020, https://becketnewsite.s3.amazonaws.com/Opp-to-MTD.pdf.

14. George M. Marsden, *Reforming Fundamentalism: Fuller Seminary and the New Evangelicalism* (Grand Rapids: Eerdmans, 1987), 53.

15. Alan Rifkin, "Jesus with a Genius Grant," *Los Angeles Times*, November 23, 2003.

16. R. Middendorf, P. A. Robertson, N. M. Delano, K. J. Mitchell, and K. T. Wang, "Student Voices: A Student-Led Survey on Fuller's Community Standards and LGBTQ+ Attitudes," paper presented at the 2023 Clinical Psychology Student Research Colloquium, Pasadena, CA, May 2023.

17. Kathryn Post, "Fuller Seminary Senior Director Fired for Refusal to Sign Non-LGBTQ Affirming Statement," Religion News Service, February 2, 2024. https://religionnews.com/2024/02/02/fuller-seminary-senior-director -fired-for-refusal-to-sign-non-lgbtq-affirming-statement/.

18. One can now learn a great deal about the politicization of gender and sexuality within evangelicalism, and about the hardening of the American Christian mindset, from Kristin Kobes Du Mez, *Jesus and John Wayne: How White Evangelicals Corrupted a Faith and Fractured a Nation* (New York: W. W. Norton, 2020).

19. Authors' translation.

20. C. S. Lewis, *Mere Christianity* (New York: HarperCollins, 2001), 102–3.

21. There are numerous reading lists available as starting points in the extensive literature on LGBTQ approaches to theology and biblical studies, including one compiled and hosted by Duke Divinity School (https://sites .duke.edu/divlib/2022/06/03/reading-list-queer-theology/). This book is not meant to take the place of that literature; rather, it is meant to complement those significant perspectives.

22. There may be a hint of this in 1 Cor 3:2, but it flourishes especially in early Christian literature such as the Odes of Solomon. Classical Christian theologians such as Clement of Alexandria, Augustine of Hippo, and Julian of Norwich all used explicit feminine imagery for God. See Christopher B. Hays, "'Can a Woman Forget Her Nursing Child?': Divine Breastfeeding and the God of Israel," in Collin Cornell, ed., *Divine Doppelgängers: YHWH's Ancient Look-Alikes* (University Park: Pennsylvania State University Press, 2020), 201–18, and literature cited there. On Paul's allusion to Isaiah's image of divine labor pains in Rom 8, see Richard B. Hays, *Reading with the Grain of Scripture* (Grand Rapids: Eerdmans, 2020), 215–18. See also Beverly Roberts Gaventa, *Our Mother Saint Paul* (Louisville: Westminster John Knox, 2007), 32–34, 56–59.

23. See the Ugaritic Baal Myth (KTU^3 1.3 ii 3–30), translated by Dennis Pardee in William W. Hallo and K. Lawson Younger, eds., *The Context of Scripture, vol. 1: Canonical Compositions from the Biblical World* (Leiden/ Boston: Brill, 2003), 250.

1
Widening Through Creation

1. Of the Sierras: John Muir, Letter from John Muir to Emily [O. Pelton], May 15, 1870, https://oac.cdlib.org/ark:/13030/kt8g50387d/?order=3&brand =oac4; of Tahoe: John Muir, *Letters to a Friend Written to Mrs. Ezra S. Carr, 1866–1879* (Boston: Houghton Mifflin, 1915), from letter dated November 3, [1873] at Tahoe City, https://vault.sierraclub.org/john_muir_exhibit/writings /letters_to_a_friend/default.aspx

2. Ps 86:9; Isa 60:21; Rom 11:36; 1 Cor 6:20, 10:31; Rev 4:11; Ps 16:5–11, 144:15; Isa 12:2; Luke 2:10; Phil 4:4; Rev 21:3–4.

3. Not to mention the early problems with *keeping* humans a little lower than the gods, as discussed in Gen 6:1–4 and 11:1–9!

4. I have in mind here the more ancient Semitic-language myths such as the Babylonian *Atra-ḫasis* or the Sumerian *Enki and Ninmaḫ*.

5. I am indebted to Prof. Sang Hyun Lee of Princeton Seminary for introducing me to Edwards's work.

6. Jonathan Edwards, "Dissertation I: Concerning the End for Which God Created the World" (originally published 1765), Jonathan Edwards Center at Yale University (http://edwards.yale.edu), *Ethical Writings*, WJE Online Vol. 8, ed. Paul Ramsey, http://edwards.yale.edu/archive?path=aHRoc DovL2Vkd2FyZHMueWFsZS5lZHUvY2dpLWJpbi9uZXdwaGlsby9n ZXRvYmplY3QucGw/Yy43OjU6Mi53amV.

7. Richard Gardiner, "The Presbyterian Rebellion: An Analysis of the Perception That the American Revolution Was a Presbyterian War," PhD diss., Marquette University, 2005. A popular presentation developed by the Presbyterian Historical Society may be found online at https://www.history.pcusa.org /history-online/exhibits/presbyterians-and-american-revolution-page-1.

8. Kenneth P. Minkema, "Jonathan Edwards's Life and Career: Society and Self," in Gerald R. McDermott, ed., *Understanding Jonathan Edwards: An Introduction to America's Theologian* (New York: Oxford Academic, 2009), 19. Minkema adds: "His civic sermons abound with words of support for the king and his ministers and, more to the point, with condemnations of those who question authority and ordained power."

9. Jonathan Edwards preached this famous sermon in 1741; the text is available several places online, including at https://digitalcommons.unl.edu /cgi/viewcontent.cgi?article=1053&context=etas.

10. Available several places online, including at https://www.jonathan -edwards.org/Narrative.html.

11. Author's translation.

12. The only other two are the promised land (in Judg 18:9) and the first Babylonian exiles (in Jer 24:2–3).

13. Translation: NJPS.

2

Mercy for God's People

1. Author's translation.

2. For a brief overview, see James L. Kugel, *Traditions of the Bible: A Guide to the Bible As It Was at the Start of the Common Era* (Cambridge, MA: Harvard University Press, 1998), 94–97. The texts that make this explicit are extrabiblical, though 2 Pet 3:8 also pertains to the postponement of judgment.

3. Author's translation.

4. Emphasis added. Throughout this book, italics within biblical quotations are added by the authors.

5. The translation of the Hebrew divine name with Greek *kyrios* ("Lord") is itself an ancient tradition and need not occupy us here. As far as we can tell, however, the name Yahweh is derived from a verb "to be," which is why at the revelation of the name in Exod 3:14, translators render "I Am Who I Am." Translation is insufficient to the divine name, and, to be perfectly frank, scholars do not fully understand it. But it seems to be about being itself, which is a very different semantic sphere from kingship or lordship. If the first line of Exod 34:6 were translated "The LORD! The LORD!—a God merciful and gracious," etc. (as in many modern translations), one might hear medieval trumpet fanfare in the background, which creates a different image from the repetition of a personal name.

6. On Hagar and Ishmael as examples of God's action on behalf of the marginalized, see Elsa Tamez, "The Woman Who Complicated the History of Salvation," in John S. Pobee and Barbel von Wartenberg-Potter, eds., *New Eyes for Reading: Biblical and Theological Reflections by Women from the Third World* (Geneva: World Council of Churches, 1986), 5–17. For the complex reception of this interpretation among African-American scholars, see Nyasha Junior, *Reimagining Hagar: Blackness and Bible* (Oxford: Oxford University Press, 2019), esp. 101–31."

3
Widening Justice

1. Katharine Doob Sakenfeld, "Zelophehad's Daughters," in James L. Crenshaw, ed., *Perspectives on the Hebrew Bible: Essays in Honor of Walter J. Harrels* (Macon, GA: Mercer University Press, 1988), 40.

2. For some examples, see J. Weingreen, "The Case of the Daughters of Zelophehad," *Vetus Testamentum* 16 (1966): 518–22.

3. Author's translation.

4. On the tendency of interpreters to flatten the complexity of biblical texts, see Carolyn J. Sharp, *Irony and Meaning in the Hebrew Bible* (Bloomington: Indiana University Press, 2009).

5. These examples can be multiplied: Exod 21:2–11 and Deut 15:12–17 have different rules for how one may treat male and female slaves; Exod 22:16–17 and Deut 22:28–29 give different options to the father of an unmarried woman who is seduced, as well as to the seducer; and so on. . . .

6. Another criticism of a liberating reading of this story is that, from the standpoint of the Canaanites, the women are part of an occupying force, so

their ability to claim land is based on the dispossession and oppression of others. Nevertheless, recent authors in the global South have found this narrative a positive case study for present societies. See, e.g., Emmanuel O. Nwaoru, "The Case of the Daughters of Zelophehad (Num 27:1–11) and African Inheritance Rights." *The Asia Journal of Theology* 16, (2002): 49–65; Amadi Ahiamadu, "Assessing Female Inheritance of Land in Nigeria with the Zelophehad Narratives (Numbers 27:1–11)," *Scriptura* 96 (2007): 299–309.

7. Dennis T. Olson, *Numbers* (Louisville: Westminster John Knox, 1996), 167.

8. Sakenfeld, "Zelophehad's Daughters," 47.

9. Sifre to Numbers 133; see Yael Shemesh, "A Gender Perspective on the Daughters of Zelophehad: Bible, Talmudic Midrash, and Modern Feminist Midrash," *Biblical Interpretation* 15 (2007): 101.

10. Author's translation.

4
"I Gave Them Statutes That Were Not Good"

1. Hyginus, *Fabulae* 69; Euripides, *Iphigeneia in Aulis,* passim.

2. The long-running debate over this statement has recently been settled: see Brien Garnand, "Phoenician Synthesis: Patterns of Human Sacrifice and Problems with Ritual Killing," in Karel C. Innemée, ed., *The Value of a Human Life: Ritual Killing and Human Sacrifice in Antiquity,* Papers on Archaeology of the Leiden Museum of Antiquities 26 (Leiden: Sidestone, 2022), 69–93.

3. Author's translation.

4. Jon D. Levenson, *The Death and Resurrection of the Beloved Son: The Transformation of Child Sacrifice in Judaism and Christianity* (New Haven: Yale University Press, 1993), 4.

5. Søren Kierkegaard, *Fear and Trembling,* tr. Howard V. Hong and Edna H. Hong (Princeton: Princeton University Press, 1983), 33.

6. Garry Wills, "Our Moloch," *New York Review,* December 15, 2012.

7. Stephanie Pappas, "Sexual Minority Teens and Suicide," American Psychological Association, July 1, 2020, https://www.apa.org/monitor/2020/07/numbers-sexual-minority-suicides. The rates of actual suicide are not clear because of limitations in the way suicides are (or are not) investigated: Azeen Ghorayshi, "No One Knows How Many L.G.B.T.Q. Americans Die by Suicide," *New York Times,* June 1, 2023, https://www.nytimes.com/2023/06/01/health/lgbtq-suicide-data.html.

8. This argument is complicated and is better made elsewhere; it de-

pends on a detailed historical analysis of social contexts, of the sort that we have decided not to repeat here.

9. Bereshit Rabbah 55:7.

10. Miroslav Volf, *Exclusion and Embrace: A Theological Exploration of Identity, Otherness, and Reconciliation* (Nashville: Abingdon, 1996), 296–300.

5
Widening the Borders

1. The Bible also ends with images of violence, in the book of Revelation. Miroslav Volf's book *Exclusion and Embrace: A Theological Exploration of Identity, Otherness, and Reconciliation* (Nashville: Abingdon, 1996) is a touchstone work for me in its emphasis on judgment as a divine prerogative and its affirmation that even though humans may, in extreme cases, resort to the use of force in pursuit of justice, we must never confuse our provisional and limited justice with God's ultimate judgment and justice.

2. The Greek word translated "family" here (γένος) can be rendered in various other ways (e.g., "offspring," NRSV), but the kinship of all nations is clearly in view here (see Acts 17:26).

3. Author's translation.

4. Translation: NJPS.

5. Gale A. Yee, "'She Stood in Tears Amid the Alien Corn': Ruth, the Perpetual Foreigner and Model Minority," in Randall C. Bailey, Tat-Siong Benny Liew, and Fernando F. Segovia, eds., *They Were All Together in One Place?: Toward Minority Biblical Criticism* (Atlanta: Society of Biblical Literature, 2009), 119–40.

6. Translations often render the Hebrew *Cush* as "Ethiopia," which is derived from the Greek word for the region. But this is somewhat confusing to us today, because the land in question is actually now Sudan. Even more confusing, different books in the same translation use different terms in some cases (e.g., NRSV).

7. There is no indication that racism in the biblical period was equivalent to racism in the present day; Cushites played significant roles in the biblical story alongside people of other nations (e.g., 2 Sam 18:21–32; Jer 38–39; Acts 8:27–39) and do not seem to have been singled out in any way. Nevertheless, differences in appearance were noted (Isa 18:2, 7; Jer 13:23) and may have played a role in this story.

8. See David A. Graham, "Rumsfeld's Knowns and Unknowns: The Intellectual History of a Quip," *Atlantic Monthly,* March 27, 2014.

9. On the protective aspect of anointing, see also Pss 28:8, 105:15; 1 Chr 16:22.

10. Author's translation.

6
"I Knew That You Are a Gracious God, and Merciful"

1. Author's translation.

2. See Pss 86:5, 15; 103:8; 145:8; Deut 5:9–10; Jer 30:11, 32:18–19, 46:28, 49:12; Mic 7:18–20; Nah 1:2.

3. Scholars of Isaiah will know that this is an uncommon word, but this interpretation of it (adopted by both the NRSV and NJPS translations) is almost certainly correct.

4. Author's translation.

5. Author's translation, which is a bit closer to the Hebrew than most translations.

6. John T. McNeill, ed., *Calvin: Institutes of the Christian Religion,* Library of Christian Classics 20–21 (Louisville: Westminster John Knox, 2001), 226 (2.xvii.12).

7. *Institutes,* 226–27.

8. The verb here is *shanah,* and not *nacham.*

9. Jonathan Lear, *Open Minded: Working Out the Logic of the Soul* (Cambridge, MA: Harvard University Press, 1998), 43.

7
Besides Those Already Gathered

1. For the sake of simplicity, in this chapter I use the name Isaiah to refer to the postexilic prophet who carried on the tradition from Isaiah ben Amoz, since we do not know his name.

2. Castration may seem unthinkable today, or at least disturbing, but it has been practiced widely in world history. One reason for its use in nations under dynastic rule was to reduce the number of sexually potent men in proximity to the royal harem. Any questions about who was the heir, or who had fathered the heir, were a potential threat to a dynasty.

3. This concern for living on in the memory of future generations is directly pertinent for understanding the story of the Ethiopian eunuch in Acts 8. See Chapter 12, below.

4. It is probably a confusion of οἰνοχόος "cupbearer," with εὐνοῦχος, "eunuch," that has led to Nehemiah being called a eunuch in Neh 1:11 of

Codex Vaticanus, but it nevertheless reflects this long tradition of interpretation. For a nuanced discussion of eunuchs at the Persian court, with many references to primary texts, see Pierre Briant, *From Cyrus to Alexander: A History of the Persian Empire* (Winona Lake, IN: Eisenbrauns, 2002), 268–77, esp. the discussion of Nehemiah on 276. See also Durrell Watkins, "Ezra-Nehemiah," in Robert E. Goss and Mona West, eds., *The Queer Bible Commentary*, 2nd ed. (London: SCM, 2022), 254–60.

5. Translation: NJPS.

6. Since the possibility was noted above that Nehemiah himself was a eunuch, it bears reflection that he nevertheless leads the way in excluding other disadvantaged groups. This situation will not be unfamiliar from that of the present day.

7. The Levites were sometimes said to "sojourn" within Israel, using a verb cognate with the term "resident alien" (Deut 18:6, Judg 17:7). The Levites are not called resident aliens, but the two groups both lacked their own land (Josh 13:14), and so both required special consideration in the law (e.g., Deut 14:29: "the Levites, because they have no allotment or inheritance with you, as well as the resident aliens, the orphans, and the widows in your towns, may come and eat their fill").

8. See further D. W. van Winkle, "An Inclusive Authoritative Text in Exclusive Communities," in Craig C. Broyles and Craig A. Evans, eds., *Writing and Reading the Scroll of Isaiah*, 2 vols., Supplements to Vetus Testamentum 70 (Leiden: E. J. Brill, 1997), 1:423–40.

9. When Jesus quotes this, he uses a word that means more specifically "poor" (Greek *ptōchos*), which is based on the Septuagint translation. That is a perfectly viable interpretation of the more general Hebrew term (*ʿănāvîm*), which is often associated with poverty (e.g., Isa 11:4, 32:7; Amos 2:7, 8:4). In several particulars, the citation in Luke 4:18–19 differs from Isa 61, most notably by adding the phrase "to let the oppressed go free" (Isa 58:6).

10. Matt 1:23, 3:3, 4:15–16, 8:17, 12:18–19, 13:14–15, 15:8–9, 24:29.

11. British journalist Brian Redhead, quoted in John F. A. Sawyer, *The Fifth Gospel: Isaiah in the History of Christianity* (Cambridge: Cambridge University Press), 4.

8

Jesus Upsets People

1. Josephus, *History of the Jewish War Against the Romans*, 2 vols., trans. H. St. J. Thackeray, Loeb Classical Library (Cambridge, MA: Harvard University Press, 1956–1957; London: William Heinemann, 1957).

2. The passage that Jesus is said to have read is not a precise quotation

of any one passage in Isaiah; it appears to be an artful mash-up of Isa 61:1–2, 35:5, and 58:6.

3. Author's translation.

4. As we shall see, this becomes a major theme in the Acts of the Apostles, the second volume in Luke's narrative of the emergence of the early Christian movement.

5. Among the Gospels, only Mark includes "for all the nations" in the quotation from Isaiah.

6. See Jer 26 for an account of this conflict. Cf. also Amos 7:10–17.

7. In contrast to Luke's clear references to literal poverty and hunger, Matthew's version of the Beatitudes (Matt 5:1–12) appears to offer a spiritualized interpretation of Jesus's words ("poor *in spirit*," "hunger and thirst *for righteousness*"). But Matthew's addition of *tēn dikaiosynēn* (rendered in most English translations as "righteousness") is perhaps better translated as "justice."

8. Variations of this saying are found also in Matt 20:16; Mark 9:35, 10:31; and Luke 13:30.

<h1 style="text-align:center">9</h1>

Sabbath as a Time for Healing

1. The Greek word for a person suffering from this condition is *hydrōpikos*, rendered by traditional English Bible translations as "dropsy." It refers to swelling in the body due to excess fluid retention. It is often a sign of congestive heart failure.

2. According to the evidence of the Mishnah (compiled in the second century CE), the rabbis debated in minute detail what sort of healing or health-promoting activities were to be allowed or forbidden on the Sabbath. See, e.g., m. Shab. 14:3–4: "Greek hyssop may not be eaten on the Sabbath since it is not the food of them that are in health, but a man may eat pennyroyal or drink knotgrass-water. He may eat any foodstuffs that serve for healing or drink any liquids except purgative water or a cup of root-water, since these serve to cure jaundice; but he may drink purgative water to quench his thirst, and he may anoint himself with root-oil if it is not used for healing. If his teeth pain him he may not suck vinegar through them but he may take vinegar after his usual fashion, and if he is healed, he is healed. If his loins pain him he may not rub thereon wine or vinegar, yet he may anoint them with oil but not with rose-oil." (Translation from Herbert Danby, *The Mishnah* [Oxford: Oxford University Press, 1933], 113.) Note that in the healing story in John 5:1–18, the complaint of the authorities focuses not on Jesus's act of healing but on his instruction to the healed man to take up his mat and walk, thus performing "work" on the Sabbath.

3. For extended treatment of this issue, see the mishnaic tractate Shabbath. On defining what animals were permitted to do on the Sabbath, see m. Shab. 5:1–4. And on the debate about what counts as permissible tying and untying of knots on the Sabbath, see m. Shab. 15:1–2. For example, "R. Meir says: None is accounted culpable because of any knot which can be untied with one hand."

10
Mercy, Not Sacrifice

1. Later tradition ascribes authorship of the Gospel of Matthew to the tax collector named in this story, but nothing in the text suggests this explicitly. The Gospels of Mark and Luke tell the same story (Mark 2:13–17, Luke 5:27–32) but identify the tax collector as Levi and add the detail that the controversial dinner occurred in Levi's house.

2. For the historical context, see Fabian E. Udoh, *To Caesar What Is Caesar's: Tribute, Taxes, and Imperial Administration in Early Roman Palestine (63 B.C.E.–70 C.E.)*, 2nd ed., Brown Judaic Studies 343 (Providence: Brown Judaic Studies, 2005). While emphasizing the paucity of clear evidence for the mechanisms of tax collection in Roman Judea, Udoh concludes: "There were, it would seem, no Roman tax collectors in the Jewish parts of the province of Judea. Tribute was collected by Jewish agents. . . . There can be no certain conclusions about the manner in which Rome collected direct and indirect taxes in the region, although in general it might be said that the Jewish aristocracy was responsible for collecting (direct) tribute" (241–42).

3. The aversion to association with sinners is analogous to the social practice of shunning people afflicted with the terrible disfiguring skin disease called leprosy, or Hansen's disease. The Gospels tell several stories of Jesus's willingness to reach out and touch the victims of this malady and to heal them. These accounts present a symbolic parallel to Jesus's action of associating himself with others who were outcasts for different reasons.

4. The same story appears in parallel accounts in Mark 2:13–17 and Luke 5:29–32, but without Matthew's citation of Hos 6:6.

5. See also Prov 21:3: "To do righteousness and justice / is more acceptable to the LORD than sacrifice."

6. This is the theme expounded at length by the apostle Paul in his Letter to the Romans.

7. The story of Zacchaeus surely bears some relevance for contemporary debates about paying reparations to the descendants of enslaved people in the United States, or others who are the victims of past injustices. Some interpreters have suggested that Zacchaeus is not making a repentant prom-

ise, but rather offering a self-justification. This interpretation rests on the fact that the verbs "give" (*didōmi*) and "pay back" (*apodidōmi*) in the Greek text are in the present rather than the future tense. But this reading of Zacchaeus's words in v. 8 is incongruous with Jesus's response in vv. 9–10, which clearly suggests that "today" salvation has come to Zacchaeus and that Jesus's encounter with him exemplifies Jesus's mission "to seek out and save the lost." In *koinē* Greek, as in many languages, the present tense verb can signify an intention by the speaker to act in the immediate future.

8. Some traditional interpretations have also conjecturally identified this woman as Mary Magdalene, but again, there is no basis for this identification in Luke's text.

9. It is noteworthy that Simon does not articulate his disapproval; he judges sternly but silently.

10. The Greek verb translated here as "filled with compassion" is *esplagchnisthē;* it literally refers to the feeling of being moved in one's guts.

11
Mercy to Foreigners and Outsiders

1. That is the picture broadly sketched in many of the New Testament documents, though recent scholarship has cautioned that for many Jewish communities, association with gentiles was both more common and less restrictive than the New Testament writings would suggest. On this topic, see E. P. Sanders, "Jewish Association with Gentiles and Galatians 2:11–14," in R. T. Fortna and B. R. Gaventa, eds., *The Conversation Continues: Studies in Paul and John in Honor of J. Louis Martyn* (Nashville: Abingdon, 1990), 170–88; Paula Fredriksen, "What Does It Mean to See Paul 'Within Judaism'?," *Journal of Biblical Literature* 141 (2022): 359–80. Be that as it may, we are concerned here with the stories told in the New Testament texts; these stories unquestionably represent the particular social realities within which these texts arose and were first received. On these issues, see John Barclay, *Jews in the Mediterranean Diaspora* (Edinburgh: T & T Clark, 1996), 434–37. Citing a wide range of sources, both Jewish and pagan, on "Jewish meal-separatism," Barclay concludes: "Even if not every Jew maintained this demarcation, it typically served to bind the Jewish community together in distinction from others and thus to solidify Jewish ethnic identity on a daily basis" (437). He also observes that "it seems that the Jewish population in general was more conservative on such matters than the educated élite" (436). Certainly, the New Testament writings did not emerge from communities that represented the "educated elite."

2. On this command's significance within Matthew's overall theological

program, see Amy-Jill Levine, *The Social and Ethnic Dimensions of Matthean Social History,* Studies in the Bible and Early Christianity 14 (Lewiston, NY: Edwin Mellen, 1988).

3. Quotation from Josephus, *Ant.* 18.27.

4. Mark A. Chancey (*The Myth of a Gentile Galilee,* Society for New Testament Studies Monograph Series 116 [Cambridge: Cambridge University Press, 2002], 69–83) cautions that much of the archaeological evidence for Greco-Roman culture at Sepphoris derives from the second century CE and later. He emphasizes that in Jesus's day the population of the town was almost certainly predominantly Jewish. These cautions are well taken, but the point remains that this major Galilean town likely would have had significant cultural and economic contacts with the wider Roman world.

5. Luke's version of the story of the centurion lacks this saying about the eschatological banquet. Luke places that saying in a different context, in which Jesus is answering the question of whether only a few will be saved (Luke 13:22–30). In that context, Jesus's reference to "many coming from east and west" is not specifically related to the inclusion of gentiles. It could refer, instead, to the ingathering and return of Jewish people living in diaspora.

6. In a parallel version of the story (Mark 7:24–30), Mark tells us that Jesus was trying to escape public attention and "did not want anyone to know he was there" (7:24).

7. W. D. Davies and D. C. Allison Jr., *The Gospel According to Saint Matthew,* Vol. 2, International Critical Commentary (Edinburgh: T & T Clark, 1991), 547.

8. On the face of it, this is a disturbing story. Jesus likens the pleading woman to a dog and rudely rebuffs her desperate entreaties for help. Christian tradition has sought various ways to defuse the offense of the story, most commonly by hypothesizing that Jesus intended all along to help but that he was just testing her faith—as though such an interpretation could mitigate the story's apparent offensiveness. For different approaches, see Gail O'Day, "Surprised by Faith: Jesus and the Canaanite Woman," in Amy-Jill Levine, ed., *A Feminist Companion to Matthew* (London: T & T Clark, 2001), 114–25; Glenna S. Jackson, *"Have Mercy on Me": The Story of the Canaanite Woman in Matthew 15:21–28,* Journal for the Study of the New Testament Supplement Series 128 (New York: Continuum, 2002), 132–44; Kathy Barrett Dawson, "Matthew's Authoritative Jesus: Reading Matthew 15 Through a Deuteronomic Lens," in David M. Moffitt and Isaac Augustine Morales, eds., *A Scribe Trained for the Kingdom of Heaven* (Lanham, MD: Lexington/Fortress, 2021), 3–23.

9. The Greek verb here (*sygchrōntai*) might mean either "have dealings with" or, more specifically, "share vessels [for eating or drinking] with."

10. Interestingly, the Greek verb translated as "stay" in 4:40 (*menō*) is the same verb translated as "abide" in John 15:1–11 ("Abide in me as I abide in you," and so forth).

11. Some translations have "lawyer," which is probably a bad translation. The Greek word, *nomikos*, does not refer to what we would call an attorney or barrister. In Luke's usage, it consistently refers to someone who is a Torah scholar, learned in the study of *ho nomos*, i.e., the Torah.

12. I should say, the first human figure other than Jesus himself. Cf. Mark 14:61–62.

13. Author's translation in italics, emphasizing that the Greek word *ethnē*, often translated in this passage as "nations," is elsewhere ordinarily rendered as "gentiles."

12

The Holy Spirit Begins to Change the Church's Mind

1. The author of Acts is unnamed, but the address to Theophilus in Acts 1:1 links this book to the Gospel of Luke (see Luke 1:1–4) as the second part of a continuous narrative.

2. For an account of how the four Gospels "read backwards" to reinterpret Israel's scripture in fresh and surprising ways, see Richard B. Hays, *Reading Backwards: Figural Christology and the Fourfold Gospel Witness* (Waco, TX: Baylor University Press, 2014).

3. On these narrowly nationalistic tendencies in Israel's scriptures and counter-impulses in other scriptural texts, see Chapter 7, above.

4. Translation: NRSVue.

5. Translation: NRSVue.

6. In the Hebrew text, Joel 3:1.

7. In Acts 6:1–7, the "Hellenists" in Jerusalem were not gentiles; they were Greek-speaking Jews from the diaspora. Nonetheless, the dissension in the community over charitable distribution to widows from these different cultural and linguistic groups had already begun to expose a fault line that would come more fully into view in Acts 15. On this issue, see Craig C. Hill, *Hellenists and Hebrews: Reappraising Division Within the Earliest Church* (Minneapolis: Fortress, 1992).

8. This brief account raises difficult questions about the relationship between water baptism and the gift of the Spirit. There is a lengthy history of theological debate about these issues, and exploring this matter would take us beyond the scope of our present concerns. For a helpful exegetical study, see James D. G. Dunn, *Baptism in the Holy Spirit*, Studies in Biblical Theology, 2nd series, 15 (Naperville, IL: Alec R. Allenson, 1970), 55–72.

9. Luke notes the queen's royal title, *Kandakē*, in Greek. English translations usually render this title as "Candace," and some readers erroneously assume that this is her name. The term *Aithiopia* was generally used to designate all of Africa south of Egypt.

10. Translation: NRSVue.

11. It is not clear how the Jerusalem temple authorities in the early first century would have resolved the tension between Deut 23:1 and Isa 56:3–5. On the Isaiah text, see Chapter 7, above.

12. See Josephus, *War* 2.409–16. Josephus indicates that it had been a long-standing tradition for gentiles to make offerings to Israel's God in the Jerusalem temple. The success of zealous Jewish nationalists in prohibiting this traditional practice was one of the precipitating factors that triggered the war against Rome and the destruction of the temple.

13. Author's translation.

14. The standard lexicon for New Testament Greek suggests, I think rightly, that *genean* in Acts 8:33 (translated in the NRSV as "generation") should be "taken in the sense of *family history*" (*Greek-English Lexicon of the New Testament and Other Early Christian Literature*, 3rd ed., ed. F. W. Danker, W. Bauer, W. F. Arndt, and F. W. Gingrich [Chicago: University of Chicago Press, 2000]). If so, I would translate the question—as I have done in the quotation above—as "Who will tell [*diēgēsetai*] his family history?" Nothing in the Greek text suggests the addition of the auxiliary verb "can." The verb *diēgēsetai* is a simple future tense ("will tell").

15. On the profound importance of having descendants who will preserve one's name in memory, see the discussion of Isa 56 in Chapter 7, above.

13
The Conscripted Apostle

1. For further discussion of this interpretation, see N. T. Wright, *Paul: A Biography* (New York: HarperOne, 2018). The first chapter of Wright's account of Paul's life is titled simply "Zeal" (pp. 27–39).

2. See Chapter 16 below for more on how Paul appealed for unity in these communities.

3. Translation: NRSVue.

14
"Who Was I That I Could Block God?"

1. The Greek text uses the word *anthrōpos* ("human being"), not "mortal," as in the NRSV.

2. Translation: NRSVue.

3. On this important topic, see E. P. Sanders, "Jewish Association with Gentiles and Galatians 2:11–14," in R. T. Fortna and B. R. Gaventa, eds., *The Conversation Continues: Studies in Paul and John in Honor of J. Louis Martyn* (Nashville: Abingdon, 1990), 170–88.

4. The issue continued to be a sensitive one for early Christian communities, as shown by Paul's extended grappling with the problem in 1 Cor 8:1–11:1 and Rom 14:1–15:13. For discussion of Paul's response to the issue in Rome, see Chapter 16, below.

5. See John M. G. Barclay, *Jews in the Mediterranean Diaspora from Alexander to Trajan (323 BCE–117 CE)* (Edinburgh: T & T Clark, 1996), 434–37.

6. Translation: NRSVue.

7. See also Lev 19:15, 2 Chr 19:7, Sir 35:14–16.

8. See also Rom 2:11.

9. Author's translation.

10. The term translated as "step by step" is *kathexēs,* the same adverb Luke used in the prologue to his Gospel (Luke 1:3) to describe his own narrative intentions in retelling the story of Jesus.

11. So, for example, it would be an apt verb to describe the actions of Senate Majority Leader Mitch McConnell in blocking the US Senate from considering President Barack Obama's nomination of Merrick Garland to the Supreme Court in 2016.

15
The Jerusalem Council

1. One thinks of Paul Simon's line from his song "Graceland": "I've reason to believe we all will be received in Graceland." Simon's song refers in the first instance, of course, to Elvis Presley's Graceland mansion in Memphis, Tennessee, but the inchoate longing of Simon's lyric suggests that to be "received" in Graceland signifies some deeper, mysterious acceptance into a place of grace and mercy.

2. On this topic, see Richard B. Hays, *Reading Backwards: Figural Christology and the Fourfold Gospel Witness* (Waco, TX: Baylor University Press, 2014).

3. There are complex critical issues here about the form of the citation and its possible relation to different textual antecedents. Some of these issues bear upon the historical accuracy of Luke's account. Would James, a pillar of the Aramaic-speaking Jerusalem church, be pinning his judgment on a Greek version of the text? For discussion of the problem, readers may consult the commentary literature. For a clear and accessible summary, see Bev-

erly Roberts Gaventa, *Acts,* Abingdon New Testament Commentaries (Nashville: Abingdon, 2003), 217–20.

4. If so, this would be a clear example of the trope of *metalepsis:* the allusive evocation of elements of an earlier text beyond the words explicitly cited. On this rhetorical technique, which is pervasive in the New Testament, see Richard B. Hays, *Echoes of Scripture in the Letters of Paul* (New Haven: Yale University Press, 1989), and Hays, "'Who Has Believed Our Message?': Paul's Reading of Isaiah," in *The Conversion of the Imagination: Paul as Interpreter of Israel's Scripture* (Grand Rapids: Eerdmans, 2005), 25–49.

5. The NRSV's translation ("I have reached the decision") is an overinterpretation of the verb *krinō,* which simply means "I judge." There is no indication in the text, here or elsewhere, that James possesses unilateral authority to decide the issue. As Luke presents the outcome, the final decision is communicated by "the apostles and elders, *with the consent of the whole church*" (Acts 15:22; emphasis added). James's speech should be read as a *proposal* to the assembly, a compromise proposal that successfully elicits agreement.

6. Translation: NRSVue.

7. Translation: NRSVue.

8. *The Moral Vision of the New Testament: Community, Cross, New Creation* (San Francisco: HarperSanFrancisco, 1996), 298–306. For further reflection on this point, see the Epilogue, below.

9. One of the earliest and most influential articulations of this proposal was offered by Luke Timothy Johnson, "Disputed Questions: Debate and Discernment, Scripture and the Spirit," *Commonweal* 121/2 (January 28, 1994): 11–13.

10. This represents a change of mind from what I wrote in *The Moral Vision of the New Testament.* See my reflections in the Epilogue to the present book.

11. Johnson ("Disputed Questions") carefully delineates the significance of these three factors, giving particular attention to the importance of listening to stories of how God is actually at work in people's lives.

16
Mercy All the Way Down

1. The finest account of the adaptations and innovations of the early Christian communities within the cultures of the Roman Empire remains Wayne A. Meeks, *The First Urban Christians: The Social World of the Apostle Paul* (New Haven: Yale University Press, 1983).

2. Whether these letters were written before or after the events that

Luke narrates in Acts 15 is a complicated historical question—too complicated to address here. My own view is that these letters were written later; if
so, they indicate that vigorous debate over circumcision and legal requirements continued in various local settings apart from and/or subsequent to
the Jerusalem meeting. Be that as it may, the main point is that Paul's letters
persistently indicate the presence of widespread conflicts in the churches
that he founded.

3. For discussion of these issues in Corinth, see Richard B. Hays, *First
Corinthians,* Interpretation Commentaries (Louisville: Westminster John
Knox, 1997).

4. On this theme, see Richard B. Hays, *The Conversion of the Imagination: Paul as Interpreter of Israel's Scripture* (Grand Rapids: Eerdmans, 2005).

5. The authorship of the Letter to the Ephesians is disputed; modern
scholars have often hypothesized that this epistle was composed not by Paul
but by a later author representing a Pauline "school." On either view, the
letter eloquently articulates themes at the heart of Paul's theological vision.

6. These translation issues carry wide-ranging implications for the interpretation of Paul's theology. For further discussion, see Richard B. Hays,
The Faith of Jesus Christ: The Narrative Substructure of Galatians 3:1–4:11, 2nd
ed., Biblical Resource Series (Grand Rapids: Eerdmans, 2002); Hays, "Justification," in *Anchor Bible Dictionary,* Vol. 3 (New York: Doubleday, 1992),
1129–33.

7. On Rom 4, see Richard B. Hays, "Abraham as Father of Jews and
Gentiles," in *Conversion of the Imagination,* 61–84.

8. I highly recommend that readers listen to Mary Gauthier's song
"Mercy Now" on her album of the same title. For those interested in background to the song, see her book *Saved by a Song: The Art and Healing Power
of Songwriting* (New York: St. Martin's Essentials, 2021).

9. Translation: NRSVue.

10. Paul had not yet been to Rome, but he must have received reports,
perhaps from some of the people he mentions in the extensive list of his ac-
quaintances in ch. 16 of the letter.

11. Josephus, *Life* 14. For this and further references, see Leander E. Keck,
Romans, Abingdon New Testament Commentary (Nashville: Abingdon, 2005),
337.

12. Cicero, *Tusc.* 4.23, 26. For this reference and further discussion of this
theme in Hellenistic philosophy, see Stanley K. Stowers, *A Rereading of Romans: Justice, Jews, and Gentiles* (New Haven: Yale University Press, 1994).

13. Translation: NRSVue.

14. Shakespeare memorably evokes the character of God's mercy—and

its implication for how we should treat one another—in Portia's appeal in *The Merchant of Venice* (Act IV, scene 1):

> The quality of mercy is not strained;
> It droppeth as the gentle rain from heaven
> Upon the place beneath. It is twice blest;
> It blesseth him that gives and him that takes.
> . . . .
> It is an attribute to God himself,
> And earthly power doth then show likest God's
> When mercy seasons justice. . . .
> . . . .
>   . . . We do pray for mercy,
> And that same prayer doth teach us all to render
> The deeds of mercy.

Portia's speech, it should be noted, echoes Moses's proclamation in Deut 32:1–2:

> Give ear, O heavens, and I will speak;
>   let the earth hear the words of my mouth.
> May my teaching drop like the rain,
>   my speech condense like the dew;
> like gentle rain on grass.

17
Moral Re-Vision

1. Translation: NRSVue.

2. The biblical authors did not have in mind the sort of homosexual relationships that the church now considers blessing, and it is not possible to imagine what they might have said about them. As it is, many of the passages are unambiguous in their disapproval of homosexual activity. See Richard B. Hays, *The Moral Vision of the New Testament: Community, Cross, New Creation* (San Francisco: HarperSanFrancisco, 1996), 381–89. I (Richard) stand fully behind the *descriptive* exegetical judgments I made there about the meaning of all these texts. But I also draw the reader's attention to the final sentences of my discussion of Rom 1:18–32: "[N]o one should presume to be above God's judgment; all of us stand in radical need of God's mercy. Thus, Paul's warning should transform the terms of our contemporary debate about homosexuality: no one has a secure platform to stand upon in order to pro-

nounce condemnation on others. Anyone who presumes to have such a vantage point is living in a dangerous fantasy, oblivious to the gospel that levels all of us before a holy God." I now wish that I had added another clause to that final sentence, so that it would read, "the gospel that levels all of us before a holy God who welcomes all of us with infinite compassion and mercy." For more detailed exegesis of Rom 1:18–32, see Beverly Roberts Gaventa, *Romans: A Commentary*, New Testament Library (Louisville: Westminster John Knox, 2024), 55–72.

3. The text in Joel reads, "your old men shall dream dreams, / and your young men shall see visions" (Joel 2:28 = Joel 3:1 LXX). The quotation as given in Acts 2:17 reverses the order of these two clauses.

4. Paul's Greek text says literally, "let the others discern [*diakrinetōsan*]."

5. Authors' translation.

6. See the evidence gathered by Willard M. Swartley, *Slavery, Sabbath, War, and Women: Case Studies in Biblical Interpretation* (Scottdale, PA: Herald, 1983), 31–64.

7. We are mindful that some churches still forbid ordination of women and persist in mandating their subordination to men in marriage. We unapologetically state that we believe these practices to be wrong and demonstrably detrimental to the well-being of the whole body of Christ. To defend that view in detail would divert us from the matter at hand.

8. Hays, *Moral Vision*, 299.

9. Eugene F. Rogers Jr., "Sanctification, Homosexuality, and God's Triune Life," in E. F. Rogers Jr., ed., *Theology and Sexuality: Classic and Contemporary Readings* (Malden, MA: Blackwell, 2002), 217–46 (238). Rogers's percipient essay is an excellent model for gracious and theologically nuanced discussion of these questions.

10. He adds: "Anyone who derives from them an idea which is useful for supporting this love but fails to say what the writer demonstrably meant in the passage has not made a fatal error, and is certainly not a liar." Augustine of Hippo, *On Christian Teaching*, trans. R. P. H. Green, Oxford World's Classics (Oxford: Oxford University Press, 1997), 27. In Green's system of numbering paragraphs, these citations appear as Book One, 86. (In the more widely used system that appeared in the older *Select Library of Nicene and Post-Nicene Fathers*, the section is designated as 1.xxxvi.)

Epilogue

1. Richard B. Hays, *The Moral Vision of the New Testament: Community, Cross, New Creation* (San Francisco: HarperSanFrancisco, 1996), 303.

2. It is not as though I wasn't given occasions to reconsider. I have a

vivid memory of a conference at Duke back in the mid-1990s where Rowan Williams, having read a prepublication draft of my book, gently challenged me on exactly this point. At the time, I brushed off his challenge. But I never forgot it. I would also like to acknowledge a vigorous and challenging essay by one of my former doctoral students: J. R. Daniel Kirk, "The Moral Vision of LGBTQ Inclusion: Community, Cross, New Creation," in David M. Moffitt and Isaac Augustine Morales, eds., *A Scribe Trained for the Kingdom of Heaven: Essays on Christology and Ethics in Honor of Richard B. Hays* (Lanham, MD: Lexington/Fortress, 2021), 197–216. In this essay—which appeared in print while the present book was in the gestation stage—Kirk seeks to demonstrate how my own methods and categories for thinking about New Testament ethics might (and should) have led to conclusions different from the ones I drew in *Moral Vision,* particularly because of the way in which the image of "New Creation" reshapes previous understandings of gender differences and hierarchies. My contribution to the present book pursues somewhat different reasoning but is nonetheless convergent with Kirk's conclusions.

3. Luke Timothy Johnson, "Disputed Questions: Debate and Discernment, Scripture and the Spirit," *Commonweal* 121/2 (January 28, 1994): 11–13. Johnson's probing essay was subsequently adapted in his book *Scripture and Discernment: Decision Making in the Church* (Nashville: Abingdon, 1996), 144–48. It was later reprinted in Eugene F. Rogers Jr., ed., *Theology and Sexuality: Classic and Contemporary Readings* (Oxford: Blackwell, 2002), 367–72. For an argument along similar lines, see also Jeffrey S. Siker, "Homosexual Christians, the Bible, and Gentile Inclusion: Confessions of a Repenting Heterosexist," in J. S. Siker, ed., *Homosexuality in the Church: Both Sides of the Debate* (Louisville: Westminster John Knox, 1994), 178–84. The proposals of Johnson and Siker, novel at the time, have now been widely disseminated at the grassroots level in "mainline" Protestant preaching and teaching.

4. Hays, *Moral Vision,* 396.

5. This version of the prayer is taken from "The Holy Eucharist: Rite II," in *The Book of Common Prayer and Administration of the Sacraments and Other Rites and Ceremonies of the Church According to the Use of the Episcopal Church* (New York: Church Publishing, 1979), 360.

General Index

Scriptural and ancient sources are in a separate index, Index of Biblical References and Other Ancient Sources

baptism: of Ethiopian eunuch,
159–61, 163; of gentiles, 150, 160,
173–74, 209; of Jesus, 113; of
LGBTQ people, 216; of Samaritans, 156, 163; by water vs. Holy
Spirit, 173–74, 240n8
Barclay, John M. G., 238n1, 242n5
Barnabas (evangelist), 176–78, 182,
184, 185
Barth, Karl, 4, 205, 215, 227n4
Bauer, W., 241n14
Beatitudes, 118–19, 134, 236n7 (ch.8)
Benjamin (Jacob's son), 164
biblical laws: changing nature of,
2–3, 49, 55–56, 211–13; on circumcision, 66, 152, 177; conscientious obedience to, 122, 200;
dietary, 152, 167, 169–71, 182,
196–201, 212; divergent views
in, 3, 55–56, 231n5 (ch.3); ethical
issues and, 56; on head coverings for women, 12, 212;
Holiness Code, 183, 212; on
inheritance, 49, 52–55, 58; on
kosher practices, 212; Mosaic
law, 53, 62, 81; for priesthood,
103–5; on sacrifices, 55, 62,
64–67; on sexuality, 68–69; Ten
Commandments, 64, 123. See
also Sabbath; Torah
bisexuals. See LGBTQ people;
sexuality and sexual orientation
Book of the Covenant, 55, 64, 66
Briant, Pierre, 234n4 (ch.7)
Brittsan, Nathan, 13
Bromiley, G. W., 227n4
Broyles, Craig C., 235n8

Caiaphas (high priest), 112
Cain (Abel's brother), 38–40, 46, 47
Caleb (Israelite leader), 44

Calvin, John and Calvinists, 31,
89–90
Canaan and Canaanites: Archites
and, 74; child sacrifice by, 63;
famine in, 43; oppression of, 44,
71, 231n6 (ch.3); paganism and,
144
cancel culture, 133
castration, 98, 99, 159, 234n2. See
also eunuchs
celibacy, 9, 11, 213, 216, 224
Chancey, Mark A., 239n4
character of God, 2, 12, 31, 34, 88,
95, 121, 216, 225
children and adolescents: gun violence deaths, 67; Jesus's interactions with, 106; LGBTQ, 67–68;
orphans, 90, 102, 172, 215, 236n7
(ch.7); sacrifice of, 62–67, 69;
suicide and suicidal ideation,
67–68
Christ. See Jesus Christ
Christianity: conflicts in, 152–53,
189–92, 196–201, 243n2; conversion to, 156, 166, 168–69, 177–78,
185; emergence of movement
for, 176, 177, 236n4; evangelical,
12, 14, 68, 228n15; ministry of
reconciliation and, 190–92; mis-
sionaries and, 176–77, 189; persecution of believers, 156, 162–66;
progressive, 11, 14, 15, 57–58;
Roman communities, 192, 196–
201, 217, 243n1, 244n10; strong/
weak disputes in, 196–201. See
also baptism; conservatism;
specific denominations
Cicero, 198, 244n12
circumcision, 66, 141, 152, 163, 167,
169, 172–73, 177, 179, 181–82, 184,
189, 223, 243n2

judgment: codification as law, 55;
communal, 210; descriptive
exegetical, 245n2; of dietary
laws, 196–97, 199–201; impartiality of, 84, 172; inclusion of
gentiles, 179–81; mercy and, 38,
40, 85–88, 92, 222; metaphor-
making and, 185, 214; moral, 7,
22, 213, 214, 222, 223; popular
conceptions of, 26; reconsider-
ation of, 85–90, 138, 207. *See also*
punishment
Julian of Norwich, 229n22
Junior, Nyasha, 231n6 (ch.2)
justice: expansion of, 59; gender
and, 58; for gentiles, 145, 150; in
kingdom of David, 112; in lieu of
sacrifice, 237n5; maintenance of,
96, 97; principles of, 48; racial,
14; retributive, 39; revelation of,
193; slavery as incompatible with,
212; systems of, 56; violence in
pursuit of, 234n1 (ch.5); for
widows and orphans, 172; for
Zelophehad's daughters, 52,
57–58

Keck, Leander E., 244n11
Kierkegaard, Søren, 67, 70, 232n5
King, Martin Luther, Jr., 116, 211
Kirk, J. R. Daniel, 13, 228n10,
246–47n2
knowingness, problem of, 91–92
kōluō (blocking action), 174–75,
242n11
Korah (Israelite rebel), 52
kosher practices, 212
Kugel, James L., 230n2

laws, biblical. *See* biblical laws
Lear, Jonathan, 91–92, 234n9

Lee, Sang Hyun, 230n5
leprosy (Hansen's disease), 106, 115,
237n3
lesbians. *See* LGBTQ people;
sexuality and sexual orientation
Levenson, Jon D., 66, 232n4
Levi (tax collector), 237n1
Levine, Amy-Jill, 238n2, 239n8
Levites, 102–4, 148, 234–35n7
Lewis, C. S., 19, 120, 228n18
LGBTQ people: baptism of, 216;
children and adolescents, 67–68;
disapproval in biblical passages,
206, 223, 245n2; "don't ask, don't
tell" policy for, 10; at Fuller
Theological Seminary, 13–15;
inclusion of, 5–8, 12, 13, 186, 206,
207, 214–16, 221, 223; marriage
and, 7, 10, 12–14, 216, 217, 224;
monogamy standards for, 187;
ordination of, 7, 216; suicide and
suicidal ideation among, 67–68,
232n7. *See also* sexuality and
sexual orientation
Liew, Tat-Siong Benny, 233n5
love: Augustine on, 220, 246n10;
commandment to, 69, 148, 191,
196; for creation, 29–30, 35, 36;
Edwards on, 29–31, 33; equality
of, 16; expansion of, 2, 29, 36;
God as definition of, 220; mercy
and, 18, 36, 151; of neighbor, 97,
148, 167, 191, 196; restorative, 134;
steadfast, 45, 85, 88, 94, 134

Maccabean revolt, 112
Magnificat, 117–19
Mahlah (Zelophehad's daughter),
50–59, 69, 231n6 (ch.3)
males. *See* men
Manasseh (Joseph's son), 50, 63

Index of Biblical References and Other Ancient Sources